Kathrin Braun
Biopolitics and Historic Justice

Political Science | Volume 66

This open access publication has been enabled by the support of POLLUX (Fachinformationsdienst Politikwissenschaft)

and a collaborative network of academic libraries for the promotion of the Open Access transformation in the Social Sciences and Humanities (transcript Open Library Politikwissenschaft 2021)

This publication is compliant with the "Recommendations on quality standards for the open access provision of books", Nationaler Open Access Kontaktpunkt 2018 (https://pub.uni-bielefeld.de/record/2932189)

Hauptsponsor: Staats- und Universitätsbibliothek Bremen (POLLUX – Informationsdienst Politikwissenschaft)
Vollsponsoren: Universitätsbibliothek Bayreuth | Universitätsbibliothek der Humboldt-Universität zu Berlin | Freie Universität Berlin - Universitätsbibliothek | Staatsbibliothek zu Berlin | Universitätsbibliothek Bielefeld | Universitätsbibliothek der Ruhr-Universität Bochum (RUB) | Universitäts- und Landesbibliothek Bonn | Vorarlberger Landesbibliothek | Universitätsbibliothek der Technischen Universität Chemnitz | Universitäts- und Landesbibliothek Darmstadt | Sächsische Landesbibliothek Staats- und Universitätsbibliothek Dresden (SLUB) | Universitätsbibliothek Duisburg-Essen | Universitäts- und Landesbibliothek Düsseldorf | Universitätsbibliothek Erlangen-Nürnberg | Universitätsbibliothek Frankfurt/M. | Niedersächsische Staats- und Universitätsbibliothek Göttingen | Universitätsbibliothek Greifswald | Universitätsbibliothek der FernUniversität in Hagen | Staats- und Universitätsbibliothek Carl von Ossietzky, Hamburg | TIB – Leibniz-Informationszentrum Technik und Naturwissenschaften und Universitätsbibliothek | Gottfried Wilhelm Leibniz Bibliothek - Niedersächsische Landesbibliothek | Universitätsbibliothek Heidelberg | Universitätsbibliothek Kassel | Universitätsbibliothek Kiel (CAU) | Universitätsbibliothek Koblenz · Landau | Universitäts- und Stadtbibliothek Köln | Universitätsbibliothek Leipzig | Zentral- und Hochschulbibliothek Luzern | Universitätsbibliothek Otto-von-Guericke-Universität Magdeburg | Universitätsbibliothek Marburg | Max Planck Digital Library (MPDL) | Universitäts- und Landesbibliothek Münster | Universitätsbibliothek der Carl von Ossietzky-Universität, Oldenburg | Universitätsbibliothek Osnabrück | Universitätsbibliothek Passau | Universitätsbibliothek St. Gallen | Universitätsbibliothek Vechta | Universitätsbibliothek Wien | Universitätsbibliothek Wuppertal | Zentralbibliothek Zürich
Sponsoring Light: Bundesministerium der Verteidigung | Landesbibliothek Oldenburg
Mikrosponsoring: Stiftung Wissenschaft und Politik (SWP) - Deutsches Institut für Internationale Politik und Sicherheit | Leibniz-Institut für Europäische Geschichte, Mainz

Kathrin Braun, political scientist, born in 1960, has done extensive work on the politics of bioethics and biomedicine, as well as the politics of coming to terms with human rights violations related to biopolitics. She received her PhD and title of extraordinary professor from the Leibniz University Hannover and has taught at a range of universities in Germany, the US, the UK and elsewhere. Since 2018 she has been research coordinator at the Center for Interdisciplinary Risk and Innovation Studies (ZIRIUS) at the University of Stuttgart, Germany.

Kathrin Braun

Biopolitics and Historic Justice

Coming to Terms with the Injuries of Normality

[transcript]

Bibliographic information published by the Deutsche Nationalbibliothek

The Deutsche Nationalbibliothek lists this publication in the Deutsche National-bibliografie; detailed bibliographic data are available in the Internet at http://dnb.d-nb.de

© 2021 transcript Verlag, Bielefeld

Cover layout: Maria Arndt, Bielefeld
Printed by Majuskel Medienproduktion GmbH, Wetzlar
Print-ISBN 978-3-8376-4550-7
PDF-ISBN 978-3-8394-4550-1
EPUB-ISBN 978-3-7328-4550-7
https://doi.org/10.14361/9783839445501

Contents

1   Introduction: Coming to Terms with Biopolitics, Temporality and Historic Justice

1.1   From Times Believed Long Overcome

In June 2020, nine citizens filed a constitutional complaint with the Federal Constitutional Court in Germany. The complaint was directed against guideline recommendations issued by the German Society of Intensive Care Physicians together with further medical societies on the question of health care rationing and treatment in situations of scarce resources due to the Covid-19 pandemic (DIVI 2020). When intensive care units face an acute shortage of resources, the societies argued, physicians must decide who should receive intensive medical treatment and who not. The guidelines suggested criteria for making these decisions and thus prioritizing some patients over others. The medical societies stated that these decisions should not be based on criteria of age, social characteristics, disability or chronic illness but only on the chances of treatment success. The claimants, however, argued that the criteria spelled out by the guidelines for establishing the chances of treatment success, like organ dysfunctionality, frailty along the Clinical Frailty Scale, neuronal diseases and 'prognostically limited life expectancy' effectively discriminated against many people with disabilities. "The criteria presented," writes the disability rights organization AbilityWatch, which supports the constitutional claim,

> could thus become the death sentence of a large number of disabled people. The fact that the president of DIVI publicly raises the question of 'whether it really makes sense to intubate and ventilate in an intensive care unit people of very old age who have been unable to live on their own for a long time and who have severe chronic concomitant diseases' awakens the worst memories

of justification patterns from times believed long overcome. (AbilityWatch 2020)[1]

It went without saying what times these were. In July 2020, five foundations and memorial sites commemorating the Nazi 'euthanasia'[2] crimes issued a common statement to express their concern about the discussion on withholding intensive health care for people with previous illnesses or disabilities in the course of the pandemic.

> The signatory memorials to commemorate the Nazi euthanasia crimes commemorate the devaluation, exclusion and murder of people under National Socialism. [...] Against this backdrop, we view with concern the discussions about intensive medical care for elderly people and people with previous illnesses or disabilities (keyword: triage) in the corona pandemic. (Gedenkstätte Hadamar 2020)

Similar discussions popped up in other countries. Many people in the United States also felt reminded of practices associated to 'eugenics' and 'euthanasia':

> The debates on health care rationing unveil how our society devalues vulnerable populations. Draftguidelines from various states and health systems identified people with dementia, cancer, intellectual disabilities, and many other pre-existing conditions as those who will not benefit from treatment compared to younger, healthier, non-disabled people. [...] Eugenics isn't a relic from World War II; it's alive today, embedded in our culture, policies, and practices. (Wong 2020)

The Center for Public Integrity in the United States has analyzed policies and guidelines from 30 U.S. states on criteria for rationing ventilators and other resources in the case of a shortage. The Center found that all but five states had provisions in place that in effect "send people with disabilities to the back of the line for life-saving treatment" (Center for Public Integrity 2020). In Alabama, for instance, a state policy had postulated that people with "severe

---

1   My translation from the German source. Unless otherwise indicated, all translations from German to English in this book are my own.

2   I will hereafter seek to avoid the euphemism euthanasia and rather speak of institutional killings, meaning the systematic killing of children with disabilities and people in psychiatric and other institutions under Nazi rule. However, since the term euthanasia is still in common use and even these memorial sites use it, it cannot always be avoided.

mental retardation [...] may be poor candidates" for treatment with ventilators if hospitals run short during the pandemic. The states of Louisiana, Pennsylvania, Texas and Utah, the Center reports, directed hospitals to take dementia into account when allocating ventilators. After a wave of complaints, the state of Alabama withdrew the policy, if only to replace it with less specific guidelines. Ensuing protests, however, from disability rights advocates as well as numerous experts and policy-makers persuaded some states to reconsider their triage policies, as the Center for Genetics and Society (2020) reports.

Aside from manifest triage policies, more indirect selection strategies, such as that of fostering so-called herd immunity, have also evoked concerns about a return of eugenics, albeit in a more indirect, economically based form. Referring to corona policies in the United Kingdom, Norway and Sweden, Vito Romer and Louis Philippe Laterza argue:

> It is hard not to read eugenic implications in this kind of thinking: the 'herd' will survive, but for that to happen, other 'weaker' members of society need to be sacrificed. (Romer and Laterza 2020)

Policies that prioritize the stronger and sacrifice the weaker, they posit, stand in continuity with eugenics policies which were *not* confined to the Nazi state:

> The Norwegian and Swedish states have a long history of adopting policies based on eugenics that continued well after World War II. Eugenics was deployed throughout the 20th century as a branch of scientific state management, part of a social engineering project that envisioned a society made of physically healthy and 'socially fit' individuals. (Romer and Laterza 2020)

One does not have to claim that we have already entered a new form of totalitarianism to realize that policies of health care rationing, whether on the hospital or state level, that refer to an individual's capacities in terms of health, strength, or fitness are effectively establishing a system of differential value of human lives. It is the practice of calculating the value of human lives that evokes reminiscences of Nazi practices, as Lennard Davis puts it:

> Social politesse, charitable involvement, religious concern all crumble in the face of the grand bargain of choosing those who appear 'normal'—not those who are seen as weakened, abnormal, debilitated, less-than. There is a term for this demographic, and the Nazis used it with abandon: *Lives Unworthy of Living*. [...] It is easy for us to blame the Nazis for these egregious and unimag-

inable deaths, but the current calculus about which lives are worth living provides a sobering if less overtly dramatic parallel. (Davis 2020, emph. i.o.)

Maybe the times believed long overcome are not so overcome after all. In any case, we can see that debates about the past are not simply about the past. They are about the present. These debates about triage, herd immunity, Nazi eugenics, Nazi 'euthanasia', eugenics in the US, or eugenics in the Scandinavian welfare states refer to the present situation. They address the scandalous treatment of people with disabilities in the past in order to scandalize the way they are treated today; they address the injustices of the past in order to counter the injustices of today. If we want to be different, these debates say, if we want to be a different kind of society than those that allowed these things to happen in the past, we have to *act* differently. It will not do to *name* selection practices differently.

In the context of these debates, but also in the wider context of the corona pandemic and governmental politics to contain it, the term 'biopolitics' crops up again and again. It emerges in relation to life-and-death decisions, allocation of health care treatment, ableism and disability rights as well as in the contexts of quarantine and mobility restrictions, surveillance mechanisms, behavioral monitoring and control, disciplinary measures, appeals to self-discipline and more.[3] At present, as far as I can see, references to biopolitics in relation to the corona pandemic are still rather cursory. Some refer to the work of Michel Foucault, others to Giorgio Agamben, some to both, but it is too early to expect a systematic review of which concepts of biopolitics and which aspects thereof are useful to understand the politics of the pandemic. I, too, am unable to undertake this endeavor here; rather, I indicate why I consider biopolitics in the Foucauldian sense a key concept for understanding a specific political rationality that emerged alongside modernity and is still operative today; it is not necessarily dark and destructive throughout, but it is problematic in that it implies an inherent tendency toward differential valuation of human lives.

---

3   To name only a few contributions: Agamben 2020; Ahrens 2020; Davis 2020; Gerhards 2020a; Kitchin 2020; Lorenzini 2020; Sarasin 2020.

1.2   Coming to Terms with the Presence of the Past

The focus of this chapter is the nexus of biopolitical rationality, the temporality of increase and optimization, and what I term the 'injuries of normality'. I will argue that modern biopolitics is characterized by the logic of increasing the human life force and that this logic implies norms and standards of differential value of human lives. Taken to the extreme, as done under Nazi rule, it involves policies of preventing, destroying and eliminating the lives of those categorized as being deficient according to its norms and standards. Not only the systematic murder of disabled new-borns and patients in psychiatric institutions, but also Nazi selective sterilization policy, the persecution of male homosexuals and persons categorized as 'asocials', I argue, were driven by this biopolitical rationality.[4] I explain my term for these types of crimes—injuries of normality—below. Although West German efforts to come to terms with the Nazi past are often lauded as a model case of historic justice, it is less well-known, particularly outside Germany, that for a long time the Federal Republic denied the status of systematic wrongdoing that requires official acknowledgement, rehabilitation and reparations to many types of crimes, including selective sterilization and the persecution of homosexuals and 'asocials'. The victims of these injuries of normality were not entitled to reparations as victims of Nazi persecution, and it took the West German state until the 2000s to formally acknowledge that these were severe injustices committed by the state. The reason for this failure, I argue, was the unwillingness to confront the underlying biopolitical rationality that had driven these crimes in the first place. The prevailing sense among reparation policy actors was that it was—in principle—reasonable for the state to take actions against those who were mentally ill, retarded, disabled, 'work-shy', homosexual or otherwise found weak, abnormal or dysfunctional, because, after all, these people posed a threat to state and society. In short, rehabilitation and reparation

---

4   I refer here to Miller and Rose, who define political rationality as "a kind of intellectual machinery for rendering reality thinkable in such a way that it is amenable to political deliberation" (Miller and Rose 1992, 179). Political rationalities are more than a set of governing technologies; they comprise substantial goals and principles of government, and they also have an epistemic character, defining what can be known and thus become an object of government. The concept of biopolitics covers both the dimension of political technologies and the dimension of particular goals and motives revolving around the idea of increasing the life force in the collective.

claims were refuted as long as the post-war elites shared the biopolitical motives of the perpetrators, even if they may not have accepted any means used to achieve them. By denying entitlement to rehabilitation and reparations, policy actors not only represented but performatively confirmed and re-enacted the very biopolitical rationality that had driven the crimes themselves. Conversely, the pertinent struggles for historic justice challenged the legitimacy of this rationality, and in this sense, they were, and are, as much about the present as they are about the past.

In the following pages, I unfold the nexus of biopolitics, temporality and the injuries of normality. I begin with an explication of how I read the concept of biopolitics and why it is a specifically modern phenomenon. Subsequently, I lay out the temporal logic of increase and optimization that characterizes modern biopolitics and argue that it inevitably generates systems of differential valuation and differential vulnerability. Finally, I explain the concept of injuries of normality as a specific type of historic injustice that has been largely overlooked in the field of historic and transitional justice. Moreover, I argue, injuries of normality are disregarded precisely because of their presumed 'normality'; they are taken as more or less 'normal' policies and practices and not as wrongs because and to the extent that the underlying biopolitical rationality that drives them remains unchallenged.

1.3   Biopolitics and the Threshold of Modernity

Biopolitics is an ambiguous and contested concept that assumes different meanings in different theoretical traditions. Oftentimes, it is used in an unspecific sense to denote any kind of relationship between 'politics' and 'life'; sometimes it refers more specifically to the policy area concerned with medicine, biotechnology and the life sciences.[5] These bilateral conceptions, so to speak, assume that 'life' and 'politics' are universal features of human existence that may or may not be connected to each other. Biopolitics, here, is this external connection. Michel Foucault, in contrast, has shown that the notion of 'life', the modern type of state, and the type of politics he terms biopolitics are not universals; rather, they co-emerged at the threshold of modernity in a move that "made knowledge-power an agent of transformation of human life" (Foucault 1980, 143). The era of biopolitics begins when the

---

5   For a more extensive discussion, see Braun and Gerhards 2019.

human becomes the object of systematic strategies of shaping and improving. It is the historic moment when the modern state with its technologies
of governing, the focus on man as a living being, and the construct of the
population as an object of government co-emerge. What Foucault terms
biopolitics is the connection between them.

Already before he started working on biopower and biopolitics, Foucault
had shown that 'life' was not a biological fact but a relatively young category
that emerged at the particular historic moment that marked the shift between
the classical and the modern episteme around 1800 (Rentea 2017). Before that,
'life' did not exist, only living beings (Foucault 1994b, 127f.). Life as a category
and possible subject of study emerged with modern biology and the conceptual opposition between the organic and the non-organic. The same historic
moment gave birth to the secular modern state with its technologies of governing and its new area of activities called 'police' (*die Policey*) (Foucault 1994a;
2000). The modern state, Foucault argues, takes over the principle of pastoral
conduct from the church, assuming responsibility for the welfare of both the
individual and the collective, guiding, guarding and protecting them. However, the modern state combines pastoral conduct with new forms of knowledge and new means of enforcement. Moreover, it secularizes the purpose of
conduct; the aim is no longer to save any individual soul but to preserve the
general, this-worldly welfare in terms of health, longevity, wealth and pros-
perity. While salvation as an aim was absolute, individualistic and universal,
the general welfare is relative, gradual, politically confined to a certain collectivity, and open to constant improvement. Salvation was absolute in that it
was ultimately about heaven or hell, salvation or perdition; it was individualistic insofar as the goal was to save *every* human soul, no matter how weak,
corrupt, or evil; and it was universal in that it was not limited to the members of a particular collective. Promoting the general welfare, by contrast, is a
matter of gradual but in principle unlimited progress. And it is not a universal
task; the modern state takes care of its own population within the boundaries
of its own territory. It may strive to expand its territory, but it has no jurisdic-
tion over the people living beyond it. On the contrary, improving the relative
welfare and the relative strength of its own population, as compared to others, is now a way for the state to improve its own relative strength and power
in a world divided into competing states (Foucault, 2000).

The modern state, in this account, performs its pastoral power through
the 'police' (Foucault 2007, 312f.). Police—*die Policey*—was the Prussian prototype of what we now know as public policy. Police connects the welfare of the

individuals to that of the collective and vice versa; it seeks to improve the individuals' welfare through improving the general welfare and to improve the general welfare through guiding the individuals' behavior and way of living. Thus, the political rationality of early police, as Foucault describes it, was already a biopolitical one, targeting, shaping, managing and improving the life processes in the population as a means to strengthen the power of the state.

The political rationality that emerged here targets life both at the level of the individual—health, birth, death, survival, procreation, morality and way of life—and at the level of the collective—its composition, growth, development, average health status and life span, mortality and birth rates and so forth. Note, however, that it is not confined to shaping and improving life in the biological sense. The life governed according to this biopolitical rationality was not merely the life studied by medicine or biology. It was also the life that was being led, the orderly life, the way of living, the standard of living; the life that became governed through police referred to public health and well-being, but also to trade, work, public order, and even entertainment.

> In short, life is the object of the police: the indispensable, the useful, and the superfluous. That people survive, live, and even do better than just that: this is what the police has to ensure. (Foucault 1994a, 321)

Hence, Foucault does not establish an opposition of biological and social life; there is no 'life itself' underneath social and cultural life that would somehow form a more fundamental layer of human existence. Biopolitics in this sense is not the production of 'bare life', as Agamben (1998) terms it; it is not the layer of life that is laid bare after the social layer is taken off, after the social being has been stripped of its rights, social status and social relations. Unlike Agamben, Foucault does not assume a conceptual opposition between the biological and the social, between bare life or life itself and social life. There is no ahistorical, non-social, biological 'life' in Foucault. Also, in contrast to Agamben, Foucault does not conceptualize biopolitics or biopower as essentially negative forces that would operate through subtraction, taking away individuals' rights, status, social relations and ultimately lives. For Foucault, unlike Agamben, biopolitics is not quintessentially thanatopolitics. However, this does not mean that biopolitics and thanatopolitics are mutually exclusive. Rather, for Foucault, biopolitics may operate through a repertoire of political technologies ranging from more liberal to more disciplinary or even repressive or murderous ones. They may range from promoting individual self-determination via incentivizing or supporting socially desired behavior to more disciplinary technologies, control mechanisms and negative sanctions, and ultimately the use of force and actual killing. There is no causal necessity that leads from one step to the next, from fostering life to taking life, no biopolitical determinism that starts with freedom and inevitably ends with force. Many twentieth-century states had eugenics policies in place, but not all of them killed psychiatric patients and committed genocide.

The point is, however, that strategies of managing, improving, and optimizing human life are never *only* supportive. They have a dark side as well. They inevitably involve norms and standards for measuring achievement, criteria for what qualifies as better, desirable, or improved and what does not. Thus, they constitutively imply scales of differential value of humans. The more systematic such strategies are, the more they involve measurements for determining success or failure, calculating the relation of means and ends, risks and benefits, distinguishing one from the other, stating progress or stagnation, and criteria for positioning individuals at some point on the spectrum. In this sense, biopolitics includes strategies and mechanisms for preserving and improving, but also for assessing, rating and calculating the relative health, fitness, productivity and functionality of individuals and collectivities—strategies that constantly establish, apply, confirm, refine and reinforce systems of differential valuation of humans. It strives to increase the level of health, fitness and productivity in the collective and ascribes differential value to individuals according to whether and to what extent they meet these standards. Thus, biopolitics, as Lennard Davis puts it, "is always a politics of *differential vulnerability*" (Davis 2020, emph. i. o.); those individuals or groups found not to meet the standards become vulnerable to the other side of biopolitics: to strategies and mechanisms of neglect and discrimination or, in the worst case, of selection and elimination.

The Nazi state took biopolitics to the extreme, pursuing the improvement of the master race through strategies of systematically eliminating those deemed to contaminate, weaken or burden it. This does not mean that biopolitics can be equated with Nazi biopolitics. Rather, we can see a continuum of biopolitical technologies ranging from promoting, supporting and improving life by means of social policy, urban planning, public health and the like to selection and ultimately elimination practices. Biopolitics is not limited to elimination, nor is there any kind of causal mechanism that necessarily leads from more benevolent forms of biopolitics to a politics of elimination. However, it does mean that the latter is always a possibility, the reason being that biopolitical rationality inevitably implies systems of differential valuation and, accordingly, differential vulnerabilities. These systems do not necessarily refer to biological categories; in fact, it is a common misunderstanding, as the following chapters will point out, that Nazi biopolitics in general was based on biologistic assumptions and that it was biologism that made it murderous. Nazi biopolitics, I will argue, selected along the lines of qualities the Nazis deemed useful for improving the Aryan master race, such as health, strength, fitness, productivity and performance capability[6]; superiority and inferiority were ascribed along these lines. Actually, the Nazis were not particularly interested in whether what they saw as inferiority was caused by social circumstances, genetic conditions, misfortune, political opposition, insubordination or a combination thereof; what mattered was whether someone conformed to their standards or not. Liberal democratic societies also allocate social positions, life chances and value along these standards; they also valuate health, productivity, functionality and performance even if they like to think of themselves as being the antithesis to Nazi biopolitics given that their systems of differential valuation are not based on 'biologism'. Nevertheless, they may establish and apply systems of differential valuation as well. Actually, as I will argue in Chapter 7, the mode of production still underlying liberal democratic societies today, namely capitalism, is characterized by a logic of accumulation that strongly converges with the logic of biopolitics in that both are directed at optimizing the forces of life and making them productive. Thus, following the Foucauldian line of thought, I understand biopolitics as a set of strategies and mechanisms flowing from a political rationality of optimizing the vital qualities of individuals and collectivities with a repertoire of strategies and mechanisms ranging from promoting, supporting and preserving life to devaluating and destroying it.

1.4   Biopolitical Temporality

Seen from this angle, biopolitics is an essentially temporalized affair. It is constituted by temporality in three regards: it is an essentially historical phenomenon, it targets temporal objects, and it is characterized by a specific future-oriented temporal logic of increasing, improving and optimizing.

First, biopolitics is a radically historical phenomenon. It is not a universal, timeless feature of human existence, but co-emerges with the modern

---

6   *Leistungsfähigkeit* would be the German term; there is no direct English equivalent.

episteme, the modern state and the modern technologies of government at a specific historic moment: the threshold of modernity. Following Reinhart Koselleck (2003; 2004), we can go one step further and say that it is not even one historic moment among others but rather the moment at which eschatological time was superseded by historical time; one could say that it was the moment at which historical time entered history. Between 1600 and 1800, Koselleck shows, a new order of time arose. Time opened up into an unbounded this-worldly future, no longer delimited by the final judgement and the end of time. The new future was amenable to, but also required, forecast and planning; the modern, secular state adopted the responsibility of organizing it. The secular state replaced prophecy with rational prognosis and drew on the latter for policy making and planning, that is, for bringing about certain futures and preventing others. Together, the notion of an unbounded future and rational prognosis as a form of knowledge allowed for what Foucault terms the formation of the *Policey* and the corresponding technologies of government. Government as the conduct of conduct now meant to bring about desired futures and prevent undesired ones.

Second, biopolitics targets temporalized objects. As argued above, police and its technologies of governing were the first manifestation of biopolitics in the Foucauldian sense. Emerging at the threshold of modernity, police was a set of government strategies that was geared at shaping the future through governing the conduct of individuals, their way of living, working, behaving and procreating, as well as life processes in the population on an aggregate level. On both levels, that of the individual and that of the collective, biopolitics strives to govern temporal phenomena: behavior and processes both take place in time; they exist only insofar and for as long as they take place.[7] While sovereign power operates according to a territorial logic—defending the territory, expanding the territory, issuing laws for a certain territory, drawing lines between what is permitted and what is prohibited and sanctioning transgressions[8]—biopolitics operates according to a temporal logic, targeting the movement of bodies, the behavior of individuals, the way they lead their lives, their carrying out of work, family, and sexual life, and the life processes of the population on an aggregate level. On the aggregate level, it links past, present

---

7   It is a curious thing to characterize temporal phenomena as those that take *place*, but I cannot think of a better term.

8   For a more detailed outline of the various forms of power in Foucault and their respective relation to different temporal regimes, see Portschy 2020.

and future through generating statistical data in the present, constructing larger processes through ordering and articulating them, extrapolating statements from past processes into the future, informing governmental policies in the present that are geared at shaping the future. In a sense, it constitutes time by articulating past, present and future. In short, biopolitics targets temporal events and sequences and seeks to shape and direct their future course.

Third, biopolitics does so in a particularly temporalized way. Others have already pointed out that biopolitics in the Foucauldian sense is critically future-oriented and that this orientation towards 'futurity' defines it as a constitutively modern affair (Tellmann 2017). However, it is not simply its future-orientedness as such that characterizes modern biopolitics; rather, it is its specific mode of future-orientedness, namely the dynamic of constantly increasing, improving and optimizing the forces of human life. Modern biopolitics is distinct from earlier historic forms of ruling human behavior in that it does not only aspire to preserve, control or stabilize certain ways of life[9], including their sexual, procreative and otherwise bodily aspects but strives to enable and optimize both the exploitation and the growth of the human life force. It emerges at the intersection of scientific, economic and political rationalities that are all directed at increasing the vital productivity of the human. Hence, it is not simply the fact *that* biopolitics is oriented towards the future but that it is oriented towards increasing and improving the functionality of human life that we must come to terms with (Wehling 2008, 251). In the modern era, Foucault states:

> 'Deduction' has tended to be no longer the major form of power but merely one element among others, working to incite, reinforce, control, monitor, optimize, and organize the forces under it: a power bent on generative forces, making them grow, and ordering them, rather than one dedicated to impeding them, making them submit, or destroying them. (Foucault 1980, 136)

In this sense, biopolitics is about the calculated, rational, systematic improvement of the human, driven forward by means of knowledge production as well as political technologies and various combinations thereof. It includes a type of strategies and mechanisms that are directed at managing, increasing and

---

9   This is what Mika Ojakangas (2016) fails to acknowledge when he argues that biopolitics is not a specifically modern phenomenon but is already present in the writings of Plato and Aristotle.

optimizing the human life force as a means of increasing productivity and functionality in the population.

The problem, for one thing, is that strategies of optimizing human life, whether through political, medical or other technologies, involve norms and standards for measuring achievement and establish what qualifies as better, desirable, or improved and what does not. Thus, such strategies constitutively imply scales of differential human value. Therefore, there is an inbuilt danger in biopolitical rationality, a dangerous tendency that may remain latent over long periods of time and be kept in check by systems of rights and a culture of solidarity but that may linger and be actuated under changing circumstances: the tendency to sacrifice less valuable lives for the life of the collective. It is rooted in the fact that individual human life is limited but the life of the collective is not. Optimizing the life force of an individual is limited by death, but optimizing the life force of the collective is not. Thus, strategies of biopolitical optimization must capitulate in the face of individual death and shift their ambitions instead to the level of the collective. When the life of the collective is reigning supreme and/or when represented as being in danger and in need of defence, sacrificing those who do not meet the standards can appear perfectly compatible with biopolitical rationality as such. This is what happened in selective sterilization policies and in Nazi 'euthanasia', and I will argue that it also what happened in Nazi persecution of homosexuals and so-called 'asocials'. It is also what happens when calculations of future healthy, fit and productive life years determine who shall live and who not. At this point, we can approach the relationships between biopolitics, temporality, historic justice and what I term injuries of normality.

1.5   Biopolitics, Historic Justice and Injuries of Normality

The past thirty years have seen an increased preoccupation with the legacies of past atrocities and systematic human rights violations. A fast-growing field of scholarly discourse and political activity has emerged, marked by concepts such as restitution, reparations, apology, and commemoration[10]. In political science, international relations, and law the concept of transitional justice (TJ)

---

10   Indeed, the volume of the literature has undeniably become unmanageable. For an overview, see De Greiff 2006; Palmer, Clark, and Granville 2012. A classic for a conceptual outline is still Martha Minow's (1998) *Between Vengeance and Forgiveness*.

prevails. TJ has grown into a well-established field of inquiry and intervention since the late 1990s. Despite the consolidation of the field, transition is still a contested concept; there is no unanimous understanding of whether it should more narrowly refer to transitions from autocratic to democratic types of government or be expanded to include transitions from conflict to peace, from instability to stability, or any major changes in the form of exercizing authority, which would also include changes within established democracies (Winter 2014). Furthermore, a number of efforts have been made to expand the scope of transitional justice in order to cover hitherto neglected issues such as social and economic injustices including forced evictions, the destruction of homes, or long-term social inequity (Arbour 2006; Miller 2008), sexualized violence and gender-related structural inequality (Buckley-Zistel and Stanley 2012; Hitzel-Cassagnes and Martinsen 2014), or systematic harm to indigenous people (Balint, Evans, and McMillan 2014; Corntassel and Holder 2008).

Here, I want to draw attention to a further type of historic wrong that has been largely overlooked by transitional and historic justice studies: systematic harm inflicted on people categorized as abnormal, deviant, deficient or inferior with respect to norms and standards of health, fitness, functionality, productivity and usefulness. I term such violations injuries of normality. They refer to notions of normality in a threefold sense:

First, injuries of normality emerge from biopolitical strategies of detecting, marking and selecting out the 'abnormals', the weak and the unproductive, whose lives, according to this logic, pose an impediment to the enhancement of the vital capacities of the collective, whether the latter is constructed as society, the nation, the race or another entity. Within a biopolitical rationality, the lives of those deemed abnormal, deficient or inferior pose a threat or a burden to the improvement of the collective. The logic of normality and deviance may overlap or intersect with notions of race, ethnicity, gender, religion or other markers but is also distinct from these. It targets people not primarily as members of a given social or cultural group. Members of a dominant, unmarked social group can also fall victim to injuries of normality if and when they are found to deviate from the standards of normality.

Second, this type of harm is not confined to situations of exceptional crisis or regimes of exceptional evil but also occurs in situations that generally qualify as normality. The logic of marking and selecting people categorized as disabled, deviant, dysfunctional or simply useless is not limited to situations of strife or war, nor to autocratic regimes, although these may aggravate it.

Third, the norms and standards underlying injuries of normality tend to be deeply entrenched in social, political, cultural or legal practices, institutions, discourses and thought systems, so much so that practices and policies of enforcing them are largely considered normal by contemporaries, even if they involve grave harm to those who are targeted.

In this book, I refer only to some cases of injuries of normality, namely the persecution under Nazi rule of people categorized as mentally ill, disabled, hereditarily ill, homosexual, or 'asocial'. Note that this is only a small selection of extreme cases and by no means a conclusive list of this type of historic injustice. The focus here is not so much on how and why these crimes were committed in the first place but on whether and to what extent the democratic successor state, the Federal Republic was prepared to reflect upon the wrongness of these crimes.

The Federal Republic of Germany is often referred to as a model case with regard to coming to terms with the past. Post-war (West) Germany, it is said, has confronted its Nazi past through education policies, apologies and payments of compensation in ways that could serve as a model for other countries that have committed human rights violations (Buruma 1994). German Holocaust reparations have been called "the prototype of all reparations politics" (Torpey 2006, 4). Yet the history of German *Aufarbeitung und Wiedergutmachung* is also a history of denial and disregard, most notably with respect to so-called forgotten victims. The term 'forgotten victims' is a misnomer, since some groups of Nazi victims were not forgotten at all but deliberately excluded from reparations, such as communists, deserters, homosexuals, or those who had been forcibly sterilized under the Law for the Prevention of Hereditary Diseases. The 1953 Federal Indemnification Act (*Bundesentschädigungsgesetz, BEG*) clearly and conclusively defined who was to be considered a victim of Nazi persecution, namely someone who had been persecuted for "racial, religious, or political reasons or because of the victim's world view" (BEG §1(1)). Thereby, the law sharply delineated those injuries that would be identified as Nazi injustices and qualify for reparations from those that would not.[11] Victims of selective sterilization, the persecution of homosexuals and of

---

11   The wording goes back to the so-called Bermuda Conference formula of "racial, religious, and political refugees" framed by the U.S. and British Allies in 1943. Regula Ludi argues that the Bermuda formula drew heavily on the idea of the Minority Treaties that had been established in the interwar period to protect national, ethnic and religious minorities (Ludi 2012, 18f.). The West German post-war reparation scheme adopted the

those categorized as 'asocial' were deliberately excluded from this reparation scheme as they were not considered victims of typical Nazi persecution. The same applied to Roma and Sinti as the German Federal Court (BGH) ruled in 1956 that racial persecution under the Nazis did not begin until March 1943. Deportations and arbitrary incarceration prior to that date were considered as a means of criminal prevention, not as persecution (Feyen 2009, 330ff.). By way of this exclusion, and in many other ways as well, the stigma that had been inflicted on these groups of victims was reconfirmed and prolonged into the era of democracy. For survivors, the transition to democracy did not coincide with the end of stigmatization, exclusion and the experience of violence. In many cases, personal, institutional or legal continuities stretched into the age of the new republic: Experts called for a new sterilization law in order to protect public health; the paragraph of the Criminal Code that banned male homosexuality remained in place in its 1935 version until 1969; girls from socially deprived backgrounds were confined to institutional 'care' for reasons of their 'sexual depravity'.

My aim in this book is to shed light on this continuity by means of a threefold argument: First, Nazi selective sterilization policy, the persecution of male homosexuals, and the persecution of people categorized as 'asocial' were driven by a biopolitical rationality aimed at improving the vital qualities of the larger collective. They were firmly anchored in a biopolitical rationality that values normality, health, functionality, productivity and fitness. Second, this rationality did not dissolve in 1945. Third, the victims of selective sterilization policy, the persecution of male homosexuals, and the persecution of 'asocials' were denied entitlement to reparations and, for a long time, also an apology and acknowledgement of the injustice they suffered—because and for as long as the relevant policy actors in the post-war state and society shared this biopolitical rationality. Thus, struggles over the biopolitics of the past are simultaneously struggles over the power of biopolitical rationality in the present, and the incidents referred to at the outset of this chapter show that these struggles are not yet over.

Bermuda formula but included persecution for political reasons. In other words, West German post-war reparations were crucially informed by the ethnic minority protection frame, and I would argue that it has remained the dominant frame in German post-war reparations to the present time.

1.6   Outline of the Book

The chapters in this book have been written at different points in time. They should each be comprehensible as stand-alone units. The disadvantage of this structure is, of course, that repetitions, discontinuities and even discrepancies may occur. Thoughts, concepts, foci and perspectives may have shifted over time, both in my thinking and in the literature.

This chapter was intended to introduce the three themes of this book—biopolitics, temporality and historic justice—and explain how they relate to one other. I have argued that biopolitics is a specifically modern phenomenon characterized by a future-oriented logic of optimizing the human life force on the level of the collective and that this logic implies the differential valuation of human lives which, in the extreme, can involve the elimination of those deemed less valuable.

Chapter 2 reviews a paradigmatic case of modern biopolitical logic: the politics of eugenics in the twentieth century. It shows that eugenics is best understood as a modern political project encompassing knowledge production, a broad repertoire of political mechanisms and technologies and engagement of civil society actors such as professional associations, women's organizations, charities and others. The eugenic project is a pinnacle of biopolitical rationality in that it was directed at enhancing the vital qualities of the larger collective through political technologies involving systems of differential valuation, exposure und vulnerability. The chapter refutes the common misunderstanding that eugenics was basically a project of the political Right based on biologistic, sexist, and racist assumptions. In fact, historical research has provided ample evidence that eugenic thought and practices emerged from a broad range of political, cultural, and scientific orientations and existed in many different variants. What they have in common is not an anti-modern, 'reactionary', pseudo-scientific attitude but rather a modern biopolitical rationality.

The ensuing Chapters 3, 4 and 5 are devoted to the question how the Federal Republic of Germany has come to terms—or not—with the injuries of normality committed by the Nazi regime. Through three case studies—the policy of selective sterilization, the persecution of male homosexuals, and the persecution of 'asocials'—I reconstruct when, how, with what result and on which grounds victims' claims to reparations and rehabilitation were denied or approved. All three groups of victims belong to the wrongly named set of 'forgotten victims' who were excluded from entitlement to reparations according to the Federal Indemnification Act. They were only granted the right to file for compensation when, in the 1980s, new hardship compensation funds were established as a second track for compensating Nazi victims. These funds, however, were designated to compensate for damages suffered due to the war or similar circumstances, not for wrongdoing on the part of the state. In addition, no official apology was issued and no official site of commemoration established until well into the twenty-first century. I trace the struggles for reparations and rehabilitation and the responses by relevant actors such as policy-makers, courts and experts as well as the rationales given for these exclusions. The focus of these chapters is on the question of what in these crimes, if anything, state actors acknowledged as wrong. It becomes clear that state actors did not grant rehabilitation and reparations because and for as long as they were unwilling to condemn the political rationality that had motivated these crimes in the past, a rationality according to which people categorized as disabled, mentally ill, mentally retarded, work-shy or weak, sick, deviant due to their homosexuality, or otherwise unproductive, useless or worthless formed a threat or burden to society that the state was obliged to fend off. In short, it was the endurance of a biopolitical rationality of enhancing the health, strength and productivity of the population through reducing the number of the allegedly unhealthy, weak and unproductive that stood in the way of historic justice. It was considered normal rather than wrong. Of the three cases presented, we can see that the denial of wrongness persisted the longest in the case of the persecution of 'asocials'; it was not until 2020 that the Bundestag officially condemned this practice. Earlier in the century, in 2004, it had officially declared that Nazi sterilization policy had been utterly wrong, although upon close inspection, one can see that the verdict of wrongness did not refer to selective sterilization policy per se but sterilization policy as a stepping stone on the way to 'euthanasia' and the Holocaust. An exceptional case of historic justice occurred in 2017, when the Bundestag repealed the criminal convictions that had been issued for male homosexuality *after* 1945 and also granted the right to reparations to those who had suffered from them. In this case, the state not only condemned the wrongdoing of its predecessor but also its own wrongs; moreover, in the same act, it formally abandoned the biopolitical construction that male homosexuality is debilitating to state and society and must thus be curbed.

Chapters 6 and 7 examine the nexus of biopolitics, temporality and the differential valuation of human life on a social–theoretical level. Chapter 6 discusses the overlaps and intersections but also the differences between Foucault's analysis of biopolitics and Hannah Arendt's analysis of totalitarianism. Both Arendt and Foucault, I argue, problematize the nexus of the assimilation of politics to management and social engineering, the structure of processual time, and modern politics' and society's preoccupation with 'life'; both draw attention to the more sinister implications of this nexus. While Foucault, however, presents the more historicized analysis, Arendt offers an alternative, non-biopolitical understanding of politics, life, and time which she captures in the concept of natality. Chapter 7 explores the intersections and convergences between Foucault's conceptualization of biopolitics and Marx's analysis of capitalism concerning the relationship between power, life and time under conditions of modernity. I posit that both Marx and Foucault highlight the productive dimension of power and that life, for both, is a key resource for this historically specific type of power—in fact, it is *the* resource that can simultaneously be exploited and increased. Finally, in both Marx and Foucault, temporality is key: Capital and biopower/biopolitics share a temporal structure characterized by an ongoing, unlimited process of ever-increasing productivity. This process, they state, is directed at the future, but not at a future of fulfilment of needs. Rather, it is a permanent, unlimited process of optimizing and increasing the human forces of life, a process that cannot possibly come to a meaningful end. Again, we see that the quest for the constant improvement of human beings is accompanied by the constant construction of deficient life, life that does not meet the norms and standards of health and fitness, of functionality and productivity. Rendering this nexus amenable to critical reflection is the purpose of this book.

2 Biopolitics and Modernity: Revisiting the Eugenics Project

For a long time, the notion of eugenics was firmly associated with the notions of racism and biological determinism; eugenics was taken to be a reactionary, pseudo-scientific ideology, typically emerging from an authoritarian, fascist or totalitarian state. Hence, eugenics was located on one side of a binary matrix, together with racism, biological determinism, pseudo-science, coercion, control and authoritarianism as opposed to tolerance, sound science, freedom and democracy on the other. In this vein, Garland Allen, one of the first historians of eugenics in the 1970s, lamented that British eugenics

> became a reactionary programme for solving social problems through biological technology. A direct heir of the Social Darwinist philosophy of the late nineteenth century, twentieth century eugenics had a strongly racist bias which explained all differences between people in hereditarian terms. Eugenicists saw all racial and ethnic groups (what they persisted in calling 'races') in hierarchical terms, with the Anglo-Saxon on top and all other groups ranging below in a scale of decreasing whiteness. (Allen 1976, 111)

With the emergence of the new genetics in the 1980s and 90s, the picture of eugenics as a repressive, reactionary and racist ideology often served as a background against which genetics compared quite favorably. While eugenics, in this picture, put the emphasis on race, the new genetics served the purpose of health; while eugenics was state-sponsored and operated through force, genetic testing was a matter of individual freedom and self-determination. Eugenics was pseudo-science; genetics was sound science. As David Gems of the Galton Library summarizes:

> Among the numerous reasons for disapproving of 20th Century (*sic*) eugenics programmes are the fact that they were typically not only authoritarian, but

also based on an inadequate understanding of human genetics, particularly before the Second World War. Then there was the special place of eugenics in the deranged ideology of German National Socialism. Arguably, Nazi atrocities justified in terms of eugenics (principally the Holocaust) are more the consequence of the brutal, totalitarian and at times insane character of Nazism, than the desire to promote human well-being through genetics. These failings of eugenics are historically contingent and do not necessarily follow from the idea of promoting human genetic well-being. (Gems 1999, 199)

Today's genetic engineering, it has been argued, is entirely different from the eugenics of former times, given that

[...] population eugenics involves commanding people to produce desired genotypic or phenotypic traits. This sort of eugenics is not the same as allowing an individual or couple voluntarily to choose a heritable trait in their sperm, egg, embryo, or fetus, motivated by their view of what is good or desirable. (Caplan, McGeen et al. 1999, 338)

Others hold that eugenics and the new genetics are not so different after all, but that both should be approved since genetic technologies in combination with reproductive medicine may serve to select against undesired qualities in human offspring and enhance the quality of the nation, population, society or human species (Lynn 2001). In this view, eugenics was not itself a problem; only the Nazis' *abuse* of it constituted one. Even if the new genetics does bring about a return of eugenics, then, this is considered acceptable unless it is coupled with a return of Nazism.

As part of a different endeavor, namely seeking to capture the distinctively novel features of biopolitics in the 21st century, Nikolas Rose also contrasts the old eugenics to the new genetics. Contemporary biopolitics, he argues, is characterized by a molecularization of knowledge, a focus on optimizing the healthy body, new somatic identities, an expanding bioeconomy, and new forms of collectivity that he and Paul Rabinow have termed biosociality (Rose 2001; Rabinow and Rose 2006; Rose 2007). We need a new conceptual framework, he argues, to capture the configuration of contemporary biopolitics in its own right; classifying it as a new form of eugenics will not suffice. As true as this may be, the contrast between old eugenics and new genetics is misleading as it draws on a simplified and reduced understanding of historic eugenics.

Eugenics, Rose claims, "was a collective attempt imposed by a state to improve the quality of the population, in a geopolitical context often seen as a struggle between races. What we see today is something different." (Rose 2006, 13) Politically, Rose argues, eugenics was sponsored and administered by the state, whereas the new biopolitics is taking place in a variety of fields and is promoted by a variety of non-state actors such as self-help groups, ethics committees, professional associations, and not least individuals (Rose 2001). Epistemologically, eugenics relied on the notion of genetic determinism and biology as destiny, whereas contemporary biomedicine and genetics refute the view of biology as destiny and, rather, regard life as something open to modification and enhancement.

This chapter challenges the dichotomy between an old, reactionary, racist, state-sponsored, biologically deterministic eugenics and a new, scientifically sound, unideological, non-racist genetics serving the health and self-determination of the individual. It does so, however, less by questioning the genetics component of the model and more by revisiting the historic eugenics project and demonstrating that it was not necessarily reactionary, racist, deterministic and state-sponsored. At least, these were not its most significant and distinctive features. It is true that eugenics was profoundly anti-egalitarian and incompatible with notions of fundamental human rights and dignity. However, it was not confined to the reactionary, authoritarian or anti-democratic end of the political spectrum. Eugenics was a multi-facetted, international, politically diverse and essentially modern phenomenon of the early 20th century (Engs 2005; Wecker 2009; Bashford and Levine 2010).

Although eugenics aligned itself with various political rationalities, its varieties have some ideas and assumptions in common. The eugenics project revolves around two basic claims, one theoretical and one practical: first, that humans can and in fact must be classified on a scale of differential worth. In the words of Harry Laughlin, one of the founding fathers of US eugenics:

> Every science which deals with man in any way attempts to make its own classification of mankind. [...] Its [eugenics'] classification must be based upon the ability of particular stocks to function as socially valuable units and to reproduce themselves in proportion with their race values. (Laughlin 1925, 31)

Eugenics thus establishes a system of differential worth among humans based on the presence or absence of certain qualities that are, assumedly, passed down to future generations. Second, eugenics assumes that it is both necessary and possible to reduce the number of individuals of inferior quality to the benefit of those of superior quality and thereby to improve the quality of the larger social collective. To quote Laughlin again: "It is a big job to purge the race, but it is one of the principal practical tasks of eugenics" (Laughlin 1925, 34).

Whether or not eugenics aligned itself with reactionary, authoritarian, racist, biologist rationalities, it maintained these two assumptions. At its core lies the distinction between the fit and the unfit, the useful and the useless, the inferior and the superior, those who are an asset to society and those who are a burden. Combined with the assumption that individuals pass these qualities on to coming generations, this distinction constitutes a eugenic matrix as part of a larger biopolitical rationality demanding to reduce the numbers of the unfit, the dysfunctional and the unproductive in order to improve the fitness, functionality and performance of the social body at large. This biopolitical rationality informed and motivated a wide range of political, academic, social and cultural efforts in the 20th century, whether these were termed eugenics, racial hygiene, social reform, or called by another name.

2.1   A Modern Project

As is generally known, the term 'eugenics' was invented by the British anthropologist and statistician Francis Galton. The new academic discipline that Galton intended to establish was a hybrid creation, a cross between science and social engineering envisioned as useful to policy and planning. Most of all, it was fundamentally oriented towards the future. Galtung thus chose the name 'eugenics' to denote "the study of the agencies under social control that may improve or impair the racial qualities of future generations either physically or mentally" (Galton 1907).

Thus, from the start, eugenics was a field where science and politics, facts and values, practices of knowing and practices of intervening intersected and co-constituted each other. It self-identified as an applied science rather than as basic research.[1] Hence, there was never such a thing as a purely scientific, value-neutral, apolitical discipline of eugenics that eventually became corrupted, that was politically misused or instrumentalized.

---

1   For a detailed study on this aspect in the German context, see Weingart, Kroll et al. 1996.

Furthermore, it was far from being 'reactionary'; its aim was not to uphold the given social order, let alone restore that of the past. It did not draw on tradition, religion, customs or conventions but was decisively oriented towards the future. As Galton saw it, eugenics "extends the function of philanthropy to future generations" (Galton cited in Turda 2010a, 22).

Eugenics' vision for the future, however, was not one of social equality. Galton did not approve of the concept of equality:

> I have no patience with the hypothesis occasionally expressed, and often implied, especially in tales written to teach children to be good, that babies are born pretty much alike [...]. It is in the most unqualified manner that I object to pretensions of natural equality. (Galton cited in Reilly 1991, 3)

Galton's opposition to the concept of equality did not, however, entail the belief that biology was destiny. His goal was not to maintain the biological status quo and stabilize existing inequalities. For Galton, eugenics was about human improvement; the purpose of the new discipline was to accelerate the evolution of mankind under conditions controlled by men. This required a new ethics. In this respect, again, eugenics was far from being 'conservative'. Implementing eugenic ideas required overcoming extant ethical norms, conventions and traditions, which in fact formed an impediment to eugenics. In Germany around 1900, prominent eugenicists explicitly promoted a new, evolutionary, so-called generative ethics, an ethics that would further the hereditary qualities of future generations and the evolution of mankind (Weingart, Kroll et al. 1996, 141). In this vein, Wilhelm Schallmayer, a prominent co-founder of eugenics in Germany who saw himself as a democrat and socialist of sorts, explained that a generative ethics would include "moral obligations in support of the race (that is, in support of the hereditary qualities of future generations of our community)" (Schallmayer cited in Weingart, Kroll et al. 1996, 141).

Thus, for eugenics, the past provided no moral orientation or authority whatsoever; at best, it did not stand in the way. The most extreme version of eugenic politics, Nazi eugenics, consequently took the most anti-conservative stance with respect to ethics. As then-Minister for the Interior Wilhelm Frick stated:

> The scientific study of heredity (based on the progress of the last decade) has enabled us clearly to recognise the rules of heredity and selection as well as their meaning for the nation and state. It gives us the right and the moral

obligation to eliminate hereditary defectives from procreation. No misinter-
preted charity nor religious scruples, based on the dogmas of past centuries,
should prevent us from fulfilling this duty [...]. (Frick cited in Turda 2010a,
111)

From its inception in 19th century Britain to its eliminatory implementation
under the Nazi regime, eugenics took a decidedly modernist stance towards
the future. Eugenics can best be understood as a modernist politico-epis-
temic project encompassing ideas, visions, knowledges and policies promoted
by experts, policy-makers, professionals, practitioners, and an exceptionally
broad variety of civil society actors. What held the project together was the
common mission to improve the socio-biological basis of human life at the
collective level. The type of collective chosen for improvement could differ. It
could be the race, the Aryan race, society, humankind, or another group. In
all cases, though, eugenics sought to strengthen and improve some sort of
collective entity. That entity then became the object of deliberate efforts at
rational intervention. As such, eugenics can be considered the paradigmatic
case of biopolitical modernity (Braun and Gerhards 2019).

The future, however, was a creature of the present. One could not simply
wait for it; it required action—action *in time*. To refrain from intervention and
social engineering would be to open the gates to degeneration. In that sense,
eugenics epitomized modernity as German historian Reinhard Koselleck saw
it. For Koselleck, the idea that the future is open and amenable to deliberate
intervention, and that it in fact requires intervention, marks the threshold of
modernity (Koselleck 1989). Modernity, according to Koselleck, is characterized by the temporalization of history. Well into the 16th century, history was
a time of eschatological expectation, the time that remained before the second coming of Christ, the Final Judgment and the end of time. Modern time,
in contrast, was open-ended and full of possibilities. The future came to be
amenable to human intervention, but at the same time it also became uncer-
tain. Planning it became both feasible and imperative. Until then, the present
had been a long stretch—nothing much would change in any case. Now, it
shrank to the point between past and future where decisions had to be taken.
At the same time, anticipating possible futures, establishing the likelihood
of future developments, deciding which were desirable and which not, push-
ing desirable developments and preventing undesirable ones became part of
the responsibilities and the remit of the state whose legitimacy no longer
originated in a Christian cosmology. From the perspective of eugenics, not

only the economy, human morality, science and technology were amenable to enhancement; human hereditary qualities were as well. It was first and foremost, although not exclusively, the state that was now in charge of action. Importantly, as Koselleck shows, the temporalization of history implies the construction of collectivities such as 'the nation', 'humanity' or 'the race'. These imagined entities were assumed to remain the same through historical changes, thus bearing the marks of history and rendering it observable.[2] What Michel Foucault (1980, 2003) called biopolitics is very similar. Biopolitics, for Foucault, is the form of politics that co-emerged with the modern state and is directed at regulating and enhancing the composition and the qualities of the population. Biopolitics is essentially future-oriented in that it strives for future improvement; it is knowledge-based in that it relies on statistics, correlations and prognoses (Braun and Gerhards 2019). On all of these counts, eugenics can be considered the paradigmatic case of biopolitics.

2.2 Eugenics and Social Reform

Hence, eugenics was not reactionary or conservative. Nor was it typically a project of the political right. Historians of eugenics have provided ample evidence that it had adherents among a broad range of political groupings, including socialists, social democrats, anarchists, and feminists.

The view that eugenics was promoted by political conservatives, at least originally, has been sustained by Daniel Kevles' (1985) influential study on the history of eugenic ideas in Britain and the US. Kevles makes a conceptual distinction between mainline eugenics and reform eugenics. Mainline eugenics, he argues, came first and was eventually superseded by reform eugenics. Kevles refers to mainline eugenics as politically conservative, elitist, rife with racist and anti-Semitic attitudes, scientifically reductionist and politically in favor of compulsory measures. Reform eugenics, in contrast, was developed by leading biologists who objected to mainline eugenics' sexual repressiveness, its class and race prejudices, and above all its false biology. By the mid-1930s, mainline eugenics was in decline due to increasing criticism from reform eugenicists. Thus, in this narrative, sound science overcomes

---

2   Koselleck coins the term "collective singular" (*Kollektivsingular*) here.

bad science along with the latter's problematic political attitudes. After 1945, Kevles states, eugenics was discredited completely due to its Nazi legacy.

Several points have been raised against this account. First, while presented as *the* history of eugenics, it is actually a history of US and UK eugenics with some references to Germany. Furthermore, a number of scholars have questioned Kevles' periodization and shown that eugenic assumptions endured among British, US and German biologists and geneticists long after 1945 (Weindling 1993; Weingart, Kroll et al. 1996, 631ff.; Mazumdar 2002; Dowbiggin 2008). Third, Kevles studies eugenics mainly as a set of ideas, not policies and practices. Due to the focus on scientists and their views, he overlooks the continuity of eugenics after 1945. Selective sterilization laws were *not* abolished in the US after the war; many in fact lasted into the 1950s and 60s (Reilly 1991). In the Scandinavian countries, selective sterilization laws endured into the 1970s[3]. Furthermore, feminist scholars have pointed out that improving the quality of the population continued to form a US policy objective after 1945, although the emphasis was more on the voluntary and pronatalist strategies of encouraging the 'fit' to have more children (Kline 2001; Stern 2005; Ziegler 2008).

Numerous studies have by now pointed out that eugenic values and aspirations were by no means confined to the political right but were quite common on the left as well (Paul 1984; Schwartz 1995). Leading socialists and social reformers such as Sidney and Beatrice Webb (Leonard 2003), Margaret Sangers (Franks 2005; Lamp 2006; Klausen and Bashford 2010), John Maynard Keynes (Leonard 2005), Gunnar and Alva Myrdal (Spektorowski and Mizrachi 2004; Rabenschlag 2008; Kulawik 2009), and Karl Kautsky (Weingart et al. 1996, 108ff.) were proponents of the eugenics project. Conversely, many leading eugenicists such as the founder of social hygiene in Germany, Alfred Grotjahn (Weingart et al. 1996, 108ff.; Ferdinand 2009) and Swiss psychiatrist Auguste Forel (Gerodetti 2006b; Mottier 2008; Mottier and Gerodetti 2007) were sympathetic to socialist ideas or ideas of social reform.[4] Even among adherents of the anarchist movement in France and Spain, which was committed to the values of sexual reform and responsible reproductive self-determination,

---

3   On Scandinavian eugenics, see Broberg and Roll-Hansen 1996; Weindling 1999; Weingart 1999; and Tydén 2010.

4   In Germany, however, as Weingart, Kroll and Bayertz (1996) note, the leftist faction of the eugenic movement was marginal.

many supported the idea of improving the race by preventing the unfit from breeding (Cleminson 2000; Sonn 2005; Cleminson 2008).

2.3   Eugenics and the Question of Race

Another popular notion about eugenics is that it is essentially racist. It is true that race is a pervasive topic in eugenics. Nevertheless, Marius Turda is correct to contend: "Eugenics as such was not necessarily a racist movement: indeed, arguing that eugenics was 'racist' tells us very little" (Turda 2010b, 63).

The relationships between eugenics and racism are multifarious and complex; whether eugenics can be characterized as racist depends first upon the respective national, regional, or political variant of eugenics and second on the meaning of the designation 'racist'. Furthermore, I would inquire whether eugenics is despicable only if and when it ascribes differential worth to people according to the notion of race. Is it less or not at all problematic if worth is ascribed along the lines of health, productivity or fitness?

The term 'race' never had a stable meaning. At the time when the eugenics project emerged, it could refer to a broad variety of constructions of social collectives (Geulen 2007). In the course of the 19th century, the term had increasingly come under the authority of biology and anthropology and given rise to scientific racism (Barkan 1992; Foucault 2003, 43ff.). Scholars of scientific racism claimed that they could classify humans along certain innate physical, mental, or behavioral characteristics; that they could identify a (varying) number of essentially different natural units among humanity that could be ranked into systems of superiority and inferiority; and that race membership caused complex social, cultural, and behavioral phenomena. Yet this was but one use of the term. Concurrently, the word 'race' could, for instance, refer to notions of tribal, family or class lineage (Conze and Sommer 1984). To confuse things further, Galton and later eugenicists often spoke of the human race as the entity that, in their view, was in danger of degeneration or need of improvement. Galton argued that, in contrast to farm animals, the human race had been sadly neglected by breeders:

> The breeders of our domestic animals have discovered many rules by experience, and act upon them to a nicety. But we have not advanced, even to this limited extent, in respect to the human race. [...] If a twentieth part of the cost and pains were spent in measures for the improvement of the human

> race that is spent on the improvement of the breed of horses and cattle, what a galaxy of genius might we not create! (Galton 1865)

Still in 1926, on occasion of an international eugenics congress in Paris, the British Daily Telegraph titled:

> Proposals for legislation which would do for the human race what natural selection does for creatures lower in the scale of life are being discussed in Paris at an international congress of eugenicists. (cited in Gerodetti 2006a, 224)

Both the meaning and the significance of race differed across national, regional, and political strands of the eugenics project. Scientific racism was an influential but not unanimously shared belief here; its influence in different national settings varied. The same holds true for the relationship between racism and eugenics at the political level. In the US, eugenic organizations such as the American Breeders Association and the Galton Society were concerned both about hereditary differences between races and about differential breeding of the fit and the unfit (Selden n.y.). In the early 1890s, concerns about the alleged fecundity of the unfit publicly aligned with racist concerns about dysgenic effects of immigration and interracial marriage and gave rise to an advocacy coalition that successfully lobbied for immigration restrictions and marriage laws on eugenic and racial grounds (Yamin 2008). Between 1875 and 1924, a number of US states had miscegenation laws in place that made it illegal for a white person to marry someone defined as a Negro (Reilly 1991, 25; Lombardo 1996; Dorr 1999). Since the early 1900s, advocates of racist marriage restrictions had received increasing support from protagonists of the eugenics movement such as Charles Davenport and Harry Laughlin, who provided scientific rationales for their demands (Reilly and Shaw 1983; Micklos and Carlson 2000; Lombardo n.y.). Interracial marriage, they argued, would inevitably lead to degeneration and the decline of the superior, namely White race. Eugenicists also supported the demand to further restrict existing miscegenation laws and enact new ones. Eugenic efforts led inter alia to the passing of the Virginia Racial Integrity Act of 1924 (Reilly and Shaw 1983; Micklos and Carlson 2000).

Similarly, eugenicists in the US identified the immigration of certain racialized groups, in particular immigrants from Southern and Eastern Europe, as one of the main causes of degeneration and lobbied for restrictive immigration laws (Micklos and Carlson 2000; Hansen and King 2001). Their efforts were translated into the 1917 Immigration Restriction Law, which restricted the immigration of undesirables such as

> idiots, imbeciles, epileptics, alcoholics, poor, criminals, beggars, any person suffering attacks of insanity, those with tuberculosis, and those who have any form of dangerous contagious disease, aliens who have a physical disability that will restrict them from earning a living in the United States [...] (Lombardo n.y.).

In addition, Laughlin's and other eugenicists' studies fed into the 1924 Johnson-Reed Act based on national quotas (Hansen and King 2001, 253).

US selective sterilization policies were also racialized in several ways. Alexandra Stern has shown that in California (which had by far the most extended and enduring sterilization policy in the US), although the wording of the law was race- and ethnicity-neutral, implementation was not, and that sterilization disproportionately affected foreign-born immigrants, African Americans and Mexicans (Stern 2005, 1131).

Thus, in the US, the eugenic project was closely intertwined with policies that deliberately discriminated against racialized groups. Racism in this sense was supported by eugenic rationales and inscribed into immigration law, marriage restrictions and selective sterilization laws. These policies operated through negative provisions such as exclusion, restriction, violation and prohibition of racialized groups. These laws and their implementation were authored and controlled by those members of the unmarked group, namely White, Anglo-Saxon US nationals, who considered themselves hereditarily superior.

Yet, these policies could also affect White US citizens who were deemed "socially inadequate", as Laughlin put it (Wilson 2002). "Socially inadequate", Lizzie Seal shows (Seal 2013), was a common label in US eugenic, psychiatric and welfare discourses in the 1910s, 20s and 30s for the so-called dependent poor, that is, those considered unable to sustain themselves economically and meet the demands of capitalist society. The socially inadequate, for Laughlin, included "feeble-minded, insane, epileptic, inebriate, criminalistic and other degenerate persons" who were "maintained wholly or in part by public expense" (Laughlin cited in Seal 2013, 147). 'Feeble-minded' and 'socially inadequate' operated as labels that linked 'substandard whiteness' and poverty to notions of moral deficiency, signalling an urgent need for state intervention. They specifically served as markers for 'tainted whiteness' (Stubblefield 2007) or 'substandard whiteness' (Seal 2013, 154). "Whereas black people would have been regarded as automatically inferior, low quality whites needed to be identified from amongst the white population. 'Degenerate' whiteness mapped onto poverty." (Seal 2013, 154)

In Germany, relations between eugenics and race played out differently and the term 'race' was allocated a more prominent role. In 1895, Alfred Ploetz, a major founder of eugenics in Germany, deliberately coined the term racial hygiene (*Rassenhygiene*) (Ploetz 1895) to denote a body of knowledge that elsewhere would have figured under the label of eugenics. Ploetz distinguished between two concepts of race: one that denoted the multiplicity of morphologically distinct groups within the human species (*Systemrasse* or *Varietät*) and one that referred to the biological quality of entire populations (*Vitalrasse*). The programme of racial hygiene, Ploetz maintained, should refer to the latter. For him, the purpose of racial hygiene was to prevent racial degeneration and improve the hereditary quality of the population as a whole (Weingart, Kroll et al. 1996, 91f.). The aim of Ploetz and some like-minded colleagues such as Fritz Lenz was explicitly to improve the Nordic race in order to defend it against a presumed Slavic threat (Weiss 1990). Others, such as the Association for National Regeneration (*Bund für Volksaufartung*) favored the term 'eugenics' but interpreted it as a nonracist endeavor to fight national degeneration and improve the hereditary fitness of the working classes (Weiss 1990, 35).[5] Another famous eugenicist in Germany, Wilhelm Schallmayer, who considered himself a socialist and a democrat, preferred the term *Rassehygiene* to that of *Rassenhygiene* in order to dissociate it from older racial theories of Gobineauan provenance (Weingart, Kroll et al. 1996, 93f.). The term *Rassehygiene* (without *n*) indicated a single race instead of different races. As shown by Weingart, Kroll and Bayertz (1996) show, however, the majority of German racial hygiene scholars sympathized with the construction of a supposedly superior Nordic race, Aryan race, German culture or other notion.

Yet what does this tell us about the relationship between eugenics and racism in the German case? Studies that interrogate the relationship between eugenics, racial hygiene, racism and Nazism point out connections, interlinkages, and collaborations as well as personal, discursive, and institutional overlaps; tensions between these strands, though, also appear (Schmuhl 1992; Weingart, Kroll et al. 1996; Wecker, Braunschweig et al. 2009). Before 1933, the

---

5   Yet, in 1931, the *Bund für Volksaufartung* merged with the *Deutsche Gesellschaft für Rassenhygiene* (German Association for Racial Hygiene) to found the *Deutsche Gesellschaft für Rassenhygiene* (Eugenik).

eugenics project in Germany had not been the most advanced one internationally; racial hygiene was well established in the forms of professional associations, academic positions and research institutions, but unlike its counterparts in the US and Scandinavia, German eugenics had not yet been translated into policies.

However, key concepts of racial hygiene featured in the Nazi programme as early as 1924, when Hitler incorporated entire passages of the so-called Baur-Fischer-Lenz, the racial hygiene classic at the time, into *Mein Kampf* (Weingart, Kroll et al. 1996, 372f.). Already at this point, the idea of eugenic selection formed an integral element of Nazi programmatics, tightly linked to racial purification, imperialist expansion and eliminatory anti-Semitism. While racial hygiene scholars had not necessarily sympathized with Nazism before 1933, they overwhelmingly embraced the Nazi seizure of power because Hitler, as psychiatrist Ernst Rüdin declared in 1934, would now at last allow them to translate their visions into reality (Weingart, Kroll et al. 1996, 390). And indeed, within two years, the Nazi regime enacted a full series of laws and measures directed at hereditary improvement and racial purification[6].

One of the first of these was the Law for the Prevention of Offspring with Hereditary Diseases of July 1933—which I will refer to as the Hereditary Health Act—which mandated the sterilization of persons deemed to suffer from a hereditary disease, innate feeble-mindedness or alcoholism. In November 1933, the regime also mandated the castration of sexual offenders through enactment of the Law against Dangerous Habitual Criminals. In June 1935, the Hereditary Health Act was revised to allow, among other things, abortions for eugenic reasons and castration of male homosexuals. In September 1935, the Law for the Protection of German Blood and Honor (*Blutschutzgesetz*) followed, which prohibited marriages and sexual relations outside of marriages between Jews and citizens of 'German or related blood'. In October 1935, it was complemented by the Marital Health Act, which banned marriages between persons deemed hereditarily valuable and those deemed hereditarily unfit and required prospective spouses to produce a marriage certificate confirming that the marriage was hereditarily unproblematic.

In contrast to the Law for the Protection of German Blood and Honor, the Hereditary Health Act was not specifically directed against Jews and did not discriminate between persons 'of German blood' and others. The wording was

---

6   For an overview, see Schmuhl 1992; Friedlander 1995; Bock 2004.

race-neutral in the sense that it did not specifically target members of racialized groups. Although Jews were among its victims (Bock 1986, 354), they did not form the main target. On the contrary, Hitler's attitude towards sterilization of Jews was, as he told Minister Frick in 1935, that "there is no reason to improve alien races through applying sterilization" (Hitler cited in Bock 1986, 352). The fate that the Nazis planned for the Jews was elimination, not sterilization. After 1945, the question of whether Nazi sterilization policy was inherently racist would play a critical role for sterilization victims' struggle for reparations, since only those who had been persecuted "for racial, religious, or political reasons or because of the victim's world view" were entitled to reparations under the Federal Indemnification Act (BEG §1(1), see Chap. 3).

German historian Gisela Bock (1986), author of the first and still classic study on Nazi sterilization policy, argues that Nazi sterilization policy was indeed inherently racist. Bock offers a conceptual distinction between anthropological and hygienic racism. Both were based on notions of superiority and inferiority, she argues, and were constructed largely in terms of heredity and biology (Bock 1986, 356). They were not mutually exclusive but intersecting and complementary elements of 'racial upgrading' (*Aufartung*). Anthropological racism, Bock holds, was directed against other races, which were per se constructed as inferior, whereas hygienic racism targeted the unfit across racialized groups. Importantly, however, the Nazi concept of 'upgrading' did not consist simply of defending an existing, supposedly superior group against a different, supposedly inferior group, but also of actively *creating* the supposedly superior group (Bock 1986, 327). This argument, stressing the future-oriented, generative nature of Nazi racism is also made by Hannah Arendt in order to delineate Nazi racism from other types of racism (Arendt 1968, 412). The Nazis saw the master race as a project rather than an existing entity, and this project articulated strategies of selective pro-natalism with strategies of selective anti-natalism, racial purification and genocide.

Hence, there can be no doubt that Nazi sterilization policy was directed at 'racial upgrading' and was in this sense essentially racist. Several open questions still remain, though, for instance: is the concept of hygienic racism also applicable to non-Nazi variants of the eugenics project, that is, to eugenic variants *not* directed at 'racial upgrading'? Should hygienic racism be conceptualized as a unique phenomenon that cannot be separated from Nazism? And if so, what is there to gain from framing classifications of fit and unfit, socially adequate or inadequate, as racist beyond the scope of Nazi eugenics?

2.4   Welfare Eugenics

Apart from Germany and the United States, the Scandinavian countries were the 20th century's most 'eugenically developed' countries, both in terms of academic knowledge and actual policies[7]. When the State Institute for Race Biology in Uppsala opened in 1922, it was the world's first government institute of eugenic research (Rudling 2014, 42), and in the 1930s and 40s, at the same time that they launched the Scandinavian social welfare state, Denmark, Sweden, and Norway all implemented selective sterilization acts that included the possibility of both voluntary and compulsory sterilization. Lene Koch emphasises that

> [c]ompulsion was reserved for cases where social responsibility and readiness to subject oneself to reproductive control could not be expected. This was the case with groups of people considered 'asocial' or 'antisocial' such as the mentally retarded, psychopaths, tramps, and prostitutes. (Koch 2004, 320)

Historians of Scandinavian eugenics tend to agree that questions of race were of rather marginal importance in these countries and that Scandinavian eugenics was not racist, although public discourse focused to some extent on ethnic minorities deemed incapable of adjusting to modernization such as Taters, Travelers and Lapps (Broberg and Tydén 1996; Haave 2000). Broberg and Tydén point out that in the 1930s, the Taters were increasingly constructed as a genetically inferior racial group whose behavior called for a more restrictive sterilization act. Somewhat ironically, the more restrictive 1941 Sterilization Act broadened the social indications for sterilization to include mental illness, mental retardation and an "anti-social way of life" (Broberg and Tydén 1996, 124ff.). This opened up the possibility of sterilizing members of the Tater group *without* further need for scientific justification. From the 1940s onward, the heredity frame in Swedish sterilization policy was increasingly superseded by a socio-political one. However, the racialization of the 'Tater issue' had been instrumental in bringing about the latter.

In Norway, racializing the so-called 'Tater issue' also played a role in the formation of the national sterilization policy in the 1920s and 30s (Haave 2000;

---

7   Broberg and Roll-Hansen 1996; Runcis 1998; Weindling 1999; Haave 2000; Koch 2000; 2006; 2009; Spektorowski and Mizrachi 2004; Kulawik 2006; Spektorowski and Ireni-Saban 2010.

Braun, Herrmann et al. 2014). In official documents, this group was commonly described as '*omstreifere*' (itinerants) and associated with crime, avoidance of work, violence, sexual offences, drinking, and other socially undesirable behavior. The Itinerant Committee (*løsgjengerkomiteen*), appointed by the government in 1927, divided the '*omstreifere*' into two subgroups, 'the hopeless' and 'the inferior'. While 'the hopeless' were to be detained, 'the inferior' were to be sterilized (Itinerant Committee cited in Bastrup and Sivertsen 1996, 210). Thus, the construction of the 'Tater issue' linked ethnicity, poverty and an alleged inability to be a productive and useful member of society. Sterilization was considered a proper means to solve the problem. The Norwegian Sterilization Act, however, also allowed for sterilizing persons without personal consent if they were deemed mentally ill or mentally handicapped. These cases required a justification on eugenic, criminal or social grounds (Haave 2001, 2). Again, biology was but one among several possible indications for sterilization. The Norwegian Sterilization Act was in force from 1934 to 1977, with an interruption from 1942 to 1945, when the Nazi Hereditary Health Act was installed. The 1934 act allowed for three categories of legal sterilizations: sterilization of persons with full legal rights and upon application of the person concerned (§3 (1)), sterilization of minors or persons deemed insane or mentally impaired upon application of the person with the consent of a guardian (§3(2)); and sterilization of persons deemed mentally ill or mentally handicapped and incapable of providing personal consent upon application of a guardian or corresponding authority (§3(4)). Under the 1934 act, 2,123 sterilizations were reported under §3(2) or §3(4); of these, 922 were performed under §3(4), that is, without personal consent (Haave 2001, 2f.).

In the 1990s, the former sterilization policy became the subject of an intense public debate which, however, focused exclusively on the sterilization of the Taters. Involuntary sterilization was framed in terms of racial and ethnic discrimination only. Those who were involuntarily sterilized on the grounds of their alleged feeble-mindedness or mental illness were not addressed at all, as if involuntary sterilization constituted a problem only if and when performed for reasons of race but not for reasons of a person's abilities (Braun, Herrmann et al. 2014). Public reflection did not extend to injuries and the violation of those who were categorized as unproductive, unfit or incapable of leading a useful life in society. Thus, reducing sterilization policy to racial or ethnic discrimination obliterated the productivist and biopolitical dimensions of selective sterilization.

2.5   Eugenics and Feminism

Mainline eugenics, Daniel Kevles holds, was an anti-feminist affair domi-
nated by White male academics who considered it a woman's most glorious
duty to marry, stay at home, and give birth to children (Kevles 1985, 88f.).
Many prominent American eugenicists opposed women's suffrage and college education on the grounds that it would divert these valuable women
from fulfilling their procreative duty, thereby propelling the trend towards
degeneration. In Germany, around the turn of the century, this type of anti-
feminist selective pronatalism was also widespread and deeply intertwined
with the rise of racial hygiene (Allen 2000). To conclude that eugenics was an
anti-feminist project, however, would be misleading. Over the past decades,
a wealth of research on the relationship between feminism and eugenics has
produced a more nuanced picture[8]. It shows that women and women's movements have been actively involved with eugenic activities of different kinds,
although the nature, scope and motives of this involvement are a matter of
scholarly dispute. Further scholarship also shows the gendered nature of the
eugenics projects, that is, its constructions of femininity, masculinity, motherhood, gender dimorphism, heterosexuality, and not least its gendered construction of target groups (Stern 2010).

According to some analysts, the alliance between women's movement actors and eugenics was a more strategic one. Late 19th and early 20th century
feminists, seeking to fend off anti-feminist accusations of eschewing the burdens of motherhood, aligned with eugenic arguments in order to benefit from
their scientific reputation (Pedersen 1993; Gordon 2002a). Other scholars object to this view, arguing that certain women's movement actors genuinely
believed in the eugenic ideal of improving the race or nation through limit-
ing the procreation of the unfit (Bland 1995; Ordover 2003). Ann Taylor Allen
goes even further and asserts that "eugenic theory was a basic and formative,
not an incidental, part of feminist positions on the vitally important themes
of motherhood, reproduction, and the state" (Allen 2000, 479). Allen shows
that British and German women's movement leaders in the 1900s to 1930s,

---

8   For an overview see Klausen and Bashford (2010) and Stern (2010). For specific case
    studies see Bucur (1994) for Romania, Gerodetti (2006) for Switzerland, Ladd-Taylor
    (1997), Dorr (1999) and Kline (2001) for the U.S., Allen (2000) for Germany and the UK
    and Allen (1988), Grossmann (1995), and Zimmermann (1988) for Germany.

including those who employed eugenic arguments, fiercely opposed contemporary pronatalism and its aggressive misogyny. In any case, a number of studies have pointed out that feminist affiliations with eugenics were heavily textured by relations of race and class as well as standards of social adequacy and fitness. Upon close inspection, feminist notions of reproductive rights and self-determination were often tied to notions of reproductive responsibility, which in turn were charged with notions of differential social worth or social adequacy. In the US, birth control movement leader Margaret Sanger, who founded the American Birth Control League in 1921, aligned her case for birth control and free and voluntary motherhood to the eugenics project of racial improvement (Sanger 2007). In Germany, the Association for the Protection of Mothers (*Bund für Mutterschutz*), a radical feminist organization for social and sexual reform founded in 1905, struggled for women's and children's social rights and women's sexual and reproductive self-determination and at the same time endorsed eugenic arguments and values (Grossmann 1995). Leading figures of the *Bund für Mutterschutz*, including Helene Stöcker and Lily Braun, adopted eugenic language to some extent to bolster their claims. Stöcker, in particular, called for women's sexual and reproductive self-determination but added that women must exercize it responsibly (Herlitzius 1995; Allen 2000). Ideally, for Stöcker, enjoying the right to reproductive self-determination would educate and enable women to make responsible reproductive decisions, for instance, to abort a pregnancy if the child could be expected to be mentally or physically weak (Herlitzius 1995, 350).[9] Those not able to do so, such as alcoholics, the mentally retarded or abnormal, should be prevented from procreating, if necessary by means of legal restrictions (Zimmermann 1988). Hence, the meaning of self-determination within feminist eugenics discourse was stratified along norms and standards of health, fitness, and socially adequate behavior.

A similar biopolitical rationality characterizes the thought of Margaret Sanger (Franks 2005; Klausen and Bashford 2010). Sanger advocated women's access to birth control, which she saw as absolutely necessary for racial betterment. Unlike many contemporary eugenicists, she did not adhere to biolog-

---

9   Teresa Kulawik (2009) comments: "Her vision therefore appears to have materialized when, at the time when women in many countries of Europe and the Americas in the 1970s achieved the right of self-determination over their bodies, they also were handed the means for eugenic selection in the form of prenatal diagnostics, which was invented at that time."

ical determinism but contended that poverty, mental retardation and racial decay had social causes (McCann 1994, 99ff.)—not least among them overpopulation. Sanger also objected to a widespread tendency at the time to blame White middle-class women for racial degeneration because they refused to have children. These nuances notwithstanding, Sanger articulated voluntariness to responsibility, rights to duties, and some women's individual freedom to other women's denigration:

> Birth control itself, often denounced as a violation of natural law, is nothing more or less than the facilitation of the process of weeding out the unfit, of preventing the birth of defectives or of those who will become defectives. So, in compliance with nature's working plan, we must permit womanhood its full development before we can expect of it efficient motherhood. If we are to make racial progress, this development of womanhood must precede motherhood in every individual woman. Then and then only can the mother cease to be an incubator and be a mother indeed. Then only can she transmit to her sons and daughters the qualities which make strong individuals and, collectively, a strong race [...]. (Sanger 1920, 229)

On these presuppositions, Sanger endorsed immigration restrictions and selective and compulsory sterilization for "the undeniably feeble-minded, insane and syphilitic" (McCann 1994, 117). While this may seem a rather short list of indications compared with that of mainstream eugenics at the time, as Lisa McCann (1994) argues, it still makes clear that the value of individual freedom and voluntariness for Sanger was stratified and contingent upon the individual's value in terms of racial improvement.

Concerning the translation of eugenic ideas into actual policies, research has shown that the majority of those sterilized under selective sterilization laws were women and girls—except in Nazi Germany, where the gender ratio was about equal.[10] However, gender norms intersected with norms and standards of health, fitness and social adequacy as well as poverty and class status. In the Swiss canton of Vaud, for instance, which was the first political body in Europe to pass a sterilization law, nine out of ten sterilizations in 1944 were performed on women, most of these on young, unmarried women who lived in poor conditions and were categorized as maladapted, socially deviant or

---

10   For Finland see Hietala (1996), for Norway Roll-Hansen (1996, for Denmark Hansen (1996), for Switzerland Mottier and Gerodetti (2007), and for Nazi Germany Bock (1986).

of low intelligence (Mottier and Gerodetti 2007). Maija Runcis (1998) argues that in Sweden, concerns about the number of mentally retarded and persons leading an anti-social way of life focused primarily on women.[11] More specifically, the verdict of an 'anti-social way of life' often meant transgressing sexual norms, which were more rigid for women than for men; as a result, the verdict was more often imposed on women. Implementation, thus, was gendered through gender-specific norms of sexual and social conformity. In addition, the medical indication introduced into Swedish as well as Norwegian sterilization legislation at some point applied to women only. In Sweden, a medical indication for sterilization was mainly advised in cases of so-called 'exhausted mothers', a concept denoting lower-class women living in impoverished living conditions and considered to be in danger of becoming dysfunctional mothers or wives (Etzemüller 2000).

Nazi sterilization policy, in contrast, affected men and women in equal measure; some 50 percent of those forcibly sterilized under the Law for the Prevention of Hereditarily Diseased Offspring were men or boys. Gisela Bock (1986, 372) argues that, on several grounds, the law was nonetheless gendered. First, 90 percent of the estimated 5,000 individuals who died from sterilization were women (Bock 2004, 80). More problematic is Bock's position that involuntary childlessness affected women in a more devastating way than it did men. Bock refers to data indicating that women protested more often against the sterilization verdict than men and that many women purportedly attempted to become pregnant before the intervention was performed (Bock 1986, 12, 371f., 384f.). However, it is difficult to discern what the equivalent signs of suffering would have been for men, since they could not become visibly pregnant. Moreover, it is remains unclear that refraining from formal protest would indicate an absence of suffering.

2.6   Biologist Determinism and Social Engineering

That eugenics was based on biologism is a truism in both public and academic discourse. Eugenicists, according to the common narrative, were convinced

---

11   This was partly due to the fact that only women could be legally sterilized on the basis of a medical indication; the number of sterilisations for medical reasons rose sharply after the war. However, among those sterilized for being 'mentally retarded', women were heavily overrepresented as well (Broberg and Tydén 1996).

that all major pathologies that plagued modern society, such as criminality, alcoholism, prostitution and poverty, were caused by genetically inherited defects and these defects would proliferate because of the dysgenics' increased fecundity. Today, we know better, namely that modern science has largely refuted these biologist explanations as unfounded or wrong.

Again, this is not the full story. Presenting eugenics as a consequence of biologism may account for many of its features, but it omits others. Neither eugenic scholarship nor eugenic policies necessarily referred to biologist assumptions; selective interventions into reproduction could be articulated within rationalities of biologist determinism as well as rationalities of social reform and social engineering. In some cases, abandoning a biologist framework actually allowed for an expansion of eugenic interventions.

A number of studies have drawn attention to the fact that a significant share of scholarship did not subscribe to the Mendelian paradigm but followed a Lamarckian line of thought. According to Lamarckism, living beings could pass acquired characteristics on to their offspring. Thus, Lamarckians did not believe in biological determinism as Mendelians did; for them, biological heredity was amenable to socio-political intervention in a more direct sense. Lamarckism was popular among eugenicists in France (Schneider 1990), Brazil (Stepan 1991), and Russia (Adams 1990) as well as Japan (Otsubo and Bartholomew 1998) and the Czech Republic (Simunek 2007). Both Lamarckians and Mendelians were concerned with heredity. For Lamarckians, however, social policy, health care and education were proper means to improve the biological quality of present and future generations, since socially acquired betterment would be passed down. Moreover, Lamarckians were not necessarily opposed to compulsory measures to fight degeneration (Adams 1990, 218). French Lamarckian eugenicists, for instance, believed that the lower classes were biologically inferior because of poverty, not the reverse. Yet, as Schneider points out, many strongly believed that the numbers of the poor must be reduced, if necessary through more restrictive immigration laws, marriage restrictions, or compulsory sterilization (Schneider 1986, 86). Thus, the scientific case for selective anti-natalism was not always based on biological determinism.

Eugenic policies, in particular sterilization policies, were also not entirely founded on an exclusively biologist framework. The Swedish Sterilization Acts of 1935 and 1941, for instance, included a eugenic *and* a social indication. The social indication in the 1935 Act permitted sterilization without personal consent in case of "mental illness, feeble-mindedness, or other mental defects" when the person concerned was declared legally incompetent and "incapable of caring for children" (Broberg and Tydén 1996, 102f.). The 1941 Swedish Sterilization Act actually broadened the social indication to include "an anti-social way of life" (Broberg and Tydén 1996, 108). The new clause arose from a recommendation by the Commission on Population, which had proposed to introduce a social indication in order to be able to sterilize persons whose 'deficiency' was *not* hereditary (Broberg and Tydén 1996, 106). According to the official statistics, between 1942 and 1975—when the law was repealed—some 20 to 100 sterilizations per year were performed in Sweden on the basis of a social indication. However, the categories of eugenic, medical and social grounds were never clearly defined, neither in theory nor in practice. What did and what did not qualify as 'hereditary' was very much at the discretion of those in power to decide. In this vein, a member of the Swedish National Board of Health, which was the committee that made sterilization decisions, explained in 1940 how the Board defined eugenic grounds:

> [O]ur basis is the general statistical probability that a disease, abnormality, or defect (epilepsy, feeble-mindedness, etc.) is hereditary or predominantly hereditary, or, from a slightly different viewpoint, the probability that it will appear in children or other relatives (the risk of morbidity). Thus, when a case is to be decided (sterilization, abortion, marital capacity), the statistical probability is decisive. That is to say, when the rate is sufficiently high, the burden of proof rests upon the person whose claim it is that, for him or her, the disease or quality...has an extrinsic cause so that his or her case is not to be judged by the general statistical risk. (Swedish National Board of Health cited in Broberg and Tydén 1996, 110f.)

The Board determined that assuming a ten percent risk of inheritance was sufficient to establish a eugenic indication. In Norway, the 1934 Sterilization Act permitted sterilization if there was a likelihood that a person would pass a hereditary disease on to any children he or she might have *or* if the person was deemed unfit to take care of a child (Roll-Hansen 1996, 172). Similarly, in Finland, the 1935 Sterilization Act stipulated that individuals could be submitted to compulsory sterilization if they were diagnosed as idiots, imbeciles or insane and there was a risk that they could transmit their disease to their children; if it was probable that their children would not be cared for; or if the individual had been proven guilty of a crime demonstrating an 'unnatural sexual drive' (Hietala 1996, 232). The 1929 Danish Sterilization Act remained relatively vague, stipulating that sterilization was permissible '...where suppression of reproduction must be regarded as being of great importance to society' (Hansen 1996). According to a review of the law in 1935, implementation was based on eugenic, social or individual considerations, with 'social' meaning that sterilization was in the interest of society, whereas 'individual' considerations meant, for instance, that the individual concerned had the option of being released from institutional confinement should they consent to undergo sterilization (Broberg and Roll-Hansen 1996, 38). Similarly, a 1937 amendment to the Alberta (Canada) Sterilization Act sanctioned the sterilization of persons "incapable of intelligent parenthood" (Grekul, Krahn et al. 2004, 363). Hence, sterilization policies referred to biologistic concerns as well as socio-political concerns about socially dysfunctional behavior or ways of life.

Similarly, the Nazi Sterilization Act of 1933 allowed the coercive sterilization of alcoholics without categorizing alcoholism as hereditary. In addition, the Act used the term 'innate' in lieu of 'hereditary' in connection to feeblemindedness so that it would encompass, for instance, people who had suffered brain damage during birth.

In practice, the category of 'mentally retarded' or 'feeble-minded'—a core category in almost all sterilization laws—was sufficiently malleable and ambiguous to allow for sterilization of those whose behavior, sexuality, or way of life was deemed socially inadequate, undesirable or dysfunctional. In short, selective sterilization laws, like other instruments of selective politics of reproduction, manifested and executed a biopolitical rationality that sought to reduce the number of people who were perceived as a burden to society, whether for reasons of their bodily or mental abilities or for their behavior or way of life.

2.7   Eugenics, Progress and Productivism

Alberto Spektorowski and Elisabet Mizrachi show that, in the case of Sweden, eugenic policies grew out of a political mindset that combined humanist Marxist ideas about social reform with a Fabian concept of industrial democracy and an exclusionist concept of social welfare (Spektorowski and Mizrachi 2004, 334). Sterilization, within this framework, was a mechanism of welfare eugenics. "The basic idea of eugenic socialism", Spektorowski and Mizrachi argue, was to engineer a welfare community for 'the fittest' or a 'welfare eugenics', built on parameters of 'right-living' destined to exclude those individuals defined as non-productive. In this sense this new scientific socialism was built on concepts such as efficiency, productivism and social margins. (Spektorowski and Mizrachi 2004, 334)

Social rights, within this framework, were universal, but individual rights to physical integrity and personal life were not; they were made contingent upon the individual's conformance to standards of 'right-living' and productivity: "Non-productive elements were denied not social welfare, but their right to procreate" (Spektorowski and Mizrachi 2004, 334).

A similar argument is made by Thomas Leonhard (2005) concerning progressivist economics in the US. Although he does not use the term 'productivism', the political rationality that Leonhard interrogates displays significant similarities to productivist welfarism as analyzed by Spektorowski and Mizrachi. Leonard argues that eugenics was mainstream in the Progressive Era. It was appealing to social conservatives as well as progressivists. The core idea of Progressive Era eugenics, he argues, was "that the labor force should be rid of unfit workers, whom they labelled 'parasites,' 'the unemployable,' 'low-wage races' and the 'industrial residuum.' Removing the unfit, so the argument went, would uplift superior, deserving workers". (Leonard 2005, 207f.)

What attracted progressive eugenicists, according to Leonhard, was a disenchantment and a mounting impatience with the laissez-faire approach to politics around the turn of the century. Overcoming the pathologies of modernity, as progressives saw it, required the concerted effort of science, social science expertise, and governance, applying the combined policy instruments of social inquiry, social control, and expert management.

Thus, progressivist eugenics shared with Scandinavian welfare eugenics a belief in biopolitical social engineering committed to values, norms and standards of productivity and social functionality. In fact, I would conclude, the belief in a biopolitical type of social engineering geared at improving productiveness, conformity and social functionality in the population constitutes the key characteristic shared by any variant of eugenics, whether feminist or antifeminist, left- or right-wing, more or less racialized, based on or independent of biological determinism. Denouncing eugenics as sexist, racist, biologist or reactionary merely obscures this distinctively modern productivist biopolitical rationality.

2.8   Conclusion

The purpose of this review was not to explain the rise and fall of the eugenics project—that would have required more comprehensive comparisons. To this point, comparative analyses exist only in some cases, such as country comparisons (Adams 1990; Allen 2000; Hansen and King 2001). What should have become clear, however, is that we cannot capture eugenics' complexity by categorizing it as reactionary, sexist, racist, biologistic. Eugenic ideas and practices were promoted by a broad range of political actors, including social reformers, women's rights activists, socialists and progressives. Gender norms and stereotypes strongly influenced the formation and implementation of eugenic policies, but they did not operate separately from race, class, and norms of social conformity, usefulness and productivity. Eugenic anxieties concerning degeneration did intersect with constructions of inferior races and racialized targeting, and members of racialized groups were disproportionately affected by eugenic policies, but constructions of inferior races did not fully coincide with categorizations of the defective, dysgenic, unfit or socially inadequate. Members of the supposedly superior, unmarked race or ethnic group could be targeted as well if deemed defective according to norms of conformity, fitness, productivity or usefulness. Biological determinism was a prevalent, but not an indispensable, feature of eugenic arguments and strategies.

Framing eugenics as a reactionary, repressive, racist, and biologist affair misses not only the heterogeneity of eugenics projects and their multifold strands and variations, but above all the biopolitical rationality they all shared, namely the distinction between the fit and the unfit, the socially adequate and the socially inadequate, the adapted and the maladapted, the functional and the dysfunctional, the useful and the useless. At the core of eugenics lay the belief that unfit, dysgenic, unproductive, deficient or socially inadequate persons constituted a burden to society and that this burden must be reduced through social engineering. While it is true that this logic was encoded in ablist categories such as feeblemindedness, mental illness, hereditary disease and the like, it would be misleading to say that eugenic policies targeted 'the disabled'. Firstly, categories of disability and abledness are themselves the product of categorizing, labelling, and marking practices; they are not given entities. Second, categorizing people as disabled, feeble-minded, mentally ill and the like cannot be separated from categorizing them as unfit, useless, dysfunctional and unproductive. Eugenic policies linked notions of race, gender, class and abledness to notions of adequacy, fitness, usefulness, productivity and normality, and it is this linkage that made them popular and powerful.

Any effort to come to terms with eugenic policies in the past and addressing the injustices, encroachments and suffering they caused must therefore confront this inherently modern biopolitical rationality. Reparation schemes and government apologies may form important elements to confront it. They may grant satisfaction to those whose rights, bodies and souls have been injured, provide moral and legal rehabilitation and, ideally, a promise of non-repetition. If, however, we as a society want to understand how and why these injuries and infringements were possible in the first place, it is mandatory to interrogate the productivist biopolitical rationality that informed and motivated them.

3 Nazi Sterilization Policy, Second-Order Injustice and the Struggle for Reparations

On 24 May 2007, the German *Bundestag* passed a declaration that ostracized the Nazi Law on the Prevention of Offspring with Hereditary Diseases of 14 July 1933. The declaration had been preceded by decades of struggle over an entitlement to reparations for those who had been forcibly sterilized under this law and over nullifying or ostracizing it. The terminological difference matters, as explained below.

The law, the MPs declared, was an "expression of the inhuman Nazi conception of 'life unworthy of living'" (BT Drs. 16/3811 2006, 3) and the first step on the way to the "'euthanasia' mass murder program" (BT Drs. 16/3811 2006, 4). It had provided a legal basis for forced sterilizations and therefore constituted Nazi injustice. Seventy-two years after the end of the Nazi regime, it was the first time that a high-ranking German constitutional body declared the Nazi sterilization act itself, and not only the way it was applied, to be an injustice committed by the state. In 1988, the *Bundestag* had already proclaimed the rulings under this law to be Nazi injustice. The verdict then, however, did not apply to the law as such. This was now different:

> The law itself is an expression of the Nazi ideology, which denies the inviolable dignity of every human being by subordinating the individual to the racist delusion of 'purifying the body of the people' [*Volkskörper*] and, as a final consequence, 'eradicating' it. Not only the violent measures based on this law, but also the 'Hereditary Health Act' as such, which legalized these violent measures, must therefore be regarded an expression of the inhuman Nazi notion of 'life unworthy of living'. (BT Drs. 16/3811 2006, 3)

The *Bundestag*, the declaration went on, "is doing so on the assumption that by ostracizing the 'Hereditary Health Act' as such, it has removed any doubts about its willingness to provide full satisfaction and rehabilitation to those affected" (BT Drs. 16/3811 2006, 4).

For the victims, the declaration finally provided the official moral rehabilitation they had been awaiting for so long: Now "they are no longer considered 'not worth of living'", Margret Hamm, managing director of the Association of Victims of "Euthanasia" and Forced Sterilization (*Bund der „Euthanasie"-Geschädigten und Zwangssterilisierten*, BEZ) told us in a personal communication. However, the declaration did not entail recognition of those affected as victims of Nazi persecution in the sense of the Federal Indemnification Act (*Bundesentschädigungsgesetz*, BEG); thus, the persons concerned still were not entitled to reparations under BEG until this point.

The faction of the Greens in Parliament (*Bündnis 90/Die Grünen*) had submitted an alternative motion proposing not to ostracize but to annul the Hereditary Health Act, thereby supporting the BEZ's central demand to declare the Act null and void (BT Drs. 16/1171). The majority in the *Bundestag*, however, rejected this motion, arguing that the Act could no longer be annulled as it had been automatically invalidated in 1949 for being incompatible with the Basic Law. Yet, Margret Hamm explained, historically this was not correct. The Act was never officially repealed. On the contrary, after 1945 and even after 1949, it remained in effect in various ways as German administrations, courts and governments continued to apply it. Courts and government bodies used the Hereditary Health Act well after 1949 as a reference for decisions on revision trials and reparation claims for persons who had been forcibly sterilized, thereby actively confirming its validity. We have called this practice, which reified the stigmatization of the victims, a second-order injustice (Braun and Herrmann 2015). In the following pages, we shall see that the 2007 declaration failed to address this second-order injustice.

This chapter reviews the politics of coming to terms with Nazi sterilization policy—or failing to do so—in the Federal Republic. More precisely, it examines the politics of reparations for victims of Nazi sterilization policy and reconstructs what was and was not subject to critical reflection in this process. I use the term 'politics of reparations' to refer to the politics of coming to terms with historic injustice in a broad sense, comprising acts of rehabilitation or redress, reparation schemes, public apologies and inquiries. This may lead to the adoption of reparation policies or the rejection thereof, take place in formal political arenas such as parliaments or courts or in the media and other public spaces, and involve state as well as civil society actors. I take a performatist approach to reparation policies here, understanding them as performative acts, as something that is being done—or not. From this per-spective, the questions are: What is it that actors are actually doing when they are crafting reparation policies? What distinctions are made, what bound-aries drawn, what value judgements implied, what responsibility assumed and what audience addressed? I draw on the approaches of Nicholas Tavuchis (1991) and Aaron Lazare (2004), both of whom worked with the concept of apol-ogy. According to their understandings, an apology is a performative act that involves certain things being done, or in fact requires they be done, in order to constitute a proper apology. These are: making a factual statement about what happened, issuing a moral verdict, determining that wrongdoing has taken place, accepting responsibility for it, and promising non-repetition. In-sofar as rehabilitation and reparation policies are intended as acts of making amends for an historic injustice—and not merely compensation for damage caused by force majeure—they involve and require acts similar to those that constitute proper apologies. Taking a performatist approach also allows us to see that rehabilitation and reparation policies do not simply address matters of the past but constitutively connect the past, the present and the future: Actors engaging in reparation policies[1] make factual statements about acts in the past; they convey a moral judgement about these acts and determine whether wrongdoing took place; they specify what was wrong about it; they accept responsibility in the present, thereby referring to normative principles or values that were violated; and they make a commitment to these norms and principles and promise non-repetition. Thus, establishing what should and should not qualify as a systemic injustice and which state actions in the past should or should not constitute an entitlement to reparations involves the confirmation of moral and legal standards for past, present and future. Therefore, struggles over reparations are struggles not only about the past but also about the present and the future as they inevitably imply the question of what kind of society we want to be: What wrongdoing has taken place? Was it so severe that it requires us to make amends? What normative principle has been violated and how important is it to us? Are we willing to commit to it? What kind of society are we now; in what way do we differ from the society that allowed these things to happen in the first place? What kind of society do we want to be in the future?

In this chapter, I interrogate the politics of coming to terms with Nazi selective sterilization policy. A note on terminology is in order: I deliberately

---

1   In the following short for rehabilitation and reparation policies.

avoid the terms 'eugenic' and 'eugenics' as well as the term 'euthanasia'. Although both acquired a more pejorative meaning after 1945, they were originally coined to denote something ostensibly positive: efforts to achieve a better-quality population (see Chapter 2) in the case of eugenics and the 'good death' in the case of euthanasia. Both terms are euphemistic and misleading. I refer instead to selective sterilization and selective sterilization policy. Selective sterilization means that certain persons or institutions claim the competence to select other persons for sterilization on the grounds that, for whatever reason, they consider these persons undesired in society. By selecting the undesired for sterilization, those who claim competence seek to reduce the number of the undesired by preventing them from having children. Note that selective sterilization does not necessarily rest on biologistic assumptions. Those who claim the authority to decide may also assume that undesired features may be passed down to future generations through procreation, education, or living conditions, as pointed out in Chapter 2.

To be sure, sterilization has not been the only practice to keep undesired people from having and raising children; institutionalization and sexual segregation, forced contraception, forced abortions, and forced removal of children are others. Sterilization policy was arguably the most widespread but by no means the only policy instrument for that purpose used by the Nazi regime. Selective sterilization, as I see it, can be understood as a biopolitical injury of normality. I use the concept of injuries of normality to denote human rights violations that refer to notions of normality in a threefold sense: First, they enact social norms and standards of health, fitness, productivity, or conformity, establish categories of differential social worth, and mark some people as socially inadequate, abnormal, deviant or deficient and ultimately being a burden or even a threat to society. Second, injuries of normality are by no means confined to situations of war, civil war or other situations of exceptional crisis. Rather, they occur also in states of normality—or what is considered by the unmarked to be normality. Lastly, injuries of normality are so ingrained and persistent because they are considered normal; as long as it goes without saying that mentally handicapped persons are a burden to society or that homosexual men endanger youth, it will be considered normal to reduce their numbers and deny them full civil rights status.

Forced sterilization is an injury in that it is both a violation of the person's physical integrity and a stigma imposed on her, a value judgement stipulating that she and persons like her are undesired and should preferably not exist at all. It is an injury of normality insofar as the value judgement refers to notions of normal vs. abnormal, deficient or deviant in relation to certain social norms and standards. It constitutes, furthermore, a biopolitical injury of normality that these norms and standards refer to notions of being a fit, healthy, functioning, productive and thus useful part of the social body. If this is accurate, then selective sterilization policies inevitably constitute biopolitical injuries of normality. Nazi sterilization policy was a particularly large-scale, systematic and violent case of selective sterilization policy, manifesting and forcefully executing a type of biopolitical rationality. The question examined in this and the following two chapters is whether and to what extent this underlying biopolitical rationality was subject to critical reflection in West German reparation politics. I argue that the biopolitical rationality that drove Nazi sterilization policy did not vanish in 1945. Moreover, it not only did not vanish; it informed the politics of reparations for decades, manifesting in the persistent failure to acknowledge victims' claims to rehabilitation and reparation. In 2007, the *Bundestag* finally managed to condemn the biopolitical logic that had driven Nazi sterilization policy, but it failed to condemn or even reflect upon the enduring power of this logic in the Federal Republic.

In this chapter, I examine the politics of reparations for coercive sterilization under Nazi rule focusing on the question of what, if anything, was considered wrong about this policy. I suggest that we can read the relevant struggles as pertaining to the question of whether basic individual rights such as the right to physical integrity, the right to found a family, and the right to personal freedom apply universally, so that violating them on a systematic basis constitutes a severe historic injustice, or whether they apply only to persons who meet certain norms and standards. From this angle, we can see that for many decades systematic violations were not considered an undue infringement when directed against persons deemed mentally ill, mentally retarded, disabled or in some way abnormal or deficient. The 2007 declaration condemned these violations under Nazi rule. However, it declared Nazi sterilization policy despicable not because it categorized people as being biopolitically inferior but because it served the despicable racist goals of the Nazi regime. It is thus unclear whether the *Bundestag* considers selective sterilization to constitute a biopolitical injustice in any case, regardless of the type of regime that performs it.

3.1   The Hereditary Health Act and its Biopolitical Rationality

The Law for the Prevention of Offspring with Hereditary Diseases (*Gesetz zur Verhütung erbkranken Nachwuchses, GzVeN*)[2], hereafter Hereditary Health Act, came into effect on 1 January 1934. It allowed for sterilizing a person 'if, according to the experience of medical science, there is a high probability that his offspring will suffer from serious physical or mental defects of a hereditary nature' (GzVeN §1).

The Act explicitly mentions "1. congenital mental deficiency, 2. schizophrenia, 3. manic depression, 4. hereditary epilepsy, 5. hereditary St. Vitus' Dance (Huntington's chorea), 6. Hereditary blindness, 7. hereditary deafness, 8. serious hereditary physical deformity" (GzVeN §1).

In addition to hereditary conditions, alcoholism served as an indication for sterilization. An amendment in 1935 also allowed for the termination of a pregnancy, formally with the woman's consent, if the woman was sentenced to sterilization but already pregnant at the time (GzVeN §10a(1)). Further, the amendment allowed males to be castrated, formally with their consent, to "free them from a degenerate sexual drive" (GzVeN §14(2)). This was primarily directed against homosexuals.

The decisions rested with the newly established Hereditary Health Courts (*Erbgesundheitsgerichte*), consisting of a district court judge, a state physician, and another physician trained in 'hereditary health' (*Erbgesundheitslehre*) (GzVeN §6). Once a verdict was passed, the sterilization was required to be carried out, even against the will of the person concerned, meaning that the Act explicitly sanctioned the use of force. Notably, there was no mention of race in the law. Sinti and Roma were disproportionally affected as they were disproportionally categorized as 'feeble-minded' (Riechert 1995), but the Act did not explicitly target ethno-racial groups. In fact, condemning Nazi sterilization policy for being 'biologistic' or discriminating against members of certain racial groups is a misconstrual. Even hereditariness was not strictly a biological category. As Gisela Bock has shown, 95 percent of sterilization verdicts referred to indistinct psychiatric categories. 'Mental deficiency', schizophrenia, epilepsy and manic depression together accounted for nearly two thirds of indications (Bock 1986, 302f.). None of these categories was

---

2   Available online at http://www.documentarchiv.de/ns/erbk-nws.html. For an English version see http://ghdi.ghi-dc.org/sub_document.cfm?document_id=1521 (last accessed 10 April 2020).

precise and well-defined, and the hereditariness of such conditions was difficult if not impossible to establish. However, this was of no consequence. Typically, sterilization candidates were identified by applying criteria of social behavior, conformity and functionality as indicated by school or work performance, sexual life, criminal record, receipt of welfare benefits, or records of institutionalization (Bock 1986, 306f.). The overall purpose of the policy was to improve the hereditary health (*Erbgesundheit*) and fitness (*Erbtüchtigkeit*) of the people, as Minister of the Interior Wilhelm Frick explained in 1940. Since *Erbgesundheit* was a "relative term", the identification of sterilization candidates was to take place by means of assessment of a person's performance (*Leistungsfähigkeit*), "taking into account the overall value to the community in terms of skills, talents, etc. as well as the existence of hereditary defects" (RMI quoted in Bock 1986, 236).

The Hereditary Health Act was certainly an instrument of biopolitical racism—not necessarily in the sense of systematically targeting Jews, Roma and Sinti, Poles or members of other racialized groups, but in the sense of pursuing the overall Nazi goal of racial improvement (*Aufartung*). Nonetheless, not all forced sterilizations were carried out on a legal basis. Several thousand Jews, Sinti, Roma, and Poles were sterilized in gruesome experiments in the camps on the basis of executive orders (Friedlander 1995); several hundred children of German women and Afro-French or African American soldiers who had been stationed in the Rhineland after World War I also suffered forced extra-legal sterilization (Pommerin 1979; Lauré al-Samarai and Lennox 2004). Between 1934 and 1945, approximately 360,000 people were legally sterilized under the Act (Bock 1986; Friedlander 1995); 5,000 to 6,000 women and 500 to 600 men died as a result (Bock 1986, 230ff.). The exact numbers, however, remain unknown.

Forced sterilization is a bodily violation, but it also imposes a stigma on a person, marking her as inferior and as a valueless member of the community.[3] It is a verdict on her "overall value to the community", as Minister Frick termed it. Bearing this mark entailed a series of further discriminations: people lost their jobs, they were banned from marrying non-sterilized partners, they were banned from adopting children, and they lost many other opportunities in life. Whether or not the person concerned suffered from health repercussions due to the surgery, whether or not she wanted children—the

---

3   The letters and testimonies of survivors collected by Stefanie Westermann (2010; 2017) provide ample evidence of this.

stigma and the resultant discriminations constituted a violation of her personal integrity and right to human dignity. Thus, the injustice committed is not merely a question of the physical injury that may or may not be caused by the surgery; it is inherent in the act of selective sterilization as such. Ascribing differential worth to people according to their presumed performance, functionality and usefulness for the community and depriving those deemed deficient of their dignity and status as full members of the community—that is what Nazi sterilization policy did and what the Federal Republic failed to acknowledge over the decades that followed.

3.2   No 'Forgotten Victims': Non-Reparation Policy after 1945

After 1945, the Hereditary Health Courts were abolished; consequently, no new sterilization verdicts could be passed under the Hereditary Health Act. However, the Act was not uniformly repealed. The Allied Control Council did not include it in its list of legal acts that were permeated by Nazi ideology and therefore to be invalidated (Control Council Law No. 1 1945). Only in the Soviet occupational zone was it repealed (as a Nazi law by the Soviet military administration in 1946). In the British occupational zone, by contrast, the military administration decided to maintain it, not least to enable the persons concerned to have their cases reviewed in court (Tümmers 2009b). To do so, claimants were required to demonstrate that *in their case* the sterilization was unlawful because the Act had been improperly applied. They needed to convince the court that, for instance, the earlier verdict was based on a faulty diagnosis or on procedural errors. It was not uncommon for these trials to consult the same documents and reports that had been used by the Heredity Health Courts, and sometimes the same judges and experts were even involved (Tümmers 2009b). If the courts established that the sterilization had in fact been unlawful, the claimant could in principle apply for hardship compensation or, in some cases, seek to have the sterilization reversed (Hebenstreit 1983). The legal basis of these proceedings, however, was always the Nazi Hereditary Health Act. By implication, the just or unjust, rightful or wrongful nature of the Act as such remained unquestioned; only its former applications were at stake. Quite the reverse: the courts made the Act the reference for their rulings and thereby performatively confirmed its enduring validity.

This practice continued after the Federal Republic was founded in 1949. The Act was not repealed, and throughout the 1950s and 60s, the courts continued to use it as a reference in revision trials. Until the 1980s, no federal constitutional body ever declared the Act to be incompatible with the Basic Law. On the contrary, the Higher Regional Court (OLG) of the city of Hamm decided in 1954 that the Hereditary Health Act did not violate the rule of law or natural law and that those affected therefore had no right to compensation (OLG Hamm 1954).

In the same vein, jurist Ernst-Walther Hanack concluded in an expert opinion on the "Criminal Law Admission of Artificial Infertilization" of 1959 that the Nazi Hereditary Health Act did not contravene the Basic Law because the provision of compulsory sterilization served not the purpose of discrimination, disenfranchisement or humiliation, but rather the preservation of public health. In fact, repudiating compulsory sterilization would contravene the obligation to respect the rights of others (Harnack 1959, 87f.). Thus, he argued, the Hereditary Health Act could not be considered invalid according to Article 123 of the Basic Law because it did not conflict with the Basic Law. The Article proscribes that "[l]aw in force before the *Bundestag* first convenes shall remain in force insofar as it does not conflict with this Basic Law" (Art. 123(1) GG).

In the early years of the Federal Republic, this was by no means a minority view. Medical, legal and other experts, many of whom had been involved in racial hygiene and Nazi sterilization policy or even in the systematic killing of people with disabilities or certain disorders, openly debated the need for selective sterilization for reasons of public health or social welfare (Tümmers 2009a; 2011, 84ff., 162f.). The prevailing view among experts and policy makers was that selective sterilization was a rational, if not necessary, state practice, an appropriate policy instrument to achieve legitimate policy goals. Selective sterilization, in other words, was considered a normal instrument of modern statecraft. Thus, the Hereditary Health Act was predominantly perceived as a policy instrument for safeguarding the welfare of the German people, not as Nazi injustice.[4] According to this logic, individual 'abuses' of the Act might have occurred, but the Act as such was not problematic. In this climate, the grievances of sterilization victims found no resonance in politics, in the courts, or in civil society. Reparation and rehabilitation for those affected were not on the political agenda.

---

4   For instance, Graf 1950, Nachtsheim 1950, Neukamp 1951. See also the minutes of the Parliamentary Reparations Committee of April 13, 1961 (BT 3 1961).

This did not change when the Federal Republic established a statutory entitlement to reparations for victims of Nazi persecution under the Federal Indemnification Act (BEG) of 1953. The entitlement was subject to restrictive territorial conditions; claimants were required to demonstrate that they had a spatial relationship to Germany within a certain time period (Brunner, Frei et al. 2009, 25). Among those who were in principle eligible on territorial terms, only those persons who were recognized as victims of Nazi persecution were granted the right to reparations. The BEG conclusively restricted this definition to those who had been persecuted for reasons of political opposition to the Nazi regime or for reasons of race, political opinion, religion or ideology (*Weltanschauung*) (BEG §1(1)). Thus, entitlement to reparations was not determined on the basis of what a person had suffered, nor was it contingent on what one had done, on whether one had been a 'fighter against fascism', as was the case in the GDR (Goschler 2005, 361ff., Ludi 2006). Rather, entitlement to reparations was made contingent on whether a person belonged to one of the groups listed by the BEG. Yet not all groups that suffered persecution were listed. Why were some groups included and others not? From a performatist perspective, the question to be asked would be: What is it that the BEG does? The answer is: The BEG makes distinctions—distinctions according to the motives of the persecution that took place. It distinguishes between deserving and undeserving victims of Nazi persecution based on the motives of the perpetrators. It sets out a number of 'reasons' for targeting, tormenting, detaining, killing people that are so despicable that they constitute a reason for making amends. These reasons included those of race, political opinion, religion or *Weltanschauung*, but not those of sexual orientation, abledness, health status, productivity or functionality.

Those who had been forcibly sterilized were not included, nor were homosexuals, 'asocials', 'professional criminals', deserters, forced laborers, or those who were killed in psychiatric institutions (Evangelische Akademie Bad Boll 1987, Goschler 2003; Reimesch 2003; Goschler 2005; 2009). This exclusion, however, was by no means the result of thoughtlessness or forgetfulness. Therefore, the concept of the forgotten Nazi victims that arose in the early 1980s is misleading. The discourse of forgotten victims addressed the persecution of those groups who were not included in reparation schemes and had not yet been included in discourses on *Aufarbeitung und Wiedergutmachung*, such as Roma and Sinti, forced laborers, homosexual men and sterilization victims. These men and women, however, had been not forgotten; they had, rather, been deliberately excluded from the reparation scheme. State Secretary Alfred Hartmann at the Ministry of Finance stated this unmistakably in 1957:

> The Act for the Prevention of Offspring with Hereditary Diseases of 14 July 1933 is not a typical Nazi law, since similar laws also exist in democratically governed countries—e.g. Sweden, Denmark, Finland and in some states of the USA. The Federal Indemnification Act, however, grants compensation benefits only to persons persecuted by the Nazi regime and, in a few exceptional cases, to injured parties who have suffered damage as a result of particularly serious violations of constitutional principles. (BT PLP 1957, 10876 (A))

The message to the persons concerned was clear: You are inferior, and the state has the right to reduce the number of the inferior; thus, the state was right to do this to you and you have no right to accuse it of wrongdoing. Another argument to fend off reparation claims drew on the fact that the Nazi sterilization law was based upon a draft sterilization law produced by the Prussian State Health Council in 1932. This draft had been the result of longstanding efforts by leading eugenicists and racial hygienists in Germany to translate their ideas into policy programmes (Weingart, Kroll et al. 1996). The purpose of the Prussian draft had been to reduce the procreation of the hereditarily ill and 'inferior' (Bock 1986, 51f.); in that respect, it did not differ from the subsequent Nazi law. The only difference was that the Hereditary Health Act sanctioned the use of force (Bock 1986, 51).

The argument that selective sterilization was not a 'typical Nazi injustice' was thus not entirely wrong; indeed, the idea had not been invented by the Nazis. Likewise, it is true that selective sterilization laws existed in Sweden, Denmark, Finland and many US states. Today, we know that such laws existed in many more countries and, at some point, in most states of the USA (see Chapter 2). In more conceptual language, we can say that selective sterilization policies did not originate in Nazi ideology but in a biopolitical rationality that was deeply ingrained and operative in many modern states. By reasoning that selective sterilization was not a typical Nazi injustice and *therefore* should not constitute entitlement to reparations, policy-makers effectively classified selective sterilization as a normal instrument of modern statecraft. They thereby simultaneously normalized and confirmed the biopolitical rationality that had originally informed and motivated these human rights infringements and shielded them from problematization. In short, unlike the oppression of racial or religious minorities or of political opponents (with the exception of communists), the biopolitical motive of improving the fitness of the social body was normalized, rather than condemned, by excluding sterilization victims from reparation claims. The Federal Republic would not condemn persecution on biopolitical grounds as wrongdoing, let alone promise non-repetition.

On the whole, in the 1950s and 60s, the view that selective sterilization programmes were a normal, useful, rational, science-based instrument of population policy prevailed. It was in this vein that the post-1945 debates about a possible new sterilization law continued (Tümmers 2011, 84ff.). One of the protagonists of these debates was hereditary pathologist Hans Nachtsheim. In the 1940s, Nachtsheim had been head of department for experimental hereditary pathology at the Kaiser Wilhelm Institute for Anthropology and performed, among other things, experiments on children with disabilities whom he obtained from the killing institution Brandenburg-Görden (Klee 2013, 427). He had also experimented with organs obtained from prisoners murdered in Auschwitz. After 1945, Nachtsheim continued to advocate "The Need for Active Hereditary Health Care", as he titled of one of his articles (Nachtsheim 1952; 1964).

In this mindset, courts and bureaucracies regularly refuted reparation claims on the grounds that selective sterilization was based on science rather than political violence. The justifications with which reparation claims were refuted thus resembled the justifications of Nazi sterilization policy. This is exemplified by the experience of Hans Lieser, whom we met in in 2010. Lieser told us that he had suffered coerced sterilization in 1942 and applied for reparation in the 1960s. In 1968, his application was dismissed by the district court of the city of Trier on the following grounds:[5]

> It is evident from the attached files that the proceedings were opened and conducted against the plaintiff for the sole reason that, in the opinion of the Hereditary Health Court, the plaintiff suffered from hereditary deafness. Prior to its decision, the Hereditary Health Court obtained the expert opinion of the Director of the University Ear, Nose and Throat Clinic in Frankfurt/Main dated 4 February 1941, in which the expert concluded that the plaintiff was suffering from sporadic recessive deafness, which was a hereditary disease

---

5   We visited Hans Lieser and his brother-in-law and fellow campaigner Valentin Hennig on 14 May 2010 in Kordel near Trier and obtained express permission from them to mention them both by name.

in terms of the Law for the Prevention of Offspring with Hereditary Diseases of 14 July 1933. It is obvious that this scientifically based expert opinion alone led the Hereditary Health Court to order infertility treatment. Moreover, it follows from statutory regulation—hardship compensation pursuant to §171, subsection 4, no. 1, BEG—that, as a rule, when sterilization was carried out in the National Socialist state, a violent measure according to §1, BEG can only be assumed if the intervention was carried out *without* prior procedure under the Hereditary Health Act. (Rationale quoted in Hennig 1999, 13, emph. i.o.)

This was common procedure. The majority of such applications were rejected "because the sterilizations were carried out on the basis of a procedure under the Hereditary Health Act" (BT Drs. 10/6287 1986, 37). In other words, if the injury was based on proper procedure, it by definition constituted no act of violence. Hence, the justifications with which reparation claims were refuted resembled the justifications of Nazi sterilization policy.

In 1965, the Parliamentary Committee on Reparations (*Wiedergutmachungsausschuss*), established by the *Bundestag* in 1953, officially approved this practice by declaring that the Hereditary Health Act had not been a law of injustice (*ein Unrechtsgesetz*); accordingly, victims of coerced sterilization were not to be entitled to reparations. The Committee based its statement on an expert hearing that it had conducted in 1961 (BT 3 1961). Seven experts were invited to this hearing, among them Professors Hans Nachtsheim, Werner Villinger and Helmut Ehrhardt. Nachtsheim, as previously mentioned, had used children with disabilities for his research (Klee 2013, 427); Ehrhardt had provided expert reports for Hereditary Health Courts (Klee 2013, 127); and Villinger had served as a judge on Hereditary Health Courts and was also involved in the so-called T4 programme, that is, the institutional killing programme, as a provider of medical reports (Klee 2013, 641). At the hearing, Nachtsheim maintained that the Hereditary Health Act was not to be conflated with Nazi racial policy because it was "an apolitical law intended to protect the hereditary health of the German people" (BT 3 1961, 33). Ehrhardt likewise underlined that the law "in its core content is indeed in line with the scientific convictions of the time, as well as those of today" (BT 3 1961, 25). Not all invited experts, however, were of this opinion. *Ministerialrat* Dr Karl[6], an administrative physician, argued that the very purpose of the Act,

---

6   The document does not give a first name here.

"namely to achieve a 'people's body (*Volkskörper*) purified of biologically inferior hereditary material'", was immoral and that the sterilizations ordered
under it constituted "a bodily injury emanating from a law of injustice". The
state, he concluded, had the duty to compensate this injury by means of a
special reparation law (BT 3 1961, 48). The Reparations Committee, however,
agreed with Nachtsheim, Ehrhardt and Villinger and denied entitlement
to reparations for victims of Nazi sterilization. As late as 2008, the Federal
Ministry of Finance affirmed this conclusion and the method by which it was
obtained, stating in a letter to the Petitions Committee of the *Bundestag* that
all aspects of reparation law had been "carefully examined by the Reparations
Committee after hearing leading experts in psychiatry" (BT Drs. 17/8729 2012,
7).

It was not until 1969 that essential parts of the Hereditary Health Act were
repealed. The remaining portions were repealed in the course of the 5th Criminal Law Reform in 1974, not, however, for reasons of incompatibility with
the Basic Law. It was not until 1986 that a German court, the Kiel District
Court, found that the Heredity Health Act had been incompatible with the
Basic Law (Scheulen 2005, 5). The Federal Constitutional Court, however, was
never concerned with the issue and consequently never stated an incompatibility between the Hereditary Health Act and the Basic Law.

3.3   The 1980s: The Struggle Gains Momentum

In the 1980s, the situation changed. A new phase of coming to terms with
Nazi crimes began with a surge of research and commemorative activities.
In this context, crimes against the so-called 'forgotten victims' met with new
public interest, among them Nazi medical crimes.

One important event was the famous 1985 speech by then-President of
State Richard von Weizsäcker on the fortieth anniversary of the end of the
war, in which he not only called May 8th, 1945 the day of liberation but also
commemorated several groups of 'forgotten victims', among them the victims of forced sterilization and institutional killings. Moreover, a number of
civil society initiatives began to address the 'forgotten victims'' exclusion from
reparations and demanded a revision of the reparation scheme (Die Grünen
im Bundestag & Fraktion der Alternativen Liste Berlin 1986; Deutscher Bundestag 1987; Tümmers 2011, 272ff.). In 1986, Gisela Bock's ground-breaking
book on coerced sterilization under Nazi rule was published (Bock 1986), and

civil society groups formed that began to research individual psychiatric institutions' involvement with the systematic killing of patients and persons with disabilities.

The Association of Victims of "Euthanasia" and Forced Sterilization (BEZ) played an important role in articulating these activities, as did the movement for the reform of psychiatry and the Study Group for Research into Nazi "Euthanasia" and Forced Sterilization (*Arbeitskreis zur Erforschung der nationalsozialistischen „Euthanasie" und Zwangssterilisation*). Among them, the BEZ was the only organization founded by and for citizens affected by coerced sterilization or institutional killing. Founded in 1987, it acted as a self-help group, an interest group, and an initiative for commemoration and civic education (Braun 2017). Its main objectives were to achieve full moral and legal rehabilitation, to have the Hereditary Health Act annulled by the German *Bundestag*, to achieve recognition as victims of the Nazi regime, and to receive reparations under the Federal Indemnification Act (*Bundesentschädigungsgesetz*, BEG). The overarching goal of these demands, however, was to overcome the stigma imposed on those affected and to ensure that nothing of the sort would ever take place again. In particular, the formal annulment of the Hereditary Health Act was of great importance to the BEZ, asthey assumed that the act of annulment (*Nichtigkeitserklärung*) would necessarily be followed by sterilization victims' recognition as Nazi victims and consequently by their entitlement to reparations under the BEG. For the BEZ, nothing short of reparation entitlements under the BEG would rescind the status of 'second-class' victims allotted to them. Only annulment of the Act and provision of full rights to reparations could reverse the stigma. However, the efforts of the BEZ failed. To this day, the victims of Nazi sterilization policy are entitled to no reparations under the BEG.

3.4   Reparations as the Greater Injustice?

We can thus speak of an enduring politics of denial and non-recognition that has never fully been reversed. It was bolstered by the core assumption that selective sterilization policies as such were a relatively normal, rational and science-based instrument of modern statecraft, even if the Nazi state might have used it improperly. Hence, Nazi sterilization policy was in principle considered rational and lawful. In the 1980s, a new argument emerged to refute reparation claims, referring this time not to science and the law but to nothing less than justice. If one were to grant entitlement to reparations to persons who were forcibly sterilized, as the argument went, one would in fact exacerbate existing injustices. Remarkably, this argument was first put forth by the abovementioned Prof. Ehrhardt at the public hearing on "Making Amends and Reparations for Nazi Injustice" organized by the Parliamentary Committee for the Interior in 1987 (Deutscher Bundestag 1987). The hearing marked a milestone in West German politics of coming to terms with the Nazi past insofar as it placed the so-called forgotten victims centre stage. For the first time, in addition to academic and policy experts, persons who were personally affected were invited as expert participants. Chairperson Klara Nowak and member Fritz Niemand attended and gave testimony on behalf of the BEZ. One of the academic experts invited was Prof. Helmut Ehrhardt, who argued:

> The last point of view concerns the actual victims of the Nazi regime. What will they say if, for example, an anti-social drunkard who was wrongly sterilized because of hereditary factors is now to be put on the same level as all those who, as respectable citizens, were tortured in a concentration camp for years simply because of their race, their faith or their political convictions? A compensation scheme for those sterilized would in many cases amount to a disavowal and a mockery of the genuine idea of reparation. (Deutscher Bundestag 1987, 288)

One year later, the Federal Ministry of Finance confirmed this view in a letter of reply to the BEZ, writing:

> [...] the expert hearing conducted by the German *Bundestag* in 1987 made it clear that revising the comprehensive laws on reparations and compensation for war-induced losses would not lead to greater justice but, on the contrary, to injustice in the relationship among the aggrieved parties.[7]

In the years that followed, the BEZ received a number of letters from the federal government reasoning, similarly, that improved compensation for sterilization victims or surviving victims of 'euthanasia' would be tantamount to an injustice to other Nazi victims (Braun 2017). For instance, in 1990, the Parliamentary Secretary of State at the Federal Ministry for Education and Research, Manfred Carstensen, wrote:

---

7   Federal Ministry of Finance, letter to the BEZ of 27 July 1988, LAV NRW OWL, D107/73. This and the following documents were retrieved from the BEZ archives.

Additional improvements are not possible if the principle of equal treatment is to be respected. They would lead to injustice towards the many severely affected Nazi victims who have received or are still receiving statutory benefits under the Federal Indemnification Act.[8]

Another letter from the Federal Chancellery, dated 2 February 1996, reiterates the position of the Ministry of Finance almost verbatim. Revising the law on reparations and compensation for war-induced losses, the letter says, "[...] would not lead to greater justice but, on the contrary, to injustice in the relations between the aggrieved parties."[9]

Nevertheless, the struggle for reparations made some, albeit slow, progress in the 1980s. In December 1980, the German government established a Hardship Fund for Victims of Coerced Sterilization under the General Act Regulating Compensation for War-Induced Losses of 1957. These victims could then claim one-time compensation of 5,000 DM; as of 1988, they could also apply for additional monthly payments under certain conditions[10]. Hardship compensation under the Fund, however, did not imply a recognition of wrongdoing. The purpose of the Fund was to compensate for damage suffered due to the war, not due to an injustice. In accordance with this purpose, claimants first needed to prove that they had in fact suffered significant harm to their health as a result of sterilization surgery. The health damage requirement was lifted in 1990. Until 2002, benefits were granted only if claimants were in a situation of acute social distress. Although several initiatives were launched in the 1980s and early 1990s for a new, more inclusive reparation scheme (Braun 2017), none of them found a majority in the *Bundestag*. According to the federal government, in February 2012, a total of 13,816 persons who had been forcibly sterilized had received one-time hardship compensation, and a total of 9,604 were receiving additional monthly benefits (BT Drs. 17/8729 2012, 3f.).

---

8   Parliamentary State Secretary at the BMBF, Manfred Carsten, letter to the BEZ of 27 June 1990, LAV NRW OWL, D107/73.

9   Federal Chancellery, letter to the BEZ of 2 February 1996, LAV NRW OWL, D107/73.

10   The monthly payments amounted to 100 DM at first, from 1 January 2004 they were raised to 100€, from 1 January 2006 to 120€, from 1 January 2011 to 291€ (BT Drs. 17/8729 2012, 3).

3.5   Ostracization or Annulment

The members of the BEZ and those who supported them struggled not only for reparations but also for moral and legal rehabilitation. The hardship compensation as such included neither an acknowledgement of wrongdoing nor a condemnation. Key to the struggle for rehabilitation became the question of annulment.

In 1986 and 1987, the faction of the Greens introduced a motion in the *Bundestag* proposing that the Hereditary Health Act be annulled (BT Drs. 10/4750 1986; BT Drs. 11/143 1987). The *Bundestag*, it was posited, should declare that the Act had been a Nazi law of injustice in that it categorized certain individuals as inferior and socially undesirable. It was necessary to condemn the Act because its very purpose, namely raising the hereditary quality of the German people, was reprehensible. The *Bundestag* should therefore annul the Act and all verdicts made under it.

The majority of the parliamentarians disagreed with this argument. In 1988, they adopted a declaration that condemned the rulings of the Hereditary Health Courts but not the Act as such (BT PLP 11/77). It took another ten years to pass the NS Annulment Act of 1998 (NS-AufG), which effectively cancelled the rulings. The main argument against annulling the Act was that it had never been part of German law after 1949; it was incompatible with the fundamental provisions of the Basic Law and had for this reason automatically gone out of force when the Basic Law was established. Thus, it could logically not be annulled, as argued for instance by then-Minister of Justice Klaus Kinkel (FDP) in 1987 (Kinkel 1987; Incesu and Saathoff 1988).

This, however, was merely the personal opinion of Minister Kinkel. In fact, as we have seen, the Hereditary Health Act was not ruled unconstitutional by a competent constitutional body until the 1980s. On the contrary, it was actively applied and thus constantly confirmed by the courts.

In the 1990s, the debate on annulling the Hereditary Health Act diminished. It was not revived until 2005, when a new initiative was launched, mainly by former Minister of Justice and long-standing supporter of the

BEZ Hans-Jochen Vogel (SPD)[11] and the National Ethics Council (NER).[12] The Ethics Council called on the *Bundestag* to extend its former condemnation of the sterilization verdicts to the Hereditary Health Act itself (Newsletter *Behindertenpolitik* 2006, 5). This initiative prompted the two proposals mentioned at the outset of this chapter: the proposal by *Bündnis 90*/The Greens to annul the Act (BT Drs. 16/1171 2006) and the proposal by the factions of the governing parties, CDU/CSU and SPD, to ostracize it (BT Drs. 16/3811 2006).[13]

It was the firm hope of the BEZ that having the Act annulled would provide full moral and legal rehabilitation to the victims and consequently constitute an entitlement to reparations under the BEG (Incesu and Saathoff 1988). However, the BEZ also wanted to draw attention to the injustices constituted by the fact that the Hereditary Health Act had been continuously applied after 1949. The annulment proposal by B90/The Greens at least mentioned this fact. The *Bundestag*, however, rejected the quest for an annulment on the grounds that

> [th]e Act had already ceased to be in force when the Basic Law entered into force to the extent that it violated the Basic Law, pursuant to Article 123(1) Basic Law. [...] The law thus no longer existed and can no longer be repealed. (BT Drs. 16/5450 2007, 1)

Unfortunately, this was not correct. The Act was not repealed when the Basic Law entered into force; rather, the courts continually referred to it in the course of review trials. No high-ranking court or constitutional body ever established its incompatibility with the Basic Law. The *Bundestag* refused the opportunity to confront this fact. It thus failed to address the countless bureaucratic and governmental acts, court rulings, and expert opinions in the 1950s and 1960s that not only confirmed the Hereditary Health Act by applying it but often expressly vindicated it. The *Bundestag* failed to see that the question of unconstitutionality had not been ignored but had rather been answered in the negative. By accepting the argument that the Act had ceased to

---

11   Hans-Jochen Vogel was a member of the National Ethics Council at the time and in this position motivated the Council to issue a statement on the matter, as he told us in a personal communication. Earlier, in 2004, the BEZ had turned to the Ethics Council to request support in their struggle to annul the Hereditary Health Act.

12   An abridged version of the NER statement is printed in the Newsletter *Behindertenpolitik* (2006).

13   The Left supported the call for annulment in a Question (*Kleine Anfrage*) submitted to the government on the matter (BT Drs. 16/2307, 2006).

exist in 1949, the majority denied the second-order injustice that had continued to take place until well after 1949 and failed to face the necessity for the Federal Republic to acknowledge not only its predecessor's wrongdoing but its own. In turn, they also failed to address the continuity of biopolitical reasoning underlying these performative confirmations and open justifications.

3.6   Comprehensive Rehabilitation?

The 2007 declaration by the *Bundestag* clearly condemned the Nazi sterilization law. The declaration meets all the requirements for an official apology: It names the wrong that has taken place, it names the major perpetrators, namely physicians and heads of institutions, and it names the victims, recognizes their suffering and expresses sorrow and respect. Moreover, in substance if not in wording, it confronts the biopolitical rationality that motivated these crimes, namely the delusional idea of 'purifying the body of the people' (*Volkskörper*). The *Bundestag* thereby distanced itself clearly and beyond doubt from the Nazi sterilization policy. It did not, however, condemn selective sterilization as such, and it did not confront the second-order injustices that occurred in the Federal Republic or the enduring biopolitical rationality that informed and motivated them. It treated Nazi sterilization policy as an isolated case of exceptional evil, clearly delineated in space and time, obviating the need to confront origins, overlaps, parallels or continuities that would go beyond these spatial and temporal demarcations. This is expressed quite clearly in the rationale for the declaration:

> Although eugenic ideas and eugenic sterilization laws were already widespread internationally before 1933, the Law for the Prevention of Offspring with Hereditary Diseases of 14 July 1933 (Hereditary Health Act) marks a historical caesura. This caesura is characterized by the fact that the allegedly 'hereditarily ill' persons were degraded to mere subjects of state disposal by this law. (BT Drs. 16/3811 2006, 1)

It does not suffice to condemn only the applications of the Act, so the rationale continues, given that the applications cannot be separated from the Act. The reasoning as to why this cannot be done, however, deserves closer inspection:

> A distinction between law and application requires a functioning separation of powers. This prerequisite was not met in the totalitarian Nazi state. [...]

Against the background of a totalitarian state practice, the legal orders and the forced sterilizations carried out on the basis of these orders cannot be separated from each other. (BT Drs. 16/3811 2006, 3)

Hence, only under the conditions of a totalitarian state was the Act itself determined to deserve condemnation and not only its application. Would a policy of selectively sterilizing the undesired, the 'useless', the unproductive be less despicable if pursued by a non-totalitarian state? Would it be acceptable to violate someone's bodily integrity, personal freedom, right to have and raise children if that person were declared inferior? In the context of the Nazi state, the declaration argues, the Hereditary Health Act was "the first step on the way to the 'euthanasia' mass murder program" (BT Drs. 16/3811 2006, 3). It can certainly be argued that this is correct insofar as we now know of significant personal, practical and ideological continuities between the Nazi sterilization policy and the institutional killings (Friedlander 1995). Yet it is unclear what the argument actually expresses: that selective sterilization necessarily entails mass murder—which would be historically incorrect—or that forced sterilization is unproblematic when it does not do so.

It is the merit of the *Bundestag* to have condemned Nazi sterilization policy for its—biopolitical—purpose of 'purifying the people's body' and to have stated that the purpose as such contravenes respect for human dignity. Yet it remains unclear whether, in the view of the *Bundestag*, the *practice* of selective sterilization is to be condemned, whether it is wrong for any political regime to assign a differential moral status to people according to their fitness, productivity and usefulness to the community, to make their rights to respect and state protection contingent on this status. By confining the issue at stake to the Nazi era, the *Bundestag* does several things at the same time: It acknowledges severe wrongdoing on the part of the predecessor regime and names perpetrators, victims, the wrong that occurred, the suffering it caused, and the reason why it was wrong. However, it evaded the question of whether the wrong—selective sterilization—is inherently wrong or only wrong under certain circumstances. In a certain sense, it thereby avoids making a promise of non-repetition insofar as it does not condemn the use of selective sterilization under conditions of a constitutional democracy. It further avoids addressing the second-order injustices that took place after 1945 and exonerates the Federal Republic from confronting its own wrongdoing. In short, the *Bundestag* failed to distance the Federal Republic explicitly and unambiguously from the biopolitical rationality that motivated selective sterilization policy in the past, to state that this biopolitical rationality is incompatible with who we are as a state and a society in the present, and to make a commitment to non-repetition in the future.

In hindsight, this was most probably the last word in the struggle for reparations for forced sterilization. After 2007, the debate was discontinued; given that very few of those concerned are still alive, it is unlikely to be reopened. What remains open, however, is the question of whether biopolitical rationality is considered compatible or incompatible with the kind of society we want to be.

4 Justice at Last: The Persecution of Homosexual Men and the Politics of Amends

On June 22, 2017, the German *Bundestag* passed the Act on the Criminal Rehabilitation of Persons Sentenced for Consensual Homosexual Acts after 8 May 1945 (StrRehaHomG), or Rehabilitation Act (BT PLP 18/240 2017). The Act repealed convictions under Paragraphs 175 and 175a of the FRG Criminal Code and Paragraph 151 of the GDR Criminal Code that were issued after 8 May 1945 in what became the Federal Republic of Germany and the German Democratic Republic, respectively. It rehabilitated men who had been convicted by German courts of consensual homosexual acts after the end of the Nazi regime[1]. Furthermore, it granted a right to reparations in the amount of 3,000 Euros per conviction plus 1,500 Euros per year or part thereof that those affected spent in custody. Later, the right to reparations was also extended to men who had been charged with homosexual acts but not convicted.

The Act was hailed by the government and the public alike as a major move to end discrimination against homosexuals and provide justice for those who had suffered from it in the past. The Federal Minister of Justice at the time, Heiko Maas, called the convictions "iniquities of the constitutional state" (*Schandtaten des Rechtsstaates*) (SZ 2017), maintaining: "From today's viewpoint, the former convictions are blatantly wrong. They deeply violate the human dignity of every person convicted" (SZ 2017). The Federal Family Minister, Manuela Schwesig, added that the Act was an "important signal for all homosexuals in Germany that discrimination and prejudice against them have no place in our society today or in the future" (SZ 2017).

---

1   The Law did not suspend all convictions, however: It did not rehabilitate those men who were sentenced for sexual interaction with boys under the age of 16. As the age of consent between persons of different sexes in Germany is not 16 but 14, this was seen as ongoing discrimination by some (BT PLP 18/240 2017, 24606 C).

The Rehabilitation Act, I argue, is both exceptional and paradigmatic. It is exceptional with regard to (West) German reparation policy in that it grants official rehabilitation and reparations to persons harmed by state wrongdoing *after* 1945. Thus, by enacting the Rehabilitation Act, the democratic state acknowledged its own systematic wrongdoing—and not only that of its predecessor, the Nazi state. Moreover, the democratic state acknowledged that it had in fact continued Nazi policy for decades: The Federal Republic had continued to apply a law dating back to 1935 and continued to persecute homosexuals, albeit in a mitigated form. By acknowledging this continuity, the state departed from the binary classification system that had structured West German reparation policies until then, namely the classification of reparation claims into those that referred to 'typical Nazi injustice' and those that did not. Within this system, the former counted as justified, the latter not; the former constituted an entitlement to reparations, the latter at best the possibility to apply for hardship compensation. The category of 'typical Nazi injustice' was circumscribed in temporal and semantic terms: In temporal terms, it was confined to the period of Nazi rule, demarcated by precise dates of beginning and ending. In semantic terms, 'typical Nazi injustice' referred exclusively to acts motivated by Nazi ideology. Conversely, this means that forms of repression, infringements and persecution that were not exclusively committed by the Nazi state, such as imprisoning homosexuals, by definition did not count as typical Nazi injustice and thus did not constitute entitlement to reparations. By definition, then, the post-war German state could not commit wrongs, at least not of a kind that would constitute an entitlement to reparations. The Nazi state was constructed as the state of exceptional evil, the post-war (West) German state as the state of democratic normality, and both as mutually exclusive. The Rehabilitation Act breaks with that dichotomy, which is an exceptional case in German reparation policy. There is no other case in which the Federal Republic has acknowledged a continuation of Nazi practices and granted reparations for it.

At the same time, the Act is paradigmatic insofar as it demonstrates the performative power of reparation policies: As the statements by Maas and Schwesig make clear, what is at stake is the moral, legal and political self-image of German society: What kind of society do we want to be? What kind of society do we *not* want to be any longer? What are our fundamental legal and ethical principles? Like any reparation policy, the Rehabilitation Act articulates past, present and future. By passing the Rehabilitation Act, the German state declared that consensual sex is a basic individual right that is protected

by the German constitution and that applies both to homosexual and heterosexual activities. The state confirmed the principle of equality before the law
and consequentially condemned the criminalization of male homosexuality
as an act of severe and unconstitutional discrimination. Homosexuality, it
declared, is a matter of individual freedom. It does not pose a threat to the
social and political order; on the contrary, it is discriminating against homosexuality that does so.

The path to that conclusion on the part of the state was, however, a long
one. To show how long, I will briefly recall the Nazi persecution of homosexuals and the continuation of that persecution in the Federal Republic, and then
reconstruct the struggle for reparations. I argue that the Nazi persecution of
male homosexuals was driven by a biopolitical rationality that long persisted
in the Federal Republic and that revolved around the idea that male homosexuality posed a threat to the health, strength and performance (*Leistungsfähigkeit*) of the body politic and thus had to be eradicated. The state failed
to recognize the persecution of homosexuals for what it was—a severe and
systematic state offence—for as long as this biopolitical construction of homosexuality endured. The 2017 Rehabilitation Act has made it manifest that
this is no longer the case and that the biopolitical construction of certain people as a threat to national health, strength and performance no longer applies
to homosexual men.

4.1 "Exterminating the Disease": The Nazi Persecution of Homosexual Men

When the Federal Republic came into being, it inherited inter alia Paragraphs
175 and 175a of the Criminal Code that had been enacted under Nazi rule in
1935. Before 1935, Paragraph 175 already penalized 'unnatural fornication' between males, but in 1935, the word 'unnatural' was removed so that men could
be convicted for each and every activity considered to go against a "general
sense of modesty and morality", including for instance "lewd glances" (*Reichs-
gerichtshof* 1940 quoted in Rinscheid 2013, 254). In addition, a new Paragraph
175a was created specifically to penalize certain forms of homosexual activities, namely threatening a man into homosexual acts, homosexual acts within
a relationship of dependency such as a service or employment relationship,
and homosexual acts between men over and under the age of 21 years. These
provisions were the first in German history to introduce an age of consent for

male homosexual acts that differed from that for heterosexual sex (Zinn 2018, 282). The homosexual acts specified in Paragraph 175a were punishable with up to ten years in penitentiary. In October 1936, Himmler established the Reich Central Office for Combating Homosexuality and Abortion (*Reichszentrale zur Bekämpfung der Homosexualität und der Abtreibung*) as a central instrument to detect and register homosexual men throughout the Reich. Upon the enactment of the revised Paragraph 175 and the establishment of the Office, the number of prosecutions, convictions, raids and arrests increased sharply.

Between 1935 and 1945, ordinary courts alone launched nearly 100,000 indictments according to Paragraphs 175 and 175a, and about half of the men charged were convicted (Zur Nieden 2009, 289). Some 6,500 additional convictions were issued by special courts such as martial courts (Grau 2014, 44). In 1940, moreover, Himmler decreed that the criminal police were to place all homosexual men who had seduced more than one partner in 'preventive detention' (*Vorbeugehaft*) *after* they had served their prison sentences (Bastian 2000, 58). Thousands were deported to concentration camps, and only a minority survived (BT Drs. 14/2984 (neu) 2000, 1). According to historical research, the death rate of homosexual men in the camps was about 60 percent (Zinn 2018, 319). Exact figures, however, are still lacking.

There is some dispute about the goals and the logic of this persecution[2]. Talk of a 'homocaust' among gay movements in the 1980s suggested that it aimed at a complete elimination of homosexuals, analogous to the attempt to eliminate Jews. Though historical researchers today tend to agree that this was not the case (Bastian 2000, 87ff.; Grau 2011, 145), leading Nazi functionaries, above all Heinrich Himmler, did indeed call for the extermination of homosexual men. His goal was nothing short of „exterminating the parasites of the people" (*die Ausmerzung der Volksschädlinge*) and "removing the predisposed, that is the centre of the epidemic, from the body of the people" (Himmler quoted in Zinn 2018, 295). Yet only a small fraction of homosexual men were in fact seized and detained (Bastian 2000, 88f.; Grau 2014; Zinn 2018, 304). The actual policy was directed at eliminating homosexuality as a visible way of life rather than eliminating each and every homosexual man. From 1934 onwards, Himmler made the issue a top priority. For him and other Nazi leaders, homosexuality was abnormal, deviant and sick, and homosexuals were alien to the ethnic community (*Gemeinschaftsfremde*), together with prostitutes, homeless

---

2   For a discussion about Nazi homophobia and racialisation of sexuality see Herzog 2005.

people, vagrants and others labelled as 'asocial' or 'work-shy'. However, rather than simply being treated as a subcategory of 'asocials', male homosexuals were constructed as a separate target group, persecuted by specifically designed instruments of detection, registration and extermination. What constituted his specificity?

One pervasive feature of Nazi homophobia was the preoccupation with population policy (Pretzel 2002, 25; 34). In that vein, the official rationale for revising Paragraph 175 in 1935 proclaimed: "The new state, which strives for a nation that is strong in number and strength and morally healthy, must vigorously confront all unnatural sexual activity." (Quoted in BT Drs. 14/2984 (neu) 2000, 1) Himmler in particular was obsessed with population policy, as indicated inter alia by his linking of the war against homosexuality with that against abortion (Grau 2011, 40). In February 1937, Himmler gave a speech to SS group leaders in Bad Tölz in which he laid out the grounds for eliminating homosexuality[3] and declared that tolerating the existence of one to two million homosexuals would mean "that our people will be wrecked by this epidemic" because the lack of "sexually able men will disrupt Germany's gender economy and become a disaster" (Himmler quoted in Zinn 2018, 291).

The preoccupation with population policy, however, does not explain why only homosexual men were targeted. Female homosexuality was ostracized as well (Eschebach and Ley 2012; Schoppmann 1997) and condemned as unnatural and morally unhealthy. The clubs, journals and meeting points of lesbian subculture were destroyed, but homosexual women were not systematically registered, charged, detained and murdered for same-sex activity. Female homosexuality was not constructed as a threat. Male homosexuality, in contrast, was constructed as an epidemic that threatened to undermine both the *Volksgemeinschaft* and the state. Unlike female homosexuals, male homosexuals were ascribed a seductive power, particularly among youth, and it was this power that made them so dangerous (Zur Nieden 2005). Accordingly, the Nazis concluded, the state had to:

> ... combat same-sex fornication between men particularly forcefully, as experience has shown that it has a tendency to spread epidemically and that it exerts a considerable influence on the entire thinking and feeling of the

---

3   According to the research of Alexander Zinn, this was Himmler's most important speech on this topic (Zinn 2018, 291).

circles concerned. (Official rationale for the revised Paragraph 175 of 1935 quoted in BT Drs. 14/2984 (neu), 2000, 1)

Similarly, the SS newspaper *The Black Corps* declared in 1937: "Forty thousand abnormals that could very well be eliminated from the ethnic community (*Volksgemeinschaft*), are, if left free, capable of poisoning two million" (*Das Schwarze Korps* quoted in Zinn 2018, 310).

Thus, male homosexuality was constructed as a contagious disease that, unless vigorously fought against, would spread among the male population. Notably, as Zinn points out, the Nazi state was heavily reliant on all-male organizations such as the SS, and these were imagined as being particularly vulnerable to the epidemic. Germany, Himmler insisted, was a men's state, and it was on the verge of self-destruction due to male homosexuality (Zur Nieden 2005). According to this imaginary, male homosexuality, equipped with its seductive power, was creating secret communities within organizations, a state within the state (Zinn 2018, 291f.; 295). Yet what was most disturbing for Himmler was the idea of homosexual men as soft, weak, spineless, cowardly, and mentally ill, tending to substitute an erotic principle for the principle of achievement (*Leistungsprinzip*) (Zinn 2018, 292; 294): "Homosexuality thus brings down every achievement (*Leistung*), every advancement (*Aufbau*) within the state and destroys the foundations of the state." (Himmler quoted in Zinn 2018, 292)

The word '*Leistung*' does not easily translate into English. It connotes not only achievement but also merit and performance; thus, it may refer to results but also the activity of making an effort or to the capacity for achieving results. The notion of *Leistung*, then, alludes to notions of efficiency, productivity, functionality, and strength and refers to results, activities and capabilities at the same time. For Himmler and other Nazi leaders, male homosexuality endangered the *Leistungsprinzip*, the basis of a strong, powerful, healthy state. Himmler therefore demanded that homosexual members of the SS be degraded, expelled and imprisoned. After serving their sentences they should be sent to concentration camps and "shot dead on the run" (Himmler quoted in Zinn 2018, 292). Hence, male homosexuality was constructed as a sex-related biopolitical threat, a contagious disease that undermined both the state and the *Volksgemeinschaft* and their health, strength and fitness. It was this biopolitical imaginary that motivated the Nazi persecution of homosexuals. As we shall see, it did not dissolve in 1945. Rather, it informed both the continued policy of criminalizing male homosexuality and, indirectly, the exclusion of homosexual Nazi victims from the post-war reparation scheme.

4.2   Normal Persecution: Paragraph 175 in the Federal Republic

Seventy years before the Rehabilitation Act was passed, in 1957, the Federal Constitutional Court issued a ruling on the matter of male homosexuality. The Court ruled that Paragraphs 175 and 175a of the Criminal Code did not violate the constitutional principles of personal freedom and equal protection before the law. The main rationale for this conclusion was that male homosexual acts violated moral law (*das Sittengesetz*) (BVerfGE 6 1957, 1).

The ruling rejected the constitutional complaint of two men, mentioned as Günther R. and Oskar K., who had been convicted for homosexual acts under Paragraphs 175 and 175a by the District Court of Hamburg in 1952. These paragraphs, the claimants held, dated back to 1935; thus, they were Nazi law and as such incompatible with the Basic Law, the West German Constitution. Consequently, they argued, Paragraphs 175 and 175a should be abolished and their convictions repealed. The Constitutional Court, however, refuted both claims; it denied that Paragraph 175 was Nazi law on the grounds that the 1935 law, although enacted under Nazi rule, was not a typical Nazi law. Not all laws dating back to the Nazi period were regarded as typical Nazi law. Therefore, the judges concluded that upholding Paragraphs 175 and 175a would not constitute a continuation of Nazi law and accordingly denied the two men legal rehabilitation.

Importantly, the Court did not engage with the fate of homosexuals under Nazi rule; the judges made no effort whatsoever to establish the facts of the persecution, let alone the logic behind it. Instead, they demonstrated at great lengths that banning male homosexuality had a long tradition in German law and that the Nazi ban was therefore merely one episode amongst others. They cited the Old Testament, the Constitutio Criminalis Carolina, Prussian law, various other German state laws before 1871, and others in order to bolster the claim that penalizing male homosexuality was perfectly normal for a political entity. In this way, the Court ultimately normalized the criminalization of male homosexuality, dissociated it from the Nazi past and categorized it as an exercise of normal statecraft.

In addition, the Court pointed to the fact that Paragraphs 175 and 175a were not listed in Control Council Law No.1. This law, established by the Allied

Control Council in September 1945, expressly repealed a number of Nazis laws and legal provisions for being "of a political or discriminatory nature upon which the Nazi regime rested" (Control Council Law No. 1 1945). It did not list Paragraphs 175 and 175a, Criminal Code, nor, for instance, the Law for the Prevention of Offspring with Hereditary Diseases, which had allowed for forcible sterilizations. Thus, the Constitutional Court concluded, the Allied Forces had not considered Paragraphs 175 and 175a to be specific to Nazi law.

Finally, the Court ruled, Paragraphs 175 and 175a were not invalidated by the Basic Law. The Federal Republic was the legal successor of the Nazi state and as such inherited the existing laws from the time prior to 1949—except for those found incompatible with the Basic Law (BVerfGE 6 1957, 20). Neither the Parliament nor the Constitutional Court found Paragraphs 175 and 175a to be incompatible with the Basic Law, so they remained in force.

In terms of content, the claimants argued that treating male homosexuality differently from female homosexuality violated the constitutional guarantee to equality before the law (Art. 3 GG). However, the Court denied this claim as well. It referred to a range of expert testimonies from medicine, psychiatry, social work, the police, and forensics that unanimously confirmed that male homosexuality was different from female homosexuality. The former, the testimonies agreed, was more intense, more aggressive, more visible, more promiscuous, more averse to marrying and having children, and not least more contagious and hence more dangerous to society (BVerfGE 6 1957, 21ff.). Due to its contagious power, they reasoned, male homosexuality was more widespread and more closely linked to venereal diseases, prostitution and crime and thus more dangerous to society. Unless the state took action to curb and control it, it would drain the life out of the population and debilitate it in terms of size, strength, health, and moral condition. Young people, as several of the invited experts claimed, were especially vulnerable to homosexual seduction; therefore, the state was called upon to protect its youth against this imminent threat.

Regarding the constitutional guarantee of personal freedom, the Court simply stated that it only applied within the confines of the moral law (Sittengesetz), whereas male homosexuality clearly violated the moral law (BVerfGE 6 1957, 30). In principle, then, the Court declared, personal freedom was a basic right, and, also in principle, the right to unrestricted personal development included one's sexuality, but this did not apply to homosexual men. Homosexual men were denied the right to personal freedom and equal treatment. The norm, according to the implicit logic, only applied to 'normals', not to 'abnormals'. The Court effectively stripped homosexual men of their basic constitutional rights and, as a result, of social status, their livelihood, and opportunities in life. In this sense, homosexual men in post-war Germany were *homini sacri* (Agamben 1998): governed and subjugated through law but deprived of legal status and protection. To bolster its reasoning, the Constitutional Court quoted the draft Criminal Code of 1927:

> The legislator should ask himself whether Paragraph 175, despite the hardships to which its application may lead and its limited practicability, does not constitute a barrier which may not be removed without harming the health and purity of the life of our people (*unseres Volkslebens*). [...] If this aberration continues to spread, it leads to the degeneration of the people and the decline of its strength [...] (BVerfGE 6 1957, 30f.)

We see here that the construction of male, and only male, homosexuality as a biopolitical threat did not originate in Nazi policy. The Nazis used it as a rationale for mass murder, but the construction as such neither arose nor ended with the Nazi regime.

The 1957 ruling set the tone for the following years, providing the main reference for legal and political decisions on the issue. We find all of its key elements reiterated in a draft criminal code presented by the Adenauer government in 1962. Eventually, the draft was rejected by the *Bundestag*, but it merits study as it set out the key elements of the biopolitical logic that motivated the preservation of Paragraph 175. It conceded that same-sex activity as such did not violate any legal rights or interests (*Rechtsgüter*). Nonetheless, the draft went on, the state was entitled to penalize behavior that was ethically despicable and shameful, as was the case with male homosexuality. After all, it was inherently contagious and spread particularly among young people. Consequently, homosexual communities would form and propagate within public services and institutions such as the police or the army and corrupt these from within (BT Drs. 4/650 1962, 377). Female homosexuality would not have this rampant, community-building, institution-corrupting power (BT Drs. 4/650 1962, 378). Therefore, the government concluded:

> More than in other areas of law, the legal system has the duty, vis-à-vis male homosexuality, to use the morality-forming power of the penal law to build a dam against the spread of a vicious activity which, if it were to take hold, would pose a serious threat to the healthy and natural order of the life of the people. (BT Drs. 4/650 1962, 377)

After all, historical experience had shown: "Where same-sex fornication has spread and assumed huge proportions, the result has been the degeneration of the people and the decay of its moral powers" (BT Drs. 4/650 1962, 377).

Paragraphs 175 and 175a did not exist only on paper; they were applied extensively. Criminal prosecution continued on a large scale: In the Federal Republic between 1945 and 1965, there were approximately 100,000 indictments and more than 44,000 convictions under Paragraphs 175 and 175a—near the number of criminal cases under Nazi rule (Zur Nieden 2009, 289). By way of comparison, in the fifteen years of the Weimar Republic, 'only' 9,375 convictions had taken place (Burgi and Wolff 2016, 22). It is important to note that not only a conviction, but even an indictment could be devastating. People could lose their jobs and their housing; they could be expelled from religious or other civil society associations. Self-help groups and sub-cultural or political associations were not permitted, so homosexual men were severely deprived of their civic and political rights (Burgi and Wolff 2016, 31).

Paragraphs 175 and 175a remained in place in the Federal Republic until the general revision of the Criminal Code in 1969. In 1973, further revisions reduced the list of sanctionable offences to sexual activities between men over and boys under eighteen years. The age of consent for heterosexual activities was sixteen at that time. In a ruling of October 1973, the Constitutional Court confirmed that this differential treatment was constitutional, citing the ruling of 1957. Male homosexuality, it reiterated, was fundamentally different from both lesbian and heterosexual sexuality, as several scientific experts had verified in 1957. Again, the main reason cited was that young men needed state protection from homosexual seduction, which would otherwise spread and damage their personal lives and development (Burgi and Wolff 2016, 31).

The GDR completely abolished Paragraphs 175 and 175a in 1968 and thereby, as Günter Grau points out, was the first polity in German history to decriminalize consensual sex between men (Grau 2011, 154). In the Federal Republic, Paragraph 175 remained in force until 1994. It was abolished solely in the context of German unification and the need to harmonize the two German Criminal Codes (Grau 2011, 157).

Thus, the Federal Republic deliberately maintained the 1935 Nazi law and deprived homosexual men of basic constitutional rights. Major state institutions subscribed to the biopolitical construction that male homosexuality was a contagious force that caused mental illness, weakness, venereal diseases, prostitution, and crime and that threatened to undermine the strength and fitness of state and society. In short, the institutions of the Federal Republic maintained the Nazi law because they shared the biopolitical rationality that informed it.

It was due to this continuity in biopolitical rationality that homosexual victims of Nazi persecution were excluded from post-war reparations, as I will show in the following pages.

4.3   Banned from Reparations

After 1945, homosexual men were effectively excluded from reparations. To understand how and why this happened, we need to understand the architecture of the West German reparation scheme and its inbuilt distinction between normal statecraft and exceptional evil. Within this framework, the type of violations that I have termed injuries of normality, such as the persecution of homosexuals, selective sterilization, and the persecution of 'asocials', would qualify as normal statecraft, not as exceptional evil. As explained in Chapter 1, the concept of injuries of normality refers to systematic human rights violations and acts of degradation, stigmatization and persecution of persons deemed not to conform with underlying standards of normality, health, fitness, productivity or usefulness for the community. Injuries of normality follow a biopolitical rationality of safeguarding and improving the fitness, functionality and productivity of the collective body, a rationality which, as such, was not limited to the Nazi regime. Nazi biopolitics was exceptionally murderous, but the biopolitical rationality that informed systematic injuries of normality was not utterly alien to German governments before or after 1945. In fact, the way that West German courts and governments dealt with the reparation claims of those affected by such injuries of normality demonstrates that they shared the underlying rationality and considered it quite normal for a state, for instance, to defend itself against the debilitating power of male homosexuality. This underlying attitude is reflected in the architecture of the West German reparation scheme.

There were, and still are, two possible ways for Nazi victims to achieve compensation in the Federal Republic: via the Federal Indemnification Act (*Bundesentschädigungsgesetz*, BEG) of 1953[4] and via the 1957 General Law on

---

4   The first reparation law on a federal level was the Federal Supplementary Law (*Bundesergänzungsgesetz*), passed on 18 September 1953. This law, however, proved insufficient and was replaced by the Federal Indemnification Act (*Bundesentschädigungsgesetz*,

Consequences of the War (*Allgemeines Kriegsfolgengesetz*, AKG) with the Hardship Funds established under it in the 1980s. Importantly, only the Federal Indemnification Act grants entitlement to reparations for an *injustice* suffered, subject to territorial restrictions[5], whereas the AKG was meant to provide compensation for a *damage* that occurred in the context of the war. The legislators were well aware that the BEG did not grant the right to reparations to *all* Nazi victims; this had never been their declared intention (Hockerts 2001). Thus, a distinction had to be made between what should and what should not constitute an entitlement to reparations. The legislators deliberately decided to make reparations under BEG available only for typical Nazi injustices, with only specific forms of Nazi persecution qualifying as typical Nazi injustices. For this reason, the BEG conclusively defines who qualifies as a victim of Nazi persecution, namely someone who was persecuted for reasons of political opposition to the Nazi regime or for reasons of race, religion or ideology (*Weltanschauung*) (BEG §1(1)). This definition excluded the victims of forced sterilization, homosexuals, so-called 'asocials', so-called 'professional criminals', deserters, forced laborers and many others, regardless of what they suffered. Even if they had suffered deportation, detention in a concentration camp, injuries, mutilation or murder, these acts as such did not qualify as Nazi persecution. The question for the BEG was not *whether* a persecution occurred, but *on what grounds*. The critical distinction for the BEG was not the severity of offenses but the subjective motive behind them (Giessler 1981, 9). Put differently, the law-makers in the 1950s distinguished between legitimate and illegitimate motives for persecution—a distinction which came down to the question of whether they themselves could or could not accept them.

State measures to curb homosexuality, inheritable diseases or asocial behavior were *not* considered typical Nazi injustice (Hockerts 2001, 201). Accordingly, the legal literature after 1945 explicitly justified their exclusion from reparations under BEG. After all, it was argued, Paragraph 175 had not been

---

BEG), passed on 29 June 1956, which entered into force retroactively on 1 October 1953 (Federal Ministry of Finance 2019, 10).

5   The Law is based on the so-called territoriality principle, which requires that claimants must have had a "spatial relationship" to the German Reich. This includes, roughly speaking, German citizens and persons who lived in within the 1937 German borders. It does not include persons who suffered from Nazi crimes elsewhere (Brunner, Frei, and Goschler 2009, 25ff.).

in place for reasons of race or political opposition but for reasons of expediency or security (Burgi and Wolff 2016, 33). The German government agreed. As late as 1986, a report by the Federal Government to the *Bundestag* explained:

> The penalization of homosexual activity in criminal proceedings conducted in accordance with criminal law provisions is neither Nazi injustice nor incompatible with the rule of law. [...] Therefore, convictions imposed in criminal proceedings conducted in accordance with the law and executed in the regular course of justice cannot be compensated as a deprivation of liberty. (BT Drs. 10/6287 1986, 40)

The fact that consensual sexuality was persecuted did not constitute an injustice because it was motivated by acceptable reasons—reasons that policy-makers and jurists of the Federal Republic could share. They, too, thought that male homosexuality constituted a danger to youth, that it was contagious and debilitating, caused moral weakness, physical and mental illness, prostitution and crime. In short, they shared the biopolitical construction of male homosexuality as undermining the health and fitness of state and society.

After the BEG, the General Law on Consequences of the War (AKG) formed a second possible track to reparations. It was passed in November 1957 and was intended to govern the claims of those who had been harmed by the Nazi regime but were not eligible for reparations under the BEG. However, as Hans Günter Hockerts states, the hurdles were high and the application deadlines tight; as a result, until the establishment of new hardship funds in the 1980s, the numbers of recipients from groups not mentioned in the BEG were close to zero (Hockerts 2001, 201). Under the hardship funds established in the 1980s, claimants could receive a one-time allowance of 5,000 Deutschmarks or, in particularly severe cases, monthly allowances. Yet, even then, the number of successful applications by homosexual men remained negligible. By 31 December 2018, a total of twenty applications had been submitted by persons who had suffered persecution as homosexuals, and eight of these were approved (Federal Ministry of Finance 2019, 29). A total of five applications had been submitted for monthly allowances; two were approved (Federal Ministry of Finance 2019, 30).

To conclude, the distinction between those who were entitled to reparations and those who were not ultimately rested on the new state's attitude towards the former's motives for persecution. With respect to male homosexuality, the political and legal elite of the Federal Republic predominantly shared the Nazi assumption that male homosexuality was debilitating and contagious and thus a danger to state and society. For them, criminalizing and controlling homosexuality was an entirely reasonable thing to do, even if some measures, such as detaining people in concentration camps, may have constituted an undue hardship in some cases. The construction that motivated the penalization of male homosexuality was essentially the same as that of the Nazi state; in this respect, the democratic state shared the Nazi state's motives, if not quite its methods.

4.4   Regret and Reluctance

After decades of struggle, Paragraph 175 was finally abolished in 1994. It was not until then that the Federal Republic began to distance itself from the persecution of homosexuals and to acknowledge that it had been a severe case of wrongdoing that required redress. After another four years, in 1998, the *Bundestag* passed the Law to Annul Unjust Sentences Imposed During the National Socialist Administration of Criminal Justice (NS Annulment Act; NS-AufG), which rescinded all unjust NS criminal judgements without case-by-case review. Yet the appendix to the law that specified *which* types of sentences were defined as 'unjust' did *not* include Paragraphs 175 and 175a, meaning that convictions according to Paragraph 175 and 175a, whether before or after 1945, were *not* annulled at that point.

Two years later, in December 2000, the *Bundestag* passed a unanimous resolution that stipulated that the criminalization of consensual homosexual activities after 1945 *had* been a violation of human dignity (BT PLP 14/140 2000). The *Bundestag* issued an apology:

> The German Bundestag confirms its conviction that the honor of the homosexual victims of the Nazi regime must be restored. The German Bundestag regrets that the National Socialist version of Paragraph 175 remained in force without change in the criminal law of the Federal Republic of Germany until 1969. It apologizes for the continuing criminal prosecution of homosexual citizens until 1969, whose human dignity, opportunity for personal development, and quality of life were severely impaired by the threat of criminal prosecution. (BT Drs. 14/2984 (neu) 2000, 2)

The decision, however, had no immediate consequences in terms of rehabilitation or reparations; the majority of MPs at the time were not ready to annul the convictions issued by the Nazi courts, let alone those of the Federal

Republic. One concern was that this might create a precedent for further re-habilitation claims, as MdB Jörg van Essen (FDP) explained:

> ... after 1945, too, people suffered terribly with the consequences of a convic-tion going far beyond what punishment should actually do, namely leading to the destruction of all opportunities in life, to social ostracism. We have to admit that, unfortunately, this has happened in a similar way in many other areas too. We have had terribly dismaying sentences [...] that make us clench our hands over our heads. People were sent to prison for several months for everyday crimes. There were incredibly harsh sentences in this area in par-ticular, because much of the injustice that had been sown during the Third Reich had an aftermath. That is why it is extremely difficult for us, from to-day's point of view, to judge the time after 1945 by saying: We declare this to be wrong; if we started in one area but did not extend it to other areas, we would not really achieve justice. I suspect that there are many areas in which, from today's point of view, we have to say that we cannot agree with the judgments of that time. (BT PLP 14/140 2000, 13744 A-B)

At stake, then, was the temporal-substantive demarcation that had been erected to separate the present from the past, the constitutional state from the state of injustice, ordinary statecraft from extraordinary evil. The ma-jority of Parliamentarians could not yet bring themselves to acknowledge the permeability of that demarcation line and concede that numerous forms of injustice had passed through it and continued to operate under the new democratic regime.

The men who had suffered Nazi persecution as homosexuals would wait two additional years until, in May 2002, the *Bundestag* finally passed the Act to Amend the Law to Annul Unjust Sentences Imposed during the National So-cialist Administration of Criminal Justice—against the votes of the CDU/CSU and FDP (Burgi and Wolff 2016, 34). Through this act, those who had been convicted under Paragraphs 175 and 175a by the Nazi state received rehabili-tation—but not those convicted under the same law after 1945.

In the following years, the Greens and the Left in Parliament again launched attempts to achieve rehabilitation and reparations for those con-victed for consensual homosexual acts after 1945 (BT Drs. 16/11440 2008; BT Drs. 16/10944). In 2009, their motions were rejected by the votes of the CDU/CSU, SPD and FDP in the *Bundestag*. The CDU/CSU, SPD and FDP were willing to annul the convictions passed by the Nazi courts but not those passed by the courts of the Federal Republic, even though the *Bundestag* had stated in 2000 that the convictions before and after 1945 violated human dignity. Obviously, the question was not *whether* a severe human rights violation had been committed, but *by whom*.

The arguments against repealing the post-1945 convictions mainly referred to constitutional issues. In a constitutional state, opponents argued, the parliament was not entitled to repeal the rulings of the courts, for this would amount to breaching the separation of powers and the principle of legal certainty (Senatsverwaltung für Arbeit and Integration und Frauen 2011, 41). The events of the following years, however, showed that where there is a political will, there is also a constitutional way.

4.5   From Injuries of Normality to Sexual Exceptionalism

In 2011, the Berlin Senate held a conference offering an alternative view on the constitutional issues related to rehabilitation of and reparations for men convicted of homosexual activity after 1945. The Senate submitted reasoning according to which annulling post-1945 convictions was indeed constitutional (Senatsverwaltung für Arbeit and Integration und Frauen 2011). In 2015, the Bundesrat passed a resolution calling upon the federal government to draft a new law to rehabilitate the men convicted for consensual homosexual acts after 1945 on the grounds that these convictions had violated human dignity (BR Drs. 189/15 (Beschluss) 2015).

Instrumental in this respect was also the legal opinion of Martin Burgi and Daniel Wolff on behalf of the Federal Anti-Discrimination Agency on rehabilitation for post-1945 convictions and the issue of constitutionality (Burgi and Wolff 2016). The opinion took constitutional concerns about legal certainty and separation of powers seriously, but also clarified that a general annulment would not violate either of them. The first of these concerns referred to the point that, in a constitutional democracy, neither the government nor parliament is permitted to interfere with the decisions of the judiciary. If the parliament were to issue a blanket annulment of an entire set of court rulings, this would amount to breaching the separation of powers and encroaching on the principle of legal certainty. Burgi and Wolff, however, countered that such an encroachment could be justified in this case given that it would refer to an exceptional matter. Firstly, they argued, the convictions at stake affected a clearly demarcatable group of individuals, and secondly, they constituted an exceptionally severe infringement of these individuals' basic rights, namely "an intervention in the inviolable core domain of a person's private life as covered by the fundamental right to free development of personality provided for in Article 2(1) Basic Law, in conjunction with Article 1(1) Basic Law" (Burgi and Wolff 2016, 10).

While there may have been other convictions after 1945 that referred to offenses no longer criminalized today, such as procuring and adultery, issuing a blanket rehabilitation of men convicted under Paragraphs 175 and 175a would not set a precedent and would not entail a series of further claims to rehabilitation, since the impact of these infringements differed: "The stigmatization and intense repression by and within society that was predominantly and typically suffered by individuals convicted under Section 175 StGB is in this regard unparalleled" (Burgi and Wolff 2016, 11).

Both the government and the parliament finally adopted this line of reasoning. In 2016, Federal Minister for Justice and Consumer Protection Heiko Maas (SPD) announced that the government was preparing for the legal rehabilitation and reparations for those convicted for consensual homosexual acts after 1945 (BMJ 2016). On 22 June 2019, the *Bundestag* adopted the Rehabilitation Act unanimously.

Proponents of rehabilitation and reparations could draw support from the European Court of Human Rights, which, beginning in 1981, had issued a series of rulings condemning the criminalization of consensual homosexuality (Johnson 2013). The Court had greatly contributed to framing homosexuality as a human rights issue, evoking particularly the right to a private life, freedom of expression and non-discrimination as laid out in the European Convention for Human Rights. The new approach developed by the Court revolved around the notion of sexuality as "an essentially private manifestation of the human personality" (Johnson 2010). Sexuality, in these rulings, became an essential and inalienable aspect of human life, inextricably linked to intimacy and identity and as such valuable and worthy of state protection. Consensual homosexuality was no longer a matter of morality or a danger to the state but a matter of private life. The older, biopolitical notion of homosexuality as undermining the strength of the state gave way to a liberal–expressivist one in which homosexuality was seen as an individual lifestyle that allowed for the expression of one's own authentic personality. In the 2000s, this new framework increasingly gained ground in German politics as well. Male homosexuality moved from the biopolitical register of diseases to the psycho–legal register of personhood and became a core element of gay men's personal identity, as Berlin Senator Dilek Kolat proclaimed: "Paragraph 175 threatened gay men at the core of their personalities, their sexual identities" (Senatsver-waltung für Arbeit, Integration und Frauen 2011, 6).

The notion of homosexuality as a core element of one's personality and thus as protected by the right to personal freedom formed the basis for the rationale for the Rehabilitation Act (BMJ 2016, 1). However, while the view that homosexuality was a matter of private life and not criminal law may have prevailed by then, it was still an exceptional step for the *Bundestag* to condemn its own former law, annul its consequences and grant reparations on the grounds that it had been unconstitutional. Therefore, as MdB Sabine Sütterlin-Waack (CDU/CSU) correctly proclaimed in the *Bundestag*'s plenary debate, "Today we are bringing to an end a unique and unprecedented legal–political process with which we are also, in a sense, entering new constitutional territory" (BT PLP 18/240 2017, 24606D).

Indeed, for the first time, the German Parliament had passed an act of regret and redress for the continuation of a Nazi policy. In a gesture of exceptional self-critique, the state distanced itself not only from the wrongdoing of its predecessor but from its own wrongdoing. It acknowledged that its own democratic institutions had committed severe human rights violations that differed only in degree from those of the Nazi state. It conceded that there was only a gradual difference between the state of normality and the state of exceptional evil. To this day, no other group of Nazi victims has received a similar gesture.

One could say that, in the case of Paragraph 175, the continuity was most palpable since here the *same* policy was continued; people were charged, convicted and imprisoned and their lives destroyed by means of the same law. This is true, but the post-war German state also continued to operate workhouses, maintained sterilization verdicts for decades, denied victims reparations and rehabilitation, and justified these exclusions by citing medical grounds, security reasons or reasons of expediency. The state could have retrospectively distanced itself from these choices and did not. In the case of the persecution of homosexuals, the state in fact broke with the original motives of persecution; in other cases, it did not. In 2017, the German state no longer shared the biopolitical motive that had driven the criminalization of male homosexuality for so long. This motive had become incompatible with the political identity of the present state. The biopolitical construction of male homosexuality as a threat to the health, strength and performance of state and society was no longer evoked: it was dead. Instead, as in the rulings of the European Court of Human Rights, homosexuality was framed as a matter of intimacy, private life and personal development. In that respect, according to the dominant discourse, sexuality was a special, particular, exceptional facet of human activity that was intimately connected to the core of one's personality. It was exactly this idea of sexuality as a matter of privacy and of the fundamental core of personal existence that allowed the government to annul the convictions under Paragraphs 175 and 175a without setting a precedent for possible further lawsuits.

Due to this articulation of sexuality, privacy and authentic subjectivity, it was possible to set the case of homosexuality apart from any other potential area of post-1945 state wrongdoing. As Paul Johnson (2010) has shown for the European Court of Human Rights, reinterpreting homosexuality as a matter of human rights was accompanied by, or even enabled by, the construction of a "European homosexual subject" possessing "a true, authentic and congenital self" (Johnson 2010, 72). The same interpretational move allowed the German government to resolve their concerns that blanket rehabilitation of homosexuals might set in motion a series of further rehabilitation claims by other groups. Attaching homosexuality to the inner, inviolable core of one's personality allowed the law-makers to demarcate these rehabilitation claims from possible others and to constitute an acceptable exception to the general rule of non-interference with the judiciary. What appears as a normalization of same-sex activity on the one hand thus implies a kind of sexual exceptionalism on the other that makes sexuality an essentially private aspect of personal life. The new articulation of sexuality and privacy allowed for redrawing the line between justified and unjustified reparation claims and shielding the state against a possible avalanche of further reparation claims. In this vein, MdB Sabine Sütterlin-Waack (CDU/CSU) explained that the state had indeed continued to apply Nazi law in other instances as well, for example in the cases of adultery and matchmaking, and that this had caused considerable hardship, but that "neither adultery nor matchmaking amount to a massive intrusion into the core area of the personal right to design one's own private life" (BT PLP 18/240 2017, 24608A).

Homosexuality had thus been transformed from a political into a private affair, from a danger to state and society to a valuable resource deserving their protection. In 2017, it is a resource rather than a threat to society. Correspondingly, the object of state protection is no longer the moral and physical health of state and society but rather the healthy development of the individual personality. On a more speculative note, one could add that personal development has been promoted to a key resource for a state that increasingly relies on human capacities such as knowledge, creativity, and intelligence. The new individualistic, personalized variant of male homosexuality is not a political force that drains society and the state of their strength and productivity; rather, it is itself a source of strength and productivity. Homosexual men are no longer public enemies; they are no longer the others against whom 'we' have to defend our youth, our state and our society. Rather, the others are now the other states that proclaim homosexuals the public enemy, as MdB Gudrun Zollner (CDU/CSU) declared:

> But we are also sending a signal as a society. Germany takes a stand—against discrimination and against exclusion. We also want to send a positive signal beyond our national borders to countries where homosexuality is still heavily ostracized. (BT PLP 18/240 2017, 24612 C)

Thus, the Rehabilitation Act is a message to the world: Look: Germany is a liberal, modern, democratic state; it draws strength from its citizens' sexual self-expression and personal growth. Homosexuality is no longer an epidemic but a way of life, and one that is perfectly compatible with the moral, social and political order of the present state.

4.6   Conclusion

Why have almost none of the victims of the Nazi persecution of homosexuals received reparations while the post-1945 victims of Paragraph 175 have been awarded them? Admittedly, this chapter cannot answer the questions of which struggles were fought by whom and how between 1945 and 2017—or why some of them were more successful than others. Here, I can only point out *what* it was that changed.

Homosexual victims of Nazi persecution were excluded from the postwar reparation scheme because the judicial and the political elite of the new, democratic state shared the Nazis' motives for that persecution. They may not have adopted the full array of Nazi methods (although with Paragraph 175 they maintained critical parts of those methods), but they shared the rationale that had motivated the Nazi policy against homosexual men. This rationale had not been invented by the Nazis but dates back at least to the time of the Weimar Republic. The Nazis, principally Himmler, developed it into a powerful biopolitical delusion, composed of the following assumptions: all same-sex sexuality is unnatural and shameful, but male homosexuality is particularly vicious, debilitating and aggressive; it is like an epidemic that, unless vigorously opposed, will spread and damage the people's health and sense of morality. It causes promiscuity, prostitution and crime and thereby damages society. Rather than an innate property, it is largely an acquired behavior caused by seduction, imitation and habit. Young people, according to this assumption, are particularly susceptible. In addition, homosexual men have the tendency to establish clandestine same-sex communities within existing institutions, rendering the core institutions of the men's state—the police and the military—particularly vulnerable. Sooner or later, homosexual communities will undermine the existing institutions and, given the vicious and debilitating character of male homosexuality, drain the strength and performance (*Leistungsfähigkeit*) of the state. Again, we see that Nazi biopolitics was not necessarily biologistic; its murderous force was not dependent on a biologistic epistemology.

This biopolitical construction did not dissolve in 1945. It was actively confirmed by the Constitutional Court in 1957 and by the Adenauer government in 1962 in its draft criminal code. The elites of the Federal Republic sustained the Nazi law that had served to deport, detain, degrade and kill tens of thousands of men because these elites continued to believe in the rationale that had motivated these atrocities. For the same reason, reparations to homosexual Nazi victims were denied. The West German reparation scheme was founded upon principles bound to contain the number of reparation claims in spatial, temporal and substantial terms: the territoriality principle, the restriction to the time between 1933 and 1945, and the definition of a victim of Nazi persecution as someone persecuted for reasons of political opposition, race, religion or ideology. Every reparation scheme draws distinctions between what constitutes a valid entitlement to reparations and what does not. In this case, the distinction ultimately referred to the perpetrators' motives; only those atrocities and infringements based on typical Nazi motivations should constitute an entitlement to reparations. Conversely, motives that reached beyond the Nazi regime in temporal, politico-geographical and/or substantial terms, such as motives that dated back further in time, were found operative in other countries as well, and/or were consistent with those of the ruling elites of the present state, would be excluded by design. Motives shared by the past and present elites included, for instance, the fight against communism and the fight against biopolitical threats and burdens (such as mental illness, disability, homelessness, and male homosexuality) that undermined the state's and society's strength and productivity. Within the post-war reparation scheme,

injuries of normality such as the persecution of 'asocials', of people categorized as mentally ill or disabled, or of male homosexuals did not constitute
an entitlement to reparations because and insofar as the post-war elites in
politics and law effectively shared the Nazis' motives for persecuting these
people. After 1945, they did not continue the camp system, they did not apply
the Nazi sterilization law to sterilize people, they did not kill people for being
mentally ill or homosexual, but in principle they shared the understanding
that these people posed a threat or a burden to society that needed to be cur-
tailed. Concerning homosexuality, the new state outright continued the Nazi
policy in crucial respects.

In this case, however, the state also performed the most clear-cut break to
date with former policy by acknowledging that this very continuity had constituted a systematic human rights violation that required redress. What made
this break possible was the dissolution of the previous policy rationale: Male
homosexuality is no longer conceived as a biopolitical threat. It has moved
from the underworld of crime, clubs and clandestine communities into the
core of one's personality, where it forms an essential element of personal development, self-expression and growth; this shift represents values most compatible with the contemporary, modern liberal state. The possibility, today, to
freely express one's sexual identity, whether homosexual or not, is considered
a source of, rather than a threat to, productivity and performance, and it is
thus perfectly compatible with the social, moral and political values of the liberal state. No corresponding act of self-criticism and acknowledgement has
occurred vis-à-vis 'asocials' or those who were forcibly sterilized. Concerning
the latter, the present state has never officially acknowledged or expressed
regret for the fact that it denied rehabilitation and reparation to victims for
many years on the grounds that it did not, or does not, condemn the perpetrators' motives.

5 Marginal Justice: Coming to Terms with the Persecution of the 'Asocials'

Between 1933 and 1945, tens of thousands of men and women, boys and girls were being stigmatized and persecuted as so-called 'asocials'. Reliable numbers are still not available today (Hörath 2017, 11). In a speech in October 1943, Heinrich Himmler boasted about the number of 70,000 'asocials' and 'professional criminals' who had been detained in concentration camps until then (Hörath 2017, 319; WD 2016, 15). According to the *Stiftung Brandenburgische Gedenkstätten*, by 1945, more than 11,500 persons had been detained as 'asocials' or 'work-shy' in the concentration camp of Sachsenhausen, of whom 2,600 died there, and about 9,173 detained in Dachau (WD 2016, 16). In addition, a letter by Secretary of State Monika Grütters recently gives the number of 1,680 persons detained as 'asocials' in the concentration camp of Flossenbürg, of whom 204 died there, 250 persons in Bergen-Belsen, of whom at least 38 died there, and at least 1,196 persons in Neuengamme, of whom at least 230 did not survive the camp. As Anne Alex for the civil society initiative *Arbeitskreis Marginalisierte – gestern und heute* points out, these figures, however, do not include all those detained in workhouses, work colonies, 'beggar camps' (*Bettlerlager*), penitentiaries, youth camps or psychiatric institutions, nor those imprisoned by the police or condemned to forced labor for being or being deemed homeless, 'work-shy', a prostitute or a vagrant or otherwise 'asocial' (Alex 2015, 33; WD 2016, 15). How many of these people were killed in these institutions we do not know. It is important to see, however, that there was no clear-cut definition of being 'asocial' under Nazi rule and this category overlapped with others. Among those detained for being 'asocial' were many who were also marked as Gypsies, Jews, homosexuals, mentally ill or handicapped. These Nazi victims had little in common except that they did not live up to Nazi standards of being a productive, well-adjusted member of the German *Volksgemeinschaft* (German ethnic community).

In the Federal Republic of Germany, those persecuted as 'asocials' under Nazi rule belong to the category of the so-called 'forgotten victims', a term coined in the 1980s denoting those Nazi victims who were not entitled to reparations under the 1953 Federal Indemnification Act (*Bundesentschädigungsgesetz*, BEG). The 'forgotten victims', however, had never been 'forgotten', but they had been consciously excluded from post-war reparation policy. For (West) German reparation policy, it was not decisive what someone had suffered from the Nazi state but on what grounds. Persecution on the grounds that someone did not conform to Nazi standards of health, fitness, sexual way of life, productivity or usefulness does not count as typical Nazi injustice. In this chapter, I will argue that the so-called 'asocials' still have a particularly marginal status in historic justice policy in Germany today, even compared with other groups of 'forgotten victims'. Today, there are official state-sponsored memorials for homosexuals, Sinti and Roma, and victims of the 'euthanasia' programme in Berlin, and the *Bundestag* has formally condemned the Nazi sterilisation and 'euthanasia' programme as well as the persecution of homosexuals as Nazi injustice. The victims of the Nazi persecution of the 'asocials', by contrast, have not received an official apology nor is there a state-sponsored memorial or historical site to commemorate their suffering.

The chapter examines how official state policy in the Federal Republic has addressed the Nazi persecution of the 'asocials' and how it has taken measures of compensation and commemoration – or not. I argue that official German politics has largely failed to identify and confront the distinctive features of this type of persecution, namely that it targeted victims according to Nazi standards of productivity, economic usefulness and social conformism. It can thus be understood as a type of persecution based on a biopolitical rationality of enhancing the life forces of the collective, in this case the *Volksgemeinschaft* through promoting and fostering the orderly, useful and productive lives and eliminating the useless, unproductive, or no more productive ones. In effect, the Federal Republic has declared some motivations behind the Nazi crimes to be incompatible with its own normative foundations – and others not. The motivation of disciplining and reducing the number of those found unwilling to live an orderly, useful, productive life was *not* among the incompatible ones, it was not one that constituted a severe historic injustice and thus required reparations.

This chapter takes the *Bundestag* to be a key site and a key actor in the politics of historic justice in the Federal Republic of Germany, being the only federal constitutional body directly elected by the people. It is not only the body that can adopt or reject legal reparation schemes or summarily inval-idate Nazi court rulings, but it can also condemn Nazi crimes and issue an official apology in the name of the people. Thus, the *Bundestag* has the power to actually do historic justice – or not. Therefore, I will focus on its activities concerning the persecution of the 'asocials'.[1]

The chapter is organized as follows. First, I suggest a performatist per-spective on historic justice, asking what policy-makers actually do when they 'do justice' to victims of state wrongdoing in the past, for instance in the form of reparations schemes, apologies or commemoration practices. From this perspective, I argue, policies of historic justice are performative acts that in-evitably link past, present and future in specific ways. Second, I briefly refer to the historical background to point out which infringements we are talking about when we speak of the persecution of the 'asocials'. The third section out-lines the construction of the West German reparation scheme and explains in which sense the 'asocials' have been excluded here. Fourth, I examine the ac-tivities in and by the *Bundestag* of coming to terms with the persecution of the 'asocials', and the responses by the government pertaining to this. The chap-ter concludes that historic justice to the victims of the Nazi persecution of the 'asocials' has remained marginal in German politics. There has been no offi-cial act neither by the *Bundestag* nor by the Federal Government of specifying what exactly had been wrong about the persecution of the 'asocials' and what must, consequently, not happen again. Concerning this type of Nazi injustice, the Federal Republic has not performed a clear-cut break with the past.

I will use the phrase 'persecution of the asocials' although it is problematic on at least two counts. First, the term 'persecution' (*Verfolgung*) in German is mostly used to denote acts of mass violence committed or condoned by the state against religious, ethnic or political minorities. In this case, however, there was no group, whether religious, ethnic or political. Second, the use of the term 'asocials' means adopting the Nazi term. It refers to those prison-ers in the camps marked by a black triangle; it is this triangle and the prac-

---

1   Sources are draft laws, parliamentary motions, parliamentary hearings, plenary de-bates, questions to the government in writing or questions to be discussed at a plenary session, government responses to these, and information provided to the *Bundestag* by the government. The documents are accessible through the *Bundestag's* electronic archives at http://pdok.bundestag.de/. Interestingly, a search for '*Asozialenverfolgung*' yielded no results, whereas a search for 'Homosexuellenverfolgung' yielded 28 results (on 12 June 2017).

tices that brought them there that together constitute the category of 'aso-cial', nothing else. I will therefore use the phrase 'persecution of the asocials' as shorthand for the Nazi practices of stigmatizing, deporting or detaining people in penitentiaries, workhouses or concentration camps and eventually killing them on the grounds that they were categorized as homeless or work-shy, vagrants, beggars or prostitutes, or otherwise not conforming to Nazi standards of being a valuable member of the *Volksgemeinschaft*.

5.1   Model Germany?

The Federal Republic has often been lauded as the model case for 'coming to terms with the past' (Wolfrum 2009). For Timothy Garton Ash, 'past-beating' has turned into a veritable industry since 1989 and Germany into its world-wide leader (Garton Ash 2002, 32). Post-war Germany, it is often said, has confronted its Nazi past in ways that could serve as a model for other coun-tries that have also committed large-scale human rights violations in the past (Buruma 1994; Cunningham 2004). In this vein, the German government has long lauded itself for its exemplary reparation policy: "All in all, the *Wiedergut-machung* can be considered a unique historical achievement that has received recognition from national and international organisations of Nazi victims, too." (BT Drs. 10/6287 1986, 11)

However, it is also true that German politics of *Aufarbeitung* und *Wiedergut-machung* have for a long time excluded many groups of Nazi victims for whom the term 'forgotten victims' came up in the early 1980s, referring to those who had suffered from systematic Nazi persecution but were not entitled to repa-rations under the BEG. This applies to coercive laborers, Roma and Sinti, ho-mosexuals, those who had been coercively sterilized and those who were killed in the course of the so-called 'euthanasia' programme. The 'asocials' have re-mained among the most 'forgotten' among the 'forgotten victims'. While vic-tims of 'euthanasia', coercive sterilisation and the persecution of homosexuals have received an official apology from the German government by, there have been no official acts of apology or commemoration for those who had been stigmatized, deported, imprisoned, detained in workhouses or concentration camps, or ultimately killed, for being allegedly work-shy, homeless, beggars, prostitutes or simply deemed 'asocial'.[2] In more recent years, initiatives of commemorating these Nazi victims have mushroomed in Germany, but, except for some isolated efforts by the faction of the Left in parliament, they all originate in civil society, not in the *Bundestag* or other government bodies. In short, this type of persecution still figures marginally within German politics of the past and the logic that underlined it has scarcely been addressed by official politics.

5.2 Doing Justice – or not.
The Performative Politics of Historic Justice

In German memory discourse, people who suffered from social rather than racial or political persecution are often addressed by the sociological term *gesellschaftliche Randgruppen*, marginal groups in English (e.g. Tümmers 2009). However, the discourse of *Randgruppen* is problematic here since it implies an ontological primacy of the target group; it implies that the existence of these 'groups' precedes the practices of stigmatizing and persecution such as rounding up, institutionalizing, detaining, imprisoning and killing. However, it is actually through these practices that the target 'group' has been constituted in the first place. No such 'group' existed until state actors began to distinguish between normal and abnormal, appropriate and deviant, adjusted and maladjusted, healthy and pathological, productive and unproductive, superior and inferior, valuable and worthless categories of people. In the context of reparation policies, the concept of *Randgruppen* obscures the question when, how and by whom certain categories were constructed for purposes of persecution and how these categories were still effective in reparation policies after 1945. I will not so much seek to explain why the 'asocials' have been excluded from reparation and commemoration policies, but explicate what this means. The focus is on what policy-makers do when they adopt or reject policies of historic justice. By policies of historic justice, I mean policies that self-critically address the nation's own past. Policies of historic justice in this sense may comprise political reparation programmes, official apologies, official commemoration days, state-sponsored memorials, commissions

---

2   The chapter is based on an article that had been written in 2017. See the addendum at the end for an update in 2020.

of inquiry or research programmes. Thus, policies of historic justice, as Regula Ludi (2005) states, inevitably make a set of performative distinctions: between legitimate claims for reparations and illegitimate ones, 'deserving' victims and 'undeserving' ones, condemnable abuse and justifiable acts of state power, things to commemorate and things to forget. Building on this, I suggest that policies of historic justice should be approached as performative acts in the way that theorists of apology understand apologies as performative acts (Lazare 2004; Tavuchis 1991). In this perspective, certain elements are required to make an apology: identifying the offence, the offended and the offender, taking responsibility for the offence and acknowledging the suffering it caused. Through offering an apology, offenders acknowledge that they have violated a fundamental moral or legal norm or principle, or a previous social contract with the offended. Thereby, the offender simultaneously confirms the validity of these norms, principles, contracts or promises and explicitly or implicitly promises not to violate them again. In the case of public apologies, it is the state who takes responsibility for the offence. In this case, it is critical that the person or body who speaks on behalf of the state is constitutionally entitled to do so. In a parliamentary democracy like the Federal Republic, this would certainly be the parliament, elected by the people, or possibly the chancellor, elected by the parliament.

In order to constitute proper acts of historic justice, policy measures such as reparation schemes or commemoration days have to fulfil the same requirements as public apologies, meaning they have to name the offence, the offended and the offender. In common with public apologies, policies of historic justice are performative acts through which actors make factual statements about what happened, issue a moral verdict, determine that wrongdoing has taken place, accept state responsibility for this wrongdoing, specify what was wrong about it and which norms or principles had been violated, confirm the enduring validity of these norms and principles and postulate that they are fundamental for the present political order, make a commitment to these norms and principles, offer means of making amends and promise non-repetition. Conversely, when governments decide not to condemn a certain course of state activity in the past and not to acknowledge that severe wrongdoing has taken place, they indirectly postulate that this course of action is not at odds with the present political order. Hence, policies of historic justice do not just struggle with 'the past' but at the same time they negotiate fundamental legal norms and principles and the nation's political imaginary in the present. They do all this simultaneously, within the same performative act. Thus, there is no intrinsic logic nor any quality to past atrocities that determines whether, when and to what extent governments take measures of making amends – or not; since what counts as condemnable abuse and what counts as a justifiable act of state power is a matter of moral and political judgement and political contestation (Sandner 2001; Teitel 2000; Wahl 2012). In a parliamentary democracy such as the Federal Republic, the parliament is both a key site where these contestations take place and a key actor that participates in them. Moreover, being entitled to make binding decisions about the fundamental norms and principles of the polity, the parliament has the highest authority to judge state actions in the past in light of present norms and principles and to make binding commitments with respect to the future. Parliamentary debates and decisions thus do not just reflect different views and judgements existing out there, but actually perform and enact binding judgements and commitments.

With regard to the persecution of the 'asocials' under Nazi rule, policies of historic justice have largely been incomplete or abortive. The Federal Republic has failed to issue any declaration that names the offence, the offended and the offenders and to take responsibility for the offences. Thus, it has not distanced itself from the logic that underlay the persecution of the 'asocials'; it has not condemned state violence against people on the grounds that they were being deemed work-shy, useless, homeless or otherwise maladjusted to norms and standards of productivity and economic usefulness. It has not declared such violations to be incompatible with its fundamental moral and legal order.

5.3   The Nazi Persecution of the 'Asocials'

Marginalization, discrimination and stigmatization of people for being deemed 'asocial' did not start in 1933, nor did this come to a close in 1945. Begging and vagrancy already constituted a criminal offence under the 1871 Imperial Criminal Code (*Reichsstrafgesetzbuch*, RStGB) and could be punished with imprisonment of up to six weeks (§361 RStGB) or detention in a workhouse of up to two years (§362 RStGB) (Ayaß 1995, 44). However, the use of workhouses had nearly come to a halt at the end of the Weimar Republic.

After 1933, the police made excessive use of §§361 and 362 RStGB and in the fall of 1933, big raids against homeless people, beggars and vagrants were already taking place and many thousands of people, according to Wolfgang

Ayaß at least 10,000 people, were sent to workhouses or concentration camps (Ayaß 1995, 23ff.; 41). Most of them were set free again after six weeks. The situation worsened with the 'Law against Dangerous Habitual Criminals', which came into force in January 1934 and allowed for indefinite detention in a workhouse. To the present day, we have no reliable numbers about how many people were held in workhouses, work camps or so-called *Bewahrungsanstalten* between 1933 and 1945 (WD 2016, 15). From 1934 to the end of 1940, 7,956 persons were sentenced to workhouse detainment on the basis of $42d of the 1934 law, according to official statistics (Ayaß 1988, 27).

Many inmates were imprisoned in workhouses for many years and many were sent to concentration camps over the following years. Since 1934, many municipalities also established coercive work camps (*Lager der geschlossenen Fürsorge* or *Arbeitszwanglager*) in addition to workhouses (Ayaß 2005). Furthermore, inmates of workhouses or work camps were systematically targeted for forced sterilization (Ayaß 1995, 47). In 1937, the Decree on Crime Prevention of 14 December 1937 authorized the police to circumvent the courts and imprison so-called 'asocials' 'preventively' in a concentration camp. The decree provided the pretext for major police roundups. It defined 'asocials' as persons who "without being a professional or habitual criminal endanger the public through their asocial behavior" (Decree quoted in Ayaß 1995, 139; 1998, document no. 50). In April 1938, executive guidelines for the decree declared: "Asocial is he who demonstrates through his anti-social, however not criminal behavior that he is not willing to adapt to the community." (Ayaß 1998, 142ff.)

The guidelines listed beggars, vagrants, prostitutes, alcoholics, the homeless, the work-shy, persons with a venereal disease or persons who did not pay alimonies, although this list was not supposed to be exhaustive. Many of the targeted were poor, but there was no 'social group' prior to the persecution; the group was constituted by the label imposed on people, through raids, imprisonment, detention, harassment and stigmatization, and eventually the black triangle attached to them in the camps. Based on the decree on 'crime prevention', the Gestapo and Criminal Police arrested more than 10,000 mostly male persons in April and June 1938 and sent them to concentration camps. The operation is nowadays known as *Aktion 'Arbeitsscheu Reich'*. It was mainly geared at adult males whose ability to work was exploited in the camps, among them many Sinti, Roma and Jews.

Women were targeted as 'asocials' too. According to Christa Schikorra, one in four who were deported to the women's concentration camp Ravensbrück between early 1939 and early 1940 were categorized as 'asocial' (Schiko-

rra 2005). In total, approximately 120,000 women were imprisoned in Ravensbrück from 1939 to 1945, many for reasons of alleged prostitution, some for
adultery in wartime *(Kriegsehebruch)*, some for petty crime, some after having
served a prison sentence for abortion. An estimated 25 percent of the women
detainees categorized as 'asocials' had previously been detained in residen-
tial care institutions for youth (Schikorra 2005, 110). Younger girls were also
imprisoned in a special concentration camp for girls and young women, the
Uckermark concentration camp. Between 1942 and 1945, some 1,200 girls and
young women between 14 and 21 years old and some boys were incarcerated
here, among them many girls classified as 'hopeless cases' by Nazi welfare
institutions. Girls could be classified as 'asocial' for all sorts of reasons, such
as running away from welfare institutions or 'sexual depravation' *(sexuelle Verwahrlosung)*, a term that could mean anything from having contact with Jews
or foreign workers to promiscuity or in any other way departing from sexual
norms of female behavior. Sexual depravation was a term uniquely used to
categorize women (Initiative Uckermark 2009, 5). Boys and young men who
had previously been detained in parallel institutions for male youth were sent
to the youth concentration camp Moringen. A decree issued by Himmler in
April 1944 declared that the purpose of the youth concentration camps was to:

> ...foster those who are still capable of adapting to the community so that they
> can fill in their place within the ethnic community (*Volksgemeinschaft*) and to
> detain those who are not amenable to education until their final detainment
> (in therapeutic institutions and institutions of care (*Heil- und Pflegeanstalten*),
> custody institutions, concentration camps), allowing for the use of their la-
> bor. (Himmler quoted in Ayaß 1998, 30)

'Healing and care institutions' *(Heil- und Pflegeanstalten)* was of course code for
the institutions that systematically killed mentally ill or disabled people. The
persecution of those stigmatized as 'asocials´ thus merges into the elimination of the mentally ill and disabled and we see once again the biopolitical
coupling of promoting productive lives and eliminating unproductive ones,
with both strategies being directed at enhancing the strength and fitness of
the collective body. We have to assume, says Martin Guse (2005), that one in
ten inmates of the Moringen youth concentration camp did not survive.

In the Federal Republic, begging, vagrancy and prostitution continued to
form a criminal offence until the major Criminal Code revision in the 1970s.
Even workhouses continued to exist into the late 1960s (Ayaß 1995, 210). While
people deemed to be 'asocial' were no longer sent to concentration camps, the

institutions of the Federal Republic did not officially condemn these practices either. Claims for reparations were constantly rejected, even if someone
had been detained in a workhouse for many years or imprisoned in a concentration camp. Such acts did not constitute 'typical Nazi injustice' for the
authorities and the courts.

5.4   Meaningful Work and Orderly Life

In the early 1950s, the question of continuity and discontinuity came up in the
Bundestag when the faction of the *Zentrum* launched an effort to introduce a
new Custody Law (*Bewahrungsgesetz*) that was supposed to allow the detention
of 'the mentally and morally weak' in closed institutions. In June 1951, the
faction of the Catholic *Zentrum* party sub-mitted a proposal for a draft law to
the *Bundestag* (BT Drs. 1/2366 1951). It stipulated that the purpose of detention
(*Bewahrung*) was to protect the individual from deterioration (*Verwahrlosung*)
and get him or her accustomed to meaningful work and an orderly life (BT
Drs. 1/2366 1951, 1). The target group was constructed as individuals of full
age who are deteriorating or at risk of deteriorating owing to a pathological
or extreme mental or moral weakness or to a bluntness of moral sentiment
(BT Drs. 1/2366 1951, 2). The law would have allowed the institutionalization of
these people on either a temporary or permanent basis. During the pertaining
parliamentary debate, MdB Helene Wessel presented the rationale for such a
measure, namely that there were people who were mentally or emotionally
'abnormal' and therefore incapable of adjusting to society (BT PLP 1/163 1951,
6606B). True, Wessel conceded, the Nazi state had misused the restriction of
personal freedom, but in her opinion that did not disqualify the new Custody
Law (BT PLP 1/163 1951, 6606C). In other words, what the Nazi state had done
to those categorized as 'asocial' in her view did not constitute a state crime
but, in principle, an exercise of ordinary statecraft. Violating a person's right
to personal freedom seemed acceptable when the person was incapable of
adjusting to 'meaningful work and an orderly life' in society, in short of being
a useful, productive member of the collective.

Others cautioned that the concept of deterioration was ill-defined and
thus prone to misuse (BT PLP 1/163 1951, 6610D) and that 'we in Germany' have
a special duty to prevent such misuse in order to overcome the 'bad inheritance' of the past. The sharpest criticism was brought forward by a Communist
MdB, Mrs Thiele, who referred to one million young people being unemployed

at the time of the debate. Instead of enacting a law that would amount to bringing back *Schutzhaft* (a euphemistic Nazi term for detaining people without judicial decision or control), the state should take measures against mass unemployment and social distress (BT PLP 1/163 1951, 6612A–D). The proposal for a new custody law was eventually defeated in parliament. Yet, another incident shows that the spirit behind it was still alive a few years later. In 1962, when the Federal Social Benefits Act (*Bundessozialhilfegesetz*) was enacted, included the so-called custody provisions (*Bewahrungsregeln*) that would allow the authorities to institutionalize people in a workhouse "who, despite being repeatedly ordered, persistently refuse to take up acceptable work" (quoted in Stegemann 2013, 18). The provision, however, was eventually invalidated by the Constitutional Court in 1967.

Both incidents show that the idea of denying personal rights and freedoms to people for not complying with social standards of economic usefulness, productivity and an 'orderly life' was not out of the question for the Federal Republic.

5.5   Excluded Victims

There can be no dispute that the Nazi persecution of 'asocials' amounted to massive, systematic and severe human rights violations committed by the state. Yet, in common with the institutional killings, coercive sterilization and the persecution of homosexuals, it did not meet the definition of Nazi persecution as stipulated by the 1953 Federal Indemnification Act. The Act established a right to reparations for victims of Nazi persecution, subject to very restrictive residency requirements. The Act defines who counts as a victim of Nazi persecution, namely he or she who has been persecuted "for racial, religious, and political reasons or because of the victim's world view" (BEG §1(1)). Thus, it stipulates that persecution for these reasons – but not others – is a severe breach of fundamental moral norms and principles of the Federal Republic. Thereby, it confirms that persecution for reasons of an individual's race, religion, political views or world view is incompatible with the Republic's moral, legal and political order. Conversely, the Act also defines who is not a deserving victim, namely he or she who has actively contributed to bringing about the Nazi regime, or who after 1949 has "fought against the free democratic constitution of the Basic Law" (BEG §6(1)2)). The latter was mostly applied to Communists. Fighting Communists, as per the underlying rationale, forms a legitimate exercise of statecraft, hence the present state cannot condemn its predecessor for having done the same thing in the past. The Indemnification Act singles out certain logics of state action which it considers incompatible with the present political order, namely stigmatizing, violating and killing people for being a member of a racial, religious or political group (except for the Communists) or a group that shares a certain world view.

Thereby, the post-war reparation scheme effectively excluded the 'asocials' from reparations since they had not been persecuted for any of these reasons – a fate they shared with other victims of what I termed the injuries of normality. The post-war reparation scheme of the Federal Republic has been constructed upon two basic assumptions. First, what is decisive is not what someone had suffered and what the state had done, but for what reasons it had done so. Second, it assumes that the state has the duty to respect and protect the rights of ethnic, racial, religious or political minority groups. Those categorized as 'asocial', however, did not form a 'minority' group; people were marked by the Gestapo, the police or the local authorities as presenting a burden or a threat to the Volksgemeinschaft, not for belonging to a certain group. These practices of marking and persecution reinforced, radicalized and executed biopolitical norms and standards of conformity, usefulness and productivity, thus establishing a system of differential valuation of human lives. However, these norms and standards had not been created by the Nazis. They formed part of an overarching biopolitical rationality that both predated and outlasted the Nazi regime. The German reparation scheme, however, was restricted to 'typical Nazi injustice' and thus excluded state wrongdoing that cut across the temporal confines of the Nazi period. Thereby, by definition, it ruled out the possibility of the Federal Republic continuing certain practices of the Nazi state. Yet, this was the case insofar as stigmatization, detention in workhouses and imprisonment for being homeless continued after 1945.

In the 1980s, many participants in civil society and in the *Bundestag* began to struggle for a reparation scheme that would go beyond the confines of the Federal Indemnification Act. These struggles were supported by the Greens and the Social Democrats, who formed the parliamentary opposition in the *Bundestag* at the time. The Greens proposed a new law that would have established entitlements to reparations for everyone who had person-ally suffered from Nazi persecution in Germany or the territories occupied by Germany between 1933 and 1945, proposing a broad concept of persecution based on the infringements someone had suffered, not on the group that they belonged to (BT Drs. 11/141 1987). The Social Democrats in parliament preferred the model of a new foundation 'Reparations for Nazi Injustice', funded by the government and supposed to compensate persons who had suffered from Nazi crimes but had not received compensation so far (BT Drs. 11/223 1987). The majority in parliament, however, did not adopt these propositions but established a new hardship fund in 1988 for Nazi victims who were not eligible to reparations under BEG. The institution in charge for managing the hardship fund became the Federal Ministry of Finance, not an independent body. When the *Bundestag*, again, debated reparations for Nazi victims in June 1989, oppositional MdBs complained that only 1.6 million Deutschmarks out of the 47.2 million budgeted for that year had been spent (BT PLP 11/151 1989, 11340C). The main problem, MdB Antje Vollmer from the Green Party remarked, was "...that the responsibility was given to an authority whose very own interest is saving money and whose representatives now sit on the government bench" (BT PLP 11/151 1989, 11344B).

When the hardship fund was established, people who had been persecuted as 'asocials' could theoretically apply for a one-off payment of 5,000 Deutschmarks. Few, however, tried and even fewer succeeded. In the period to 31 December 2011, a total of 354 persons categorized as 'asocial', vagrants, unwilling to work or work-shy by the Nazis had applied for hardship compensation and only 222 were successful (BMF 2012, 33).

5.6   Forgotten 'Forgotten Victims'?

When in the 1980s the new discourse about the 'forgotten victims' came up, there was some reference to the persecution of the 'asocials'. On the whole, however, the topic remained marginal. Reviewing the history of this discourse and the politics of historic justice through the lenses of the 'asocials' results in drawing up a long list of omissions. Since the 1980s the *Bundestag* was concerned with a series of initiatives to confront, commemorate, condemn and compensate Nazi crimes and those against the 'forgotten victims' in particular. One can look at these discourses from a semantic and an interlocutionary perspective, in terms of content or conversation. As regards content, we can inquire, first, whether political speech acts – draft laws, proposals, questions and inquiries sub-mitted to the government, governmental responses and reports, parliamentary debates, hearings or speeches dealing with *Aufarbeitung und Wiedergutmachung* – do mention this type of persecution at all. Second, whether they do so in a more nominal way by just listing it or in a more substantial way by specifying offences, offended and offenders, and third, whether and when we see initiatives addressing this particular type of persecution. From an interlocutionary perspective, the major question is whether policy-makers talked to people who had suffered from this type of persecution or just talked about them, that is, whether these Nazi victims were treated as active participants in political conversations or as passive beneficiaries of certain policies.

Let us begin with the latter. Survivors of the persecution of 'asocials' never entered the politics of historic justice as participants, neither individually nor collectively. When the Social Democrats in parliament submitted their initiative for a new foundation for compensating Nazi injustice in 1987, they named a number of victims' organizations supposed to be represented on the board of trustees. That foundation never came to be but it is worth noting that no association representing the 'asocial' Nazi victims was mentioned in this context (BT Drs. 11/223 1987). In June 1987, the Parliamentary Committee on Internal Affairs held an important public hearing on *Wiedergutmachung und Entschädigung für nationalsozialistisches Unrecht* in Bonn (Deutscher Bundestag 1987). It was the first public hearing where victims of Nazi persecution, including 'forgotten victims', could tell their story to members of the *Bundestag*. Two years later, when the *Bundestag* debated the allocation of resources for Nazi victims, MdBs recalled that the hearing and the testimonies had left a lasting impression on them. It was, as Antje Vollmer said, "...as if many became aware for the first time how many groups of Nazi victims were living without recognition and compensation in the Federal Republic and abroad. ... There have been tears at the hearing." (BT PLP 11/151 1989, 11344A)

Among the participants were representatives of Sinti and Roma, people who had been forcibly sterilized, surviving victims of the 'euthanasia' programme, homosexuals and forced laborers – but no representatives of 'asocials'. Only one participant, the historian Wolfgang Ayaß, represented the group. Arguably, there was no association of 'asocial' Nazi victims at that time. At least no association publicly complained that they had not been invited. Whatever the reason, the fact remains that those labelled 'asocial' by the Nazis had no voice in the politics of historical justice. In terms of content, the 'asocials' were absent for a long time too. When President Richard von Weizsäcker gave his celebrated speech on 8 May 1985 and, as first official representative of the Federal Republic, commemorated the 'forgotten victims' such as homosexuals and those who had been coercively sterilized or killed in mental institutions, he did not mention the persecution of the 'asocials' (Bundespräsidialamt 1985).

In the following years, a number of parliamentary initiatives were launched for a more comprehensive and inclusionary politics of *Aufarbeitung und Wiedergutmachung*. During the 10th and 11th *Bundestag*, the Greens launched a proposal for a draft law that would provide social benefits to all victims of Nazi persecution (BT Drs. 10/4040 1985), the Social Democrats proposed that the government submit a report on how to improve reparations for Nazi victims (BT Drs. 10/4638 1986), the Greens again proposed a draft law for adequate social benefits for all Nazi victims (BT Drs. 11/141 1987) in April 1987, the Social Democrats proposed a draft law for a foundation 'Reparations for Nazi Injustice' in May 1987 (BT Drs. 11/223 1987), the Committee on Internal Affairs submitted a report on a new hardship fund for the 'forgotten victims' in 1987 (BT Drs. 11/1392 1987) and in 1987 the Social Democrats proposed guidelines for allocating means to a more inclusive range of Nazi victims (BT Drs. 11/1413 1987). Of these motions and reports, two mention a range of 'forgotten victim' groups but not the 'asocials' (BT Drs. 10/4638 1986; BT Drs. 11/223 1987), three mention the 'asocials' or 'socially persecuted' amongst others, without, however, specifying the violations they had suffered (BT Drs. 10/4040 1985; BT Drs. 11/141 1987; BT Drs. 11/1413 1987) and the rest make no mention of specific groups.

The Social Democrats in parliament used the term socially persecuted (*Sozialverfolgte*), which at least hints at the specificity of this type of persecution. They did not say, however, what this means, who was afflicted or who the perpetrators were. More can be learned from the report provided by the government on the request of the *Bundestag* on *Wiedergutmachung* and reparations for Nazi injustice, and the situation of Roma and Sinti and related groups. The report names some of the offences and the offended, namely:

> persons who were taken to a concentration camp or another prison site for reasons of 'security' without regular trial and without sentence or after having served their prison sentence. Such measures were directed, for instance, at poachers, sexual criminals, pimps, vagrants, drunks, work-shy, dangerous criminals, so-called asocials, persons failing to pay alimonies, psychopaths, mentally distorted, and prostitutes. Homosexuals were affected as well. (BT Drs. 10/6287 1986, 39)

The report devotes a few lines on the logic that had underlined these infringements:

> Against this group of people so-called preventive measures were taken as well during Nazi rule. These measures served to subject this group to regular work and at the same time to recruit workers who, due to the tense situation in the labor market, were in short supply. [...]. In 1938, two actions were taken against the so-called work-shy and those imprisoned in the course of these actions were taken to the concentration camp Buchenwald. According to the findings of the Institute for Contemporary History, however, we have to assume that the majority of these prisoners were released in 1939 in the context of an amnesty on the occasion of Hitler's birthday. (BT Drs. 10/6287 1986, 41)[3]

Hence, what we learn from the government report is that the Nazi state violated these persons' right to the due process of law. We learn little about the logic that drove these infringements other than, apparently, it having to do with a labor shortage at the time and the strategy of the state to recruit additional labor. In short, the report suggests, the Nazi state acted out of economic rationality. It does not become clear whether the government condemns this course of action, and if so, on what grounds.

The Greens in parliament discerned a different logic at work. In 1995, they launched an initiative to establish a new foundation for reparations for Nazi crimes (*Entschädigung für NS-Unrecht*) supposed to grant reparations to all victims of Nazi persecution, not just those listed by the Federal Indemnification Act:

> The purpose of the foundation is that all persons who had been subject to Nazi persecution get acknowledged as victims of National Socialism and in principle received continuous material benefits as compensation. Nazi persecution is each measure of Nazi injustice against the life, body, health, freedom, professionalism or property. (BT Drs. 13/1193 1989, 1)

The key criteria to delineate legitimate from illegitimate reparation claims were supposed to be the acts of injustice as such, not the grounds on which they had been inflicted upon people. The proposal would have radically reorganized the West German reparation scheme. In the proposal, the Greens named as prospective beneficiaries inter alia "persons who on the grounds of

---

3   Wolfgang Ayaß, however, the leading scholar on the persecution of the 'asocials' in Germany, argues that there is no evidence that most of the detainees were set free upon Hitler's 50th birthday (Ayaß 1988, 22).

their way of living or living situation were treated as being parasitic to the community, according to Nazi ideology (e.g. 'gripers', 'work-shy', 'homeless') and harmed as such." (BT Drs. 13/1193 1989, 2)

Albeit briefly, the proposal thus addresses the specificity of this type of persecution and to some extent identifies a specific logic behind it, namely the logic of persecuting people for a way of life that, whether freely chosen or not, does not conform to Nazi ideology. Yet the Greens were a small minority faction in the *Bundestag* without a realistic chance of getting the proposal approved. Later, when they formed a coalition government with the Social Democrats in 1995–2005 and thus had a parliamentary majority, neither of them came back to their former proposals.

It was not until 2008 – the year of the *Aktion's* 70th 'anniversary' and also the year of the financial crisis – when the Left inquired about commemorating the *Aktion 'Arbeitsscheu Reich'* of 1938 that a parliamentary action addressed the persecution of the 'asocials' separately, as a stand-alone topic. The Question explicitly linked the events of 1938 to the situation in 2008 and vice versa: "Since people who have been marked as 'asocial' are increasingly exposed to aggressive acts this type of anti-human hostility should have a place within the politics of reminding and commemoration." (BT Drs. 16/9405 2008, 2)

The list of questions submitted here refers inter alia to the number of 'asocials' sterilized, imprisoned, impaired, sentenced to death, executed, detained and/or killed in prisons, penitentiaries, concentration camps or medical institutions. It further inquired about the government's plans to obtain such data, about the amount of reparations paid so far, plans to examine the role of ministries, authorities and other parts of government in these violations (*Aufarbeitung*), and further plans, projects and activities to commemorate these crimes. Albeit briefly, the inquiry names the offence, the offended and the offender, namely the *Sturmabteilung* and the police. This was the first parliamentary or governmental action to do so.

The government's response mostly states that the government had no information concerning numbers of victims or offences, no intentions to obtain them, and no plans or intentions as regards commemoration. The only concrete data provided were data on hardship compensation payments. According to these, 163 'asocials', 17 persons who had refused work (*Arbeitsverweigerer*), 24 work-shy and one vagrant had received a one-off payment of €2556.46 up to that date (BT Drs. 16/9887 2008).

In 2010, the Left in parliament again submitted a question in writing to the government, inquiring about the site of the former concentration camp

Uckermark for girls and young women categorized as 'asocial'. Most of them, the question holds, were detained because their behavior did not conform to the norms of Nazi society:

> Changing the place of residence, periods without proof of employment, refusing service in the *Bund Deutscher Mädel* [League of German Girls], or acquaintances with men who were stigmatized or discriminated against could lead to accusations of 'hanging around' or 'sexual depravation' and detainment in a concentration camp. (BT Drs. 17/1493 2010, 1)

The question also names the ordeals and injustices the inmates suffered such as malnutrition and coercive labor for the company Siemens. When the Left inquired whether the government had any plans to develop a commemoration site devoted to this group of Nazi victims, the government responded that the authority in charge was not the Federal Government but the State of Brandenburg. On the question which memorials or commemoration sites existed that were particularly devoted to those who had been stigmatized and persecuted as 'asocials', the government responded: "On the federal level, no memorial sites or sites of commemoration are known that are particularly dedicated to the group of people Nazi victims persecuted as 'asocials'." (BT Drs. 17/1721 2010, 4)

These two interventions by the Left in parliament remained isolated over the following years. In sum, over the past decades, the German government has acknowledged for a fact that thousands or tens of thousands of men and women, girls and boys had been deprived of their freedom, health, dignity and/or life because the way they lived did not conform to Nazi norms of productivity or being adjusted to society. The government did not deny the factual truth of these violations. Nor did it deny that the state had been responsible. However, it did not view these violations as typical Nazi injustice and accordingly did not grant reparations under the Federal Indemnification Act. Nor did any German government or the *Bundestag* ever issue an official apology for these violations. Neither did the Federal Government ever set up a commission of inquiry into these aspects of the Nazi past, nor sponsor any specific commemoration practices such as developing and sustaining a memorial site. The Federal Republic never officially specified what, if anything, had been wrong about stigmatizing, detaining and persecuting people as 'asocials'. There is no official declaration that names offence, offended and offenders. In the absence of such a declaration, the Federal Republic has not drawn a line between the past and the present, it has not identified or condemned the logic that under-lined this type of persecution, it has not specified the moral or legal norms and principles that had been violated, and consequently it has not committed itself to these norms and principles in the present and has not promised non-repetition.

5.7   Commemoration Beyond the State

In recent years, an impressive number of civil society initiatives have struggled to commemorate the persecution of the 'asocials'. Today, many sites of former violence such as the site of the former youth concentration camps Uckermark and Moringen, as well as the site of a former workhouse called Rummelsburg (Irmer 2013; Irmer, Reischl et al. n.y.) in Berlin-Lichtenberg, have been turned into memorials by local civil society groups. They organize conferences, talks and workshops, discover and preserve memorial sites, and provide information and analyses in form of articles, books and websites. Through placing the persecution of the 'asocials' in the context of the economic crisis, social inequality, marginalization and exclusion, they articulate commemoration and social critique. They draw a continuum between past and present and problematize the injustices of the latter in light of the former. A very active group is the *Arbeitskreis Marginalisierte – gestern und heute*, a name that deliberately articulates the past with the present. In addition, in German the name signifies both 'working group on marginalized people' and 'working group of marginalized people'; hence, it addresses the marginalized both as subject matter and as active participants. The group makes it very clear that it seeks to expose and condemn the continuity of social marginalization before, during and after the Nazi era and this continuity, in their view, is at least partly due to capitalism. It is the marginalizing effects of capitalism that they seek to bring to the fore – a project not particularly supported by the government. Nevertheless, if the government were looking for interlocutors to talk to about commemorating the persecution of 'asocials', it could find them here. These activists self-identify as people affected by social marginalization, many of them know first-hand what it means to be poor, unemployed or homeless, and thus vulnerable to stigmatization, criminalization or violence, many of them have become experts on the persecution of 'asocials' under Nazi rule, and they have made it their cause to prevent similar things from happening again.

5.8   Conclusion

Tens of thousands of men and women, boys and girls were stigmatized, deported, detained in penitentiaries, workhouses or concentration camps. Many were eventually killed on the grounds that the way they lived did not conform to Nazi norms and standards of being a productive, valuable, useful, well-adjusted member of the *Volksgemeinschaft*. Like other 'forgotten victims' of Nazi crimes, they are still excluded from reparations under the Federal Indemnification Act since their suffering does not count as Nazi persecution in the sense of the law. Only a few hundred have received a small amount of hardship compensation payment. Unlike many other groups of 'forgotten victims', those categorized and persecuted as 'asocials' have not received an official apology, nor is there a state-sponsored memorial, museum, foundation or historical site to commemorate their suffering. In their case, there has been no declaration by the *Bundestag* or the Federal Government that names offence, offended and offender. Despite the fact that the infringements, the violence and the degradation they suffered have been acknowledged as a fact and mentioned as one type of persecution amongst others since the 1980s, until 2008 no parliamentary or governmental action referred to this type of persecution in particular. Those two initiatives in the *Bundestag* that finally did so, remained marginal themselves. From a pragmatist perspective, this means that the Federal Republic has failed to specify what exactly was wrong about these infringements, whether, why and in what way this was an abuse of state power and not the exercise of statecraft. In failing to do so, the Federal Republic has failed to distance itself from the biopolitical and productivist logic that underlay the persecution of the 'asocials'. The Federal Republic has condemned state violence against people on the grounds that they were homosexual, disabled or mentally ill, but not on the grounds that they were homeless, unemployed, poor or deemed to be work-shy, useless, or just mal-adjusted to norms and standards of productivity and economic usefulness. The state has avoided clarifying which ways of treating the socially marginalized are acceptable and which are not, thereby avoiding making a commitment on how to treat the socially marginalized. The state, therefore, has not declared violations on these grounds to be incompatible with its fundamental moral and legal order. In turn, this says something not only about the past but also about the present.

5.9   Addendum

On February 13, 2020, at the beginning of the Corona crisis and largely unnoticed by the general public, the majority of the *Bundestag* adopted a declaration on the acknowledgement of 'Asocials' and 'Habitual Criminals' as victims of Nazi persecution. All MPs voted in favor of the declaration, except those from the right-wing extremist party *Alternative for Germany* who voted against. With this declaration, the *Bundestag* responded to the petition "Acknowledgement of 'Asocials' and 'Habitual Criminals' as Nazi Victims" that had been launched in April 2018. It received broad support from a number of parliamentarians, artists, scholars, and other figures from public life and was signed by over 21,000 people. It states that the Nazis persecuted, stigmatized, incarcerated and murdered homeless persons, beggars, alcoholics and migrant workers and "carried out a kind of socio-biological prevention of violence among those with criminal records" by detaining them in concentration camps after serving a prison sentence, on the assumption of the existence of criminal genes (BT Drs. 19/14342 2020, 2; 3). The fate of these victims, the *Bundestag* declared, has not yet been commemorated and this needed to change: "No one was rightly imprisoned, tortured or murdered in a concentration camp". (BT Drs. 19/14342 2020, 3)

6 Hannah Arendt and Michel Foucault on Biopolitics, Time and Totalitarianism

Although Hannah Arendt never used the term 'biopolitics', she has developed some of the most critical insights into the primacy of life in modern society and the reduction of people to mere living things in 20th-century totalitarianism. These insights, I will argue, essentially refer to a structure of temporality which I will term processual temporality, that runs from the beginnings of modernity through 20th century totalitarianism up to post-war capitalist mass society. I will show that Arendt's examination of modern temporality to large degrees overlaps with Michel Foucault's diagnosis of modern biopolitics. Unlike Foucault, however, Arendt also offers a starting point for developing a different, non-biopolitical conception of politics, based on a non-processual form of temporality: the temporality of the interval.

Recent work in philosophy and the social sciences has highlighted a number of intersections and affinities between Foucault and Arendt, although they never referred to one another (Allen 2002; Gordon 2002b). Both reject an essentialist conception of human nature and a teleological conception of history, be it of Hegelian or Marxist provenance, and both share a commitment, although spelled out differently, to a type of inquiry that combines philosophical and historical perspectives. It would not be too far-fetched to say that not only Foucault but also Arendt reconstructed the 'history of the present', to use Foucault's term. Both investigate the ideational dimension of history without reducing it to a traditional history of ideas. While in Foucault it is the body that is of particular importance to his history of the present, in Arendt it is the category of experience. It has also been noted that both Arendt and Foucault move beyond a Weberian notion of power (Allen 2002; Gordon 2002b), both stressing the relational and performative, and, as I would add, the generative character of power. However, one must not take the analogy too far because, as Richard Dana Villa (1992) remarks, when Foucault and Arendt speak about power, they speak about different things. While the Foucauldian concept of power in a specifically crypto-normative way denotes a ubiquitous, pervasive, and somewhat dark and troubling force, power in Arendt (1970) emanates from concerted political action. Power, in Arendt, is the public and visible manifestation of human action's 'weak' messianic potency, making its appearance in a specifically messianic structure of temporality: the interval.

It was Giorgio Agamben, who most influentially highlighted the aspect of biopolitics in Arendt and Foucault, bringing together the Foucauldian concept of biopolitics with Arendt's analysis of totalitarianism. In his *Homo Sacer*, Agamben (1998), who makes detailed reference to Arendt's analysis of how totalitarianism reduces persons to mere specimens, deplores the fact that Arendt did not explicitly draw a connection between her analysis of modern society in *The Human Condition* (1958) and her analysis of totalitarianism in *Origins* (1968). He concludes that *Origins* was altogether without a biopolitical perspective (Agamben 1998) whereas Foucault, he holds, has never dealt with 20th-century totalitarianism. Both statements are only partly correct. Foucault, in the last part of *The History of Sexuality* (1980) and in his lectures at the Collège de France in 1976 (Foucault 2003), albeit briefly, *did* refer to totalitarianism, and these passages, as Alan Milchman and Alan Rosenberg (1998) have shown, are perfectly in line with his other works. As far as Arendt is concerned, it is correct that in *Origins* she does not refer to the terms 'life' or 'biopolitics' and does not explicitly explain the relation between *The Human Condition* and *Origins*. However, in *The Human Condition*, she intensively examines the notion of life in connection with the emergence of the social and the decline of politics in occidental history up to the 20th century. Strangely enough, Agamben makes little or no use of these thoughts. In this chapter, I will not undertake a detailed discussion of Agamben's political theory but rather continue the project of bringing Arendt and Foucault together on the issue of biopolitics. Although the term 'biopolitics' does not appear in Arendt, I will argue that in her work we can find a rich and in-depth analysis of the specific features that constitute modern biopolitics, so that we can read Arendt as a theorist of biopolitics avant la lèttre. So far, this aspect in Arendt's work seems to have been widely overlooked. An exception is André Duarte (2005) who argues that reading *Origins* and *The Human Condition* as analyses of biopolitical violence, even though biopolitics is not an Arendtian category, enables us to find the missing link between these two works and to understand the lingering continuity between capitalist market society and totalitarian violence in our contemporary world. Duarte suggests that we live in a world in which there is a constant danger that the Arendtian animal laborans gets converted into the Agambian homo sacer. My own reading of Arendt widely corresponds to this thesis, but I will discuss in more detail the overlaps and intersections between Foucault's conception of biopolitics and Arendt's analysis of totalitarianism. These intersections, I argue, concern the analysis of certain critical features of the modern project that culminate and converge in totalitarianism: the zoefication of humans, a technocratic understanding of politics, and, not least, modern processual temporality. The issue of temporality, as I will show, is of particular significance in Arendt's political thought. Furthermore, I will focus on Arendt's specific contribution to a theory of biopolitics and modernity and point out the additional insights she can offer. Those consist, in my view, first in opening up an additional dimension of understanding in regard to biopolitics, one that refers to a debatable but also inspiring existentialist, if not theological, layer in her thought. Second, and linked to this dimension, with her concept of natality, she presents an alternative way of conceiving temporality, politics, and life that has the potential to take us beyond the spell of biopolitics.

6.1 Life and Labor

Both Arendt and Foucault belong to those thinkers who draw our attention to the dark sides of the modern project. What Jeffrey Isaac said about Arendt is equally true for Foucault: both are puzzled by the irony "that the modern age, which proclaims the value of life above all else, is also the age of genocidal mass murder" (Isaac 1996, 65). That is, both Arendt and Foucault ask the question of how the atrocities of 20th-century totalitarianism were rooted in the soil of modernity and how to unearth these roots. Whereas Arendt provides an in-depth study on the functioning principles of totalitarian rule and the nexus between shaping, regulating, and enhancing the *Volkskörper* and classifying and killing people marked as 'life not worth living', Foucault's works, as Milchman and Rosenberg (1998) point out, rather shed light on the formative stages of this nexus. Milchman and Rosenberg argue that the idea of 'life not worth living' can be seen as one possible, though not necessary, outcome of the practices of classifying and categorizing in terms of health–disease, normal–pathological, fit–unfit, which Foucault traced back to the emergence of modern medicine, psychiatry, biology and the carceral society. In the following, I will highlight some further aspects in Foucault's and Arendt's work that illuminate the threads running from the formation of the modern project to the extermination camps. To avoid misunderstandings, this is not to say that Nazism was the inevitable, necessary outcome of anything. It is only to say that Nazism was able to build on ideational and practical elements that were and are still key to modernity and that it is worthwhile studying these elements in order to be aware of the possibility that they might again grow into a real nightmare.

The first aspect I want to highlight is the observation of what might be termed the political zoefication of humans.[1] Looking at the formative stage of the modern state, Foucault observes that it was accompanied or even characterized by the move through which humans as living beings became the subject and target of political rule:

> Power would no longer be dealing simply with legal subjects over whom the ultimate domination was death, but with living beings, and the mastery it would be able to exercise over them would have to be applied at the level of life itself; it was the taking charge of life, more than the threat of death, that gave power its access event to the body" (Foucault 1980, 142f.).

The life at stake here is not so much the life people live, the life story, the biography, but rather the zoe-aspect of their existence. Public policy and the welfare state through the late 18th and 19th centuries, Foucault argues, co-emerged with practices, institutions, and new bodies of knowledge, designed to take care of the physical aspects of human life such as fertility, health, disease, longevity, or morbidity, in order to enhance the productivity of the population as well as its loyalty to the state (Foucault 1988). Foucault makes it clear that the shift towards the population was a decisive precondition for the emergence of the economy as a separate sphere which he links to the governmentalization of the state (Foucault 2000a, 220), that is, the understanding of politics as government in the sense of management.

This analysis partly overlaps with Arendt's indictment in *The Human Condition* that modern society is being based on labor rather than on work or political action. Labor, in her terminology, means the type of activity that serves the necessities of life and the ongoing circle of consumption and reproduction.

---

1   Agamben (1998) has pointed out that the Greeks had no single word for life but the two terms *bios* and *zoe*. Unlike the contemporary use of the prefix bio in terms such as biology or biopolitics, *bios* denoted the life one was living whereas *zoe* comprised the physical aspects of being an animal, a living thing.

The purpose of labor is not really to produce lasting works but to maintain the life processes of the individual, society, and the species. The Arendtian categories of labor, work, and action are certainly problematic, as Bronislaw Szerszynski (2005) argues, particularly when understood as universal, neatly separable features of human existence or as an account of the social evolution. Still, I think, if we do not share Arendt's "phenomenological essentialism" (Benhabib 1996, 123ff.) but rather understand labor, work and action as a typology of action *within modern society*, these concepts may be useful to understand some of its basic features.

From this perspective, Arendt's delineation of the role of labor as compared with work and action clearly draws from Marx's analysis of capitalist accumulation (Braun 2001); human activity merely serves as a means to feed the ongoing dynamic of a process that Marx has analyzed as the process of capitalist accumulation. Any act of work tends to get transformed into an act of labor insofar as it is neither performed for its own sake nor for the sake of creating a lasting product but merely as a means to maintain the dynamic of the economy. Arendt speaks of "repetition and the endlessness of the process itself" and of a "specifically modern acceleration", which has transformed work into labor (Arendt 1958, 125). It is not least in this sense that life in modern society has become the highest good; however, it is not the life of human individuals but rather the 'life' of society, the ongoing dynamic of the economic process, which ranks as the supreme good.

Thus, while Foucault stresses that life is a resource which gets mobilized, Arendt points out that life is constantly (re)produced. Both state that individual life functions as a force that feeds into the dynamic of a larger process, be it as a resource or as a product, and that the newly emerging sphere of the social is not least characterized by the constant consumption of life in order to maintain the dynamic of this process. They both make the diagnosis, similar to the Marxian analysis of capitalist society, that the rise of the social implies a certain degradation of individual lives to mere means of sustaining and feeding the economy. Thus, to a certain extent, we can say that the political zoefication of humans is inherent in modern society from the very beginning.

The totalitarian systems of the 20th century have taken the political zoefication of humans to the extreme in reducing certain groups of people to the status of *being* mere life. They did so through stripping these people of their civil rights, social positions and political status. The concentration camps, Arendt says, demonstrated "that human beings can be transformed into specimens of the human animal" (Arendt 1968, 455). She also makes clear, that the practice of stripping people of their legal and political status was not *invented* by the Nazis. It had already occurred in the aftermath of the First World War, when hundreds of thousands of people became refugees, homeless or stateless due to expatriation, flight, or expulsion. These people, Arendt says, belonged "to the human race in much the same way as animals belong to a specific animal species" (Arendt 1968, 302); they were reduced to a status similar to that of an animal; it did not matter what they thought or did but only what they *were* (Arendt 1981). While it was the Nazi state that declared whole categories of people to be 'life not worth living' and accordingly destroyed their lives, the Stalinist Soviet Union also, as both Arendt and Foucault remark, classified political adversaries in biological terms, as mentally ill (Foucault 2003) or "dying classes or parasitic races" (Arendt 1996, 938).[2]

6.2   Total Management

The political zoefication of humans is closely linked to another thread which, according to both Arendt and Foucault, runs through modern politics and society up to totalitarianism: the conception of politics as administration, namely the administration of life. Foucault (2003) shows that the emergence of biopolitics comes with a shift from understanding politics basically as the continuation of war to an understanding of politics as administrating, regulating, calculating, and managing the life of the population. Within this new paradigm the population was seen as a resource that can be mobilized in order to strengthen the state. Administrating and managing this resource was dependent on knowledge and gave rise to population statistics, population science, hygiene, public health, or eugenics. These bodies of knowledge were, as Foucault points out, intrinsically based on a logic of classifying, qualifying, categorizing, and ranking. Biopolitics in Foucault, as Larry Reynolds (2005) notes, actually means bio-administration. Foucault thus diagnoses a specifically technocratic understanding of politics in modernity: politics is mainly the set of technologies required to achieve certain ends such as the increase

---

2   I refer to the German version here since the German version of *Origins*, which has not so much been translated but rather rewritten by Arendt herself, is much sharper and stronger compared to the earlier English version. Whenever I refer to the German version, it is for this reason.

of the welfare and productivity of the population and the relative strength of the state as compared to other states.

Arendt, too, views modern politics mainly as administrating or managing the necessities of life. The 19th and 20th centuries, according to her, have developed an understanding of politics that equates politics with government and sees it as a sort of housekeeping. Whereas Foucault takes a non-normative view, simply stating the substitution of one unappealing understanding of politics for another, Arendt takes a decisively normative perspective, mourning the loss of the public sphere and referring to an emphatic idea of politics as an activity that forms an end in itself.

Again, we find that a general feature of modernity culminates in totalitarianism. Under totalitarian rule, there is no room for politics in the sense of expressing and debating different viewpoints and opinions and for acting in concert as opposed to exercizing command and obedience. In short, there is no space for political action as an end in itself. The sites where the utmost destruction of the ability for political action altogether took place were the camps. Hence, we find that both Arendt and Foucault see totalitarianism as the extreme case of a system that has turned politics into a knowledge-based administration of life.

In totalitarianism, according to Arendt, this knowledge-based administration of life takes on a new dimension: she depicts the system of the camps in terms of experiments and laboratories, that is, in terms of techno-scientific knowledge production. Totalitarianism, here, is seen as a gigantic experiment on human subjects, the camps being the laboratories where new technologies of turning humans into mere life are developed and tested: "The concentration and extermination camps of totalitarian regimes serve as the laboratories in which the fundamental belief of totalitarianism that everything is possible is being verified" (Arendt 1968, 437).

6.3 Politics, Life and Modern Temporality

The last observation about the relation between modernity and totalitarianism in Foucault and Arendt concerns the processual structure of time. It is here that Arendt can offer some crucial insights into the nature of totalitarianism and the modern link between politics and life. Therefore, in the following, I will reconstruct her argumentation in more detail.

Again, Foucault makes us aware of a specifically new modern feature of power and politics which, as Arendt's analysis makes clear, fully and fatally takes shape in totalitarianism. He points out that the new modern form of power which refers to 'man-as-a-living-being (Foucault 2003, 242) does not really target individuals as living beings. It does not primarily operate through exercizing direct control over the body or through intervening in individual lives. Instead, it targets collective phenomena such as the birth *rate*, or the *average* life expectancy. While on the individual level these phenomena seem ungovernable, they are not necessarily so when taken as collective phenomena. This, however, implies another characteristic new feature of biopolitics, namely that it targets *processes*, temporal phenomena, phenomena which

> occur *over a period of time*, which have to be studied *over a certain period of time*: they are *serial* phenomena. The phenomena addressed by biopolitics are, essentially, aleatory events that occur within a population that exists *over a period of time* (Foucault 2003, 246, emph. added).

Biopolitics is essentially about "taking control of life and the biological *processes* of man-as-species" (Foucault 2003, 247, emph. added); it "is a technology in which bodies are replaced by general biological processes" (Foucault 2003, 249). In other words, the processes Foucault is talking about do not take place within an individual's life time. On the contrary, they pass through individual life. The individual's birth and death do not delimitate but on the contrary mediate and facilitate the activities of modern governing. Hence, the life that biopolitics targets has a supra-individual dimension, not just in a numeric but also in a temporal sense (Gerodetti 2005). Modern politics, as Foucault depicts it, consists of a set of government technologies which act upon a target, the biological processes in the population, within which individual life is just a transitory moment.

We will rediscover this relation between politics and life and its specific temporal structure in a radicalized form in Arendt's analysis of totalitarianism. To her, it forms a key to understanding the specific nature of totalitarianism. Understanding, here, means to recognize the principle that sets this form of government in motion (Arendt 2005). However, it is also more:

> Insofar as totalitarian movements have sprung up in the non-totalitarian world (crystallizing elements found in that world, since totalitarian governments have not been imported from the moon), the process of understand-

ing is clearly, and perhaps primarily, also a process of self-understanding (Arendt 2005, 310).

Trying to understand totalitarianism, for her, includes asking the question of how it could have an appeal to people and she examines this question both in her works on totalitarianism and in *The Human Condition*. However, she does so not on a political sociology plane but on a speculative, if not theological, plane, seeking to understand the rule of processual temporality as an answer to the questions of death, finitude, and loneliness. It is at this point that Arendt and Foucault definitely part; Foucault would not concede that it made sense to deal with questions of that kind. He deliberately restricts himself to the study of when and how certain questions emerged and evolved. However, such self-restriction comes at a cost: Within these limits it is neither possible to ask the question of appeal, which certainly limits the range of understanding what was going on, nor is it possible to develop better, non-destructive answers or to distinguish between bad, worse, and better answers at all. Therefore, I think it is worthwhile to take a closer look at Arendt's analysis of the configuration of politics, life, and temporality that characterizes the nature of totalitarianism and links it to the modern predicament. Against this backdrop we can then reconstruct Arendt's concept of natality as a guidepost to break away from this still dangerous configuration.

At the core of totalitarianism, both as a form of government and as a type of ideology, Arendt argues, lies the idea that all human action is subordinated to laws of nature or laws of history. In retrospect, she sees one such line leading from Darwin to Nazi racism, another from Marx to Stalinism. What both have in common is the idea "that a superior process of movement has seized both nature and history" (Arendt 1996, 952). Totalitarianism, according to Arendt, is largely about executing the laws of nature or history. What does this mean? It essentially implies a disastrously distorted, preposterous relation between continuity and change, intransience and transience, timelessness and time. Here, Arendt in fact starts from some basic assumptions about human needs, and about the kind of relation between intransience and transience that would be more appropriate to humans. Her assumption is that, due to their capacity for freedom and spontaneity, human actions and their results unavoidably have a moment of unpredictability, instability, and transience to them. That is, transience is built into the human condition—which is a problem that men inevitably have to deal with. Positive law and political institutions, to Arendt, form something like an appropriate compensatory answer to this problem. They are able to provide continuity and stability in order to balance the essential instability and changeability of human action. Positive laws are depicted in terms of boundaries or a "framework of stability" (Arendt 2005, 341), which confines but also permits and protects the exercise of freedom. As such, positive law hedges what she calls a "common world, the reality of some transcending continuity" (Arendt 2005, 342).

Two other salient concepts in this context are home and homelessness. Arendt goes so far as to assume that "human beings need the constant trans-formation of chaotic and accidental conditions into a man-made pattern of relative consistency" (Arendt 1968, 352). The transformation of class society into mass society and the related process of atomization, in her view, have eroded such a common world and left the masses in a condition of "essen-tial homelessness" (Arendt 1968, 352). She even speaks of a "social *and spiritual* homelessness" (Arendt 1968, 352, emph. added), which underlines that she is arguing on a highly speculative plane here.

The totalitarian response to this spiritual homelessness was to twist around the relation between continuity and change so that under totalitarian rule it is human action which is made static (Arendt 2005, 342), whereas all laws are turned into laws of movement. Terror, the main instrument of totalitarian rule, stabilizes or freezes men (Arendt 1968, 342) through shutting down the spaces where freedom and spontaneity could be exercized, whereas the laws of nature or history undermine and ultimately destroy the conditions of stability and a common world. At first glance, the laws of nature or history, in contrast to positive, man-made law, seem to be characterized by their unchanging, permanent quality, their timeless presence, as Arendt puts it. At the same time, however, the laws of nature or history display an inherent dynamic linked to the political zoefication of humans. We can reconstruct Arendt's argument through discerning three ways in which the laws of nature or history form laws of movement: first, they allegedly determine the course and movement of history, much as natural laws determine the course of the planets. Second, totalitarian movements make them their highest-ranking source of authority, so they become the laws of *these* movements. Third, the totalitarian movement as such can only proceed if it avoids the establishment of any stable institutional order. In order to maintain its existence, it has to preserve its form as a political movement even after having taken seizure of the state. Arendt insists that totalitarianism is far from forming a monolithic or hierarchical state structure but is rather characterized by its shapelessness (Arendt 1968, 395). Through mechanisms such as the confusing co-existence of party and state offices, real and façade power centres, overlapping and competing jurisdictions, and not least the constant shifting of the centre of power, it avoids the establishment of stability. Keep in mind, Arendt insists, that the goal of a totalitarian movement is *not* simply to retain power within the territorial boundaries of a state but to conquer the world and to create a new mankind. The latter in particular can be seen as a dynamic goal. Whereas world conquest could theoretically be achieved—the surface of the earth is limited—this is not the case with creating the master race or the 'new man'; these are endless projects requiring an ongoing process of purge and elimination. It is here that the different dimensions of the laws of movement converge with one another *and* with the political zoefication of humans: the project of creating the new human species through the execution of supra-human laws of movement, thereby avoiding stabilization and preserving the political movement as such, according to Arendt, forms the essence of totalitarianism.

6.4 Improving Life

Creating the new mankind, or the new human race or species, through executing the laws of nature or history displays and implies the general features that Foucault ascribes to biopolitics: It targets collective and serial, temporal phenomena. Put differently, it operates on the level of the species and employs the sequence of generations, thereby transgressing, utilizing, and mobilizing individual life. Further, when Foucault highlights evolutionism as a general paradigm that emerged in the 19th century he comes very close to Arendt's analysis of processual thought:

> Basically, evolutionism, understood in the broad sense—or in other words, not so much Darwin's theory itself as a set, a bundle, of notions (such as: the hierarchy of species that grow from a common evolutionary tree, the struggle for existence among species, the selection that eliminates the less fit)—naturally became within a few years during the nineteenth century not simply a way of transcribing a political discourse into biological terms, and not simply a way of dressing up a political discourse in scientific clothing, but a real way of thinking about the relations between colonization, the necessity for wars, criminality, the phenomena of madness and mental illness,

the history of societies with their different classes, and so on. (Foucault 2003, 256f.)

Evolutionism, according to Foucault, forms an important link between classical biopolitics and what he calls the evolutionary racism developed by Stalinism and Nazism. Thus, Foucault, too, points at the specifically processual structure of modern temporality, which links the biopolitical dimension of the modern project to the totalitarian project.[3] Totalitarianism prolongs and radicalizes the features of biopolitics highlighted in Foucault to the point that it uses the elimination of humans as a means of productively consuming individual life in the production process of the new species life. The only functions individuals can have vis-à-vis the laws of movement are to execute them and/or to become "walking embodiments of these laws" (Arendt 2005, 340), which is by no means mutually exclusive. Executing them means actively applying the standards according to which certain individuals or groups do or do not allow for the unfolding dynamic of the laws of movements. Embodying them means being classified according to these standards. Laws or processes which function through transgressing and productively consuming individual lives are not served through compliance but through providing the material in which they realize themselves. This material can be of higher or lower quality and the political zoefication of humans is the outcome of a mechanism that judges the existence of individuals or groups according to the question of whether they present suitable or unsuitable material to realize and promote the project of enhancing the human race. Within this logic, being deemed a 'dying' or a 'decadent class' functions much the same way as being deemed 'unfit to live', whether the classification refers to physical qualities or not.

Compared with 19th-century processual thought, the totalitarianism as depicted in Arendt thus adds, or at least dramatically increases, the element of acceleration. The totalitarian project is not only about scientifically understanding the laws of movement but about actively promoting the process of their unfolding. Here, execution is at the same time acceleration. Its instrument is terror, which makes terror the borderline case of a technocratic, instrumentalist understanding of politics. Hence, Arendt seems to say, processual thought had a certain appeal to the masses in their spiritual homelessness

---

3   For an overview on the respective notions of temporality in the different stages of the work of Foucault see Michon (2002), for a systematic discussion of the relationship between different regimes of time and forms of power in Foucault see Portschy (2019).

because it enabled them to participate in a permanent, intransient, timeless presence. The alleged intransience or permanence of these laws, however, was a fatal error because in fact their operating principle was mobilization, dynamization, acceleration. What processual temporality really did was destroy the chance of establishing some sort of this-worldly stability, continuity, or common home. In the end, the

> supra-gigantic forces whose movements race through humanity, dragging every individual willy-nilly with them—either riding atop their triumphant car or crushed under its wheels—may be various and complicated: still, it is surprising to see how, for all practical political purposes, these ideologies always result in the same 'law' of elimination of individuals for the sake of the process or progress of the species. From the elimination of harmful or superfluous individuals, the result of natural or historical movement rises like the phoenix from its own ashes; but unlike the fabulous bird, this mankind which is the end and at the same time the embodiment of the movement of either History or Nature requires permanent sacrifices, the permanent elimination of hostile or parasitic or unhealthy classes or races in order to enter upon its bloody eternity. (Arendt 2005, 341)

The kind of eternity the totalitarian movement has to offer is a deadly eternity, the permanence it produces is the "tranquility of the cemetery" (Arendt 2005, 348). Hence, the totalitarian project is based on a specifically processual structure of temporality in which endlessness has taken a double meaning: first, the processes determined by the laws of nature or history and executed through terror cannot come to an end because their goal, the production of a new human species, can never be completed. Second, each individual and each human activity merely counts as a means to promote the process and not as an end in itself. These processes have a direction, but no end(s). To Arendt, this structure is expressed concisely by the maxim of the SS: "No task exists for its own sake" (Arendt 1968, 409). This attitude, she says, destroys "all genuine interest in specific jobs and produces a mentality which sees every conceivable action as an instrument for something entirely different" (Arendt 1968, 409).

Here, however, we also see that processual temporality is not confined to the totalitarian project, although it is within the totalitarian project that it assumes its most deadly power. Rather, the relation cited earlier between actions and ends bears considerable resemblance to Marx's analysis of the relation between exchange value and utility value under capitalist conditions, in which human productivity is essentially transformed into a mere means to advance the process of accumulation. Indeed, Arendt's later work on modern society can, arguably, be read as a study on the functioning of processual temporality before and after totalitarianism. In *The Human Condition*, as I will point out in the following, Arendt both makes an endeavor to understand the development of processual temporality and to present an alternative model, the temporality of the interval, the former crystallizing in the priority of life, the latter in the concept of natality.

6.5   Living in the Interval

In *The Human Condition*, Arendt explores the rise of 'life' to be the supreme good in occidental culture; she shows how the changing notion of 'life' is related to a pertinent transformation of temporality and how these transformations form responses to certain fundamental, traumatic historic experiences. The *polis*, in her view, had offered its citizens a kind of "worldly immortality" in that it formed the institutional framework for the possibility of remembrance (Arendt 1958, 314). Life was conceived of as a life *story* that can be passed down over generations and remembrance constitutes a response to human mortality. This response required a body politic though with a functioning context of narration and remembrance. The decline of the *polis* therefore meant a traumatic experience and the cultural response to that experience was the invention of a new form of temporality, namely eternity, which came with a revaluation of the *vita contemplativa* in relation to political action. This shift, however, came at the price of devaluating the only human capacity that is able to create a common world *before* death.

Similarly, Arendt understands Christianity and its idea of the immortal soul as a response to the decline of the Roman Empire. However, this shift meant a further devaluation of political action and the political realm insofar as the immortality of the soul did not rely on a functioning body politic. On the contrary, in order to save one's soul and attain immortality, what mattered was to turn away from worldly political life. For this reason, Arendt argues, the price for this new form of immortality was alienation from the interpersonal world.

The beginning of the modern age and the development of modern science mark a further upheaval in that science implied a model of investigation that devalued contemplation as a path to truth so that contemplation lost the status of being the most highly regarded form of life. For a short time, Arendt says, work took the place of contemplation and *homo faber* the place of the philosopher. However, to the extent that religion lost its capacity to determine the appropriate ends of work it lost its significance and was superseded by processual thought, be it evolutionism, historical materialism, life philosophy, or the belief in progress, as a new notion of temporality. This notion of temporality in turn, she argues, is modelled on the biological life process, or on a biologistical understanding of life. In terms of *bios* and *zoe*, it would be modelled on *zoe*, referring to the idea of an entity that, in analogy to the species, sustains itself through the coming and going of individuals. The species in that sense is beyond life and death and so is the assumed entity that underlies processual thought, be it termed nature, history, society, or progress.

However, we could also say that Arendt understands processual thought as a response to the 'spiritual homelessness' that has accompanied the inhabitants of the western world from the turn to metaphysics in ancient Greece to post-war capitalism. To model thought on the life process—*zoe*—therefore means a specifically immanentist endeavor of constructing immortality. Note, however, that Arendt does not consider the quest for immortality to be an essential feature of 'human nature'. In her interpretation, the quest for immortality is not a cause but rather an outcome of or a response to another human need, which she *does* assume to be essential: the need to find a home in the world, to be respected as a member of this worldly community.

Incidentally, according to Arendt, the capitalist economy of the 20th century is in no way based on work but on labor in that every human activity is directed at the maintenance of the economic dynamic. Again, we find, "no task exists for its own sake"; no activity forms an end in itself, anything and any activity merely serves to feed the automatically proceeding dynamic. From this perspective, we still live under the rule of processual temporality. It certainly does not take as murderous a shape as it has taken in Nazism and Stalinism insofar as it is not directed at the production of one new single mankind and does not use terror as its main instrument. However, to the extent that human activities are qualified and treated as mere means to feed an automatic, relentlessly proceeding paramount process, whether it is named progress or globalization, we are still under the spell of processual thought. In post-war society, Arendt says, one form the rule of supra-human processes takes is the inexorable progress of science and technology "compelling us to do whatever we can, regardless of consequences" (Arendt 1970, 86), not least in the realm of biotechnology which, in Arendt's view, is apparently driven by the desire to escape the human condition of natality and mortality.

6.6   Beyond Biopolitics: *Zur Welt Kommen*

Hence, we note that Arendt and Foucault help us discern certain critical, inter-related elements of the modern project that fatally culminated and converged in the totalitarian projects of the 20th century, but did not disappear with them. As such features we have identified the political zoefication of humans, a technocratic understanding of politics, and processual temporality. Biopolitics can be understood as the combination of these elements. As long as these elements are to be found in contemporary thought, science, technology, society, or politics, it is advisable to watch out for their impact and their possible convergence. Arendt, in my view, goes a little further than Foucault in that she decidedly outlines an alternative, non-biopolitical understanding of politics, life and temporality captured by the concept of natality. The idea of natality is meant to present a different and better response to the existential human need to find a home in the world. This response would differ from the various predominant responses we can find in occidental history which all focused on overcoming mortality. Up to now, the history of occidental thought has been preoccupied by mortality (Arendt 1958). Metaphysics, Christianity, and processual thought, in this perspective, do respond to the need of finding a home in the world and to the experience of this need being frustrated. Metaphysics and Christianity responded in developing a specific temporal form: eternity, a sphere of permanence and intransience beyond the interpersonal world and superior to it. In processual thought, however, eternity moves from transcendence into the immanence of nature or history and in this move gets dynamized so that what remains from eternity is just the constancy of the process. Processuality is the new temporal form emerging in the 19th century. Hence, to Arendt, both eternity and processuality form temporal structures that respond to the problem of homelessness in the world, a problem caused by the nature of human action itself, but they respond in a way which rather makes things worse as they devaluate and undermine those human faculties through which humans are able to create a home in *this* world. To focus on natality instead of mortality would mean to acknowledge that the only remedy to the volatility of human action and its results is human action itself, complemented by the capacity to promise and to forgive. While human action produces results that are volatile and unstable, action is also the capacity to begin anew, to create a new political community in concert with others. Arendt concludes *Origins* with the warning that totalitarianism will stay with us as an ever-present potentiality but also with the more optimistic outlook that the end of totalitarianism at the same time implies the promise of a new beginning: "Beginning, before it becomes a historical event, is the supreme capacity of man, politically, it is identical with man's freedom" (Arendt 1968, 479).

Although the concept of beginning, *initium*, is taken from Augustine, Arendt gives it a distinctive turn in linking it to the factum of birth: "This beginning is guaranteed by each new birth; it is indeed every man" (Arendt 1968, 479). In *The Human Condition*, she develops this idea further by coining the concept of natality to capture the linkage between beginning, freedom, and action. Being born—*zur Welt kommen* in German—is not just a physiological event at the beginning of life, although it is that too, but in the case of humans it also means entering the world which is already inhabited by others. For Arendt, it is the beginning of a being that is capable of beginning. Action can be understood as a kind of second birth, through which a person, again, enters the world of interactions and common projects. Unlike many other metaphors of a second birth this one does not devaluate the first birth. The second birth is not the antithesis of the first but its confirmation; it means accepting the gift of spontaneity and freedom man has received already at and through birth. While birth forms the beginning of physiological life that has to be sustained through labor and work, action is the essence of political life. Physiological life thus provides time for the good life; action fills *zoe* with *bios*. It is important to note though that political life, in Arendt, is no idyll, no paradise that had been lost and could be regained; the idea of embracing natality is not meant to lead us back to an alleged state of static timelessness. There is no denying that human action can cause mistakes and that political institutions are volatile, which is why we need promising and forgiving.

With the help of forgiveness one cannot undo mistakes caused by human action but one can prevent them from determining the future. By means of making and keeping promises human beings can bring consistency and commitment into their affairs without relinquishing their freedom. Focusing on natality, instead of mortality, means appreciating these human capacities and sustaining the institutional framework that allows them to be exercized. To focus on natality also means to break away from eternity and processuality and to introduce a new temporal form instead: the interval. Thus, it is not least a revision of our understanding of time that the concept of natality is aiming at, as Julia Kristeva (2001) has remarked.[4] Human life, then, is not understood as a transitory stage to eternity or as a means to feed the dynamic of an ongoing process nor as a timeless idyll but as "the time interval between birth and death" (Arendt 1958, 97). As such it has a beginning and an end, it is limited, and it provides time for the good life, which in turn can be remembered as a life story.

To focus on natality would thus mean putting an end to processual temporality and replacing it with the time of the interval. It is here where we can locate what Susannah Young-ah Gottlieb has called Arendt's weak or inconspicuous messianism (Gottlieb 2003, 160). Arendt frequently refers to the figure of Jesus, particularly when she wants to emphasize the significance of action and forgiveness. Jesus, she holds, was far from preaching the superiority of contemplation over action: "The only activity Jesus of Nazareth recommends in his preachings is action, and the only human capacity he stresses is the capacity 'to perform miracles'" (Arendt 1958, 318).

Hence, it is not necessarily Jesus who has messianic qualities but rather Jesus demonstrates the messianic, potentially redeeming powers of action and forgiveness. To Arendt, these amount to the human faculty to perform miracles. In many passages of the New Testament, she tells us,

> miracles are clearly not supernatural events but only what all miracles, those performed by men no less than those performed by a divine agent, always must be, namely, interruptions of some natural series of events, of some automatic process, in whose context they constitute the wholly unexpected (Arendt 1968/1993, 168).

This miraculous power of human action has a messianic quality to it as it ends one time and opens up another; it disrupts the time of the process and opens up the time of the interval. It brings the current time to a close insofar as it stops the racing of time towards the future and breaks open a time span in the present, a time between limits.

The element of messianism and the thought of redemption are alien to Foucault and it is with regard to this messianic perspective that Arendt's and

---

4   However, I do not share Kristeva's (2001) view that Arendt pursues a vehement defence of life in *The Human Condition*. Kristeva does not sort out the different meanings of the term life in this book.

Foucault's conceptions of temporality fundamentally diverge. Foucault's considerations about time do not refer to the messianic idea of an end of time, whereas Arendt's conception of human action as a messianic power that manifests itself in the public sphere bears strong affinities to what Gershom Scholem identifies as the messianic idea in Judaism:

> Judaism, in all of its forms and manifestations, has always maintained a concept of redemption as an event which takes place publicly, on the stage of history and within the community. It is an occurrence which takes place in the visible world and which cannot be conceived apart from such a visible appearance (Scholem 1971, 1).

Arendt, as well as Foucault, strictly rejects the strong messianic idea that the world could be saved once and for all, which she, as well as Foucault, considers extremely dangerous. Nevertheless, she does convey a messianic message, only that the messianic powers, the human faculties of action and forgiving, are themselves temporal; they operate within time, their results are unstable and all they can do is open up time for a new beginning in this world. Hence, messianic time in Arendt has the structure of the interval, redemption means freedom, the exercise of which in Arendt is synonymous with power, and such power takes place, quite as Scholem put it, publicly, in the community.

To Foucault, in contrast, freedom means the capacity to think differently and to conceive of ourselves differently, different from the requirements of subjectification, of becoming an autonomous subject through confessing and truth telling and thereby producing knowledge required for the biopolitical management of the living. The liberty Foucault finally leaves us with consists of *thought* practices and *self* practices; liberty to Foucault is "an attitude, an ethos, a philosophical life" (Foucault 1997, 319), "a permanent critique of our historical era" (Foucault 1997, 312), a "critical ontology of ourselves", it is "work carried out by ourselves upon ourselves" (Foucault 1997, 316). It is a liberty that remains preoccupied with the self, if not confined within the limits of the *vita contemplativa*. Foucault's way of interrogating history and exposing allegedly universal, necessary, rational or emancipatory features of modernity as being not only historical but also inherently ambiguous provides us with a tremendously helpful prerequisite to analyze the logic of modern biopolitics. It is hard to see, however, how this self-centred, philosophical conception of liberty could point at an alternative conception of politics, one that enables us not only to analyze but also to overcome biopolitics.

The concept of natality, I have argued, takes us a step further, offering an alternative understanding of politics, life, and temporality. Human life here is understood not as a moment in an endlessly racing process whose laws are to be executed on the individual, nor as a manageable entity but as the time span between birth and death. Time is not the medium for the execution of supra-human processes but the interval that provides the chance to perform activities for their own sake. Politics, finally, would be understood not as the management of populations or the acceleration of economic or scientific progress[5] but as acting in concert together with others, and the purpose of politics would not be to enhance the quality of some collective entity, to create a better species or to maintain the dynamics of the economy, but to make the world a home.

---

5   Arendt's critique of the idea of progress and processual thought clearly draws from Walter Benjamin's *Theses on the Concept of History* (1968). The affinities and differences between Arendt's and Benjamin's conception of temporality would, however, require another study. For exploring the use of Benjamin for a critical analysis of biopolitics see Wehling 2019.

7 Increasing the Forces of Life: Biopolitics, Capitalism and Time in Marx and Foucault

> It is no longer the worker who employs the means of production, but the means of production which employ the worker. Instead of being consumed by him as material elements of his productive activity, they consume him as the ferment necessary to their own life-process, and the life-process of capital consists solely in its own motion as self-valorizing value.
>
> *(Marx 1990, 425)*

> Since the classical age the West has undergone a profound transformation of these mechanisms of power. 'Deduction' has tended to be no longer the major form of power but merely one element among others, working to incite, reinforce, control, monitor, optimize, and organize the forces under it: a power bent on generating forces, making them grow, and ordering them, rather than one dedicated to impeding them, making them submit, or destroying them.
>
> *(Foucault 1980, 136)*

7.1 Missing the Link: Biopolitics and Capitalism

At the beginning of the 21st century, the biofication of terms finally entered the field of economics. Compounds such as biotechnology, biomedicine, bioethics, biolaw and, to a lesser degree, biopolitics, had already taken off in the 1980s and 90s, whereas notions of bioeconomy, biovalue, and biocapital did not proliferate until the early 2000s. Like the term biopolitics, they are being used in very disparate ways, seeking either to promote or to critique the subject they are referring to. Those who use them in a critical way customarily refer in one way or other to the concepts of biopolitics and biopower as coined by Michel Foucault.[1] Even within this tradition, however, the relationship between biopower and biopolitics on one hand and (bio-)value, (bio-)capital and (bio-)capitalism on the other is still relatively unclear. As Ute Tellmann (2017, 69) rightly notes, the nexus between liberal economics and biopolitics is often assumed but seldom explored. This holds all the more true for the relation between biopolitics and capitalism. Although there is much mention of biopolitics and liberalism, biopolitics and liberal governmentality, biopolitics and biovalue, or biopolitics and biocapital in the literature, the focus is rarely on the relationship between biopolitics and capitalism. The concept of capitalism almost never figures in this literature, and when it does, it tends to be equated either with liberalism or with a particular segment of the economy that makes use of the biosciences and biotechnology. We can thus distinguish two main approaches to relating issues of biopolitics and capitalism in the Foucauldian tradition, which I will term the 'technology-centred approach' and the 'government-centred approach'.

7.2   Biopolitics as Biotechnology

I borrow here the concept of a technology-centred approach from Lars Thorup Larsen (2007), denoting a line of work on the relationship between biopolitics and economics that focuses not so much on government but on bioscience and biotechnology. The concepts of bioeconomy, biovalue, bioproperty and biocapital here denote either a particular sector or era, or both, of 20th/21st-century economics, namely one capitalizing on the potential of life processes, from the molecular level to the human body, based on advances in technoscientific

---

1   Unfortunately, Foucault himself never clarified the relationship between the two concepts. Sometimes, he seems to use them synonymously; then again, biopolitics appears to denote a subset of ways through which biopower is exercised. The confusion is further exacerbated by the popularity of the term 'biopolitics' since about the turn of the millennium and by the fact that Foucauldian and non-Foucauldian uses often intermingle in the literature. While biopolitics is the more widespread term, biopower, in Foucault, is arguably the more fundamental one. As a counterpart to sovereign power, biopower denotes a new, epochal form of power that pervades different strata, spheres and dimensions of modern society. Since this is actually the theoretical level this chapter is aiming at, biopower would thus in many cases be the more appropriate term. Since, however, biopolitics is the more common one in the literature, I will for pragmatic reasons generally use that term here.

knowledge production (Helmreich 2008). The focus here is on studying the political economy of the biotech industry, including the disentanglement and valorization of biological objects or processes and the development of individual business models and investment strategies. On the general level, one can add to these the formation of markets, research and development strategies, economic discourses, and visions and imaginaries—as well as, importantly, the transformation of economic structures in interaction with biomedical and biotechnological knowledge production (Cooper 2008; Rose 2007; Sunder Rajan 2006; Waldby 2008; 2009; Waldby and Cooper 2010). The concepts of capital and capitalism come into play when and insofar as the valorization of bodies, life processes, biosciences and biotechnologies are analyzed as situated within a capitalist economy governed by capitalist principles of competition and profit-seeking and, though it is more rarely addressed in the literature, exploitation. For technology-centred approaches, biopolitics concerns the ways in which life processes are made accessible, mobilized and enrolled in order to utilize their vital potential (Waldby and Cooper 2008, 68). Contemporary biopolitics, in this sense, tends to coincide with biotechnology-based ways of valorizing vitality. Thus, technology-centred approaches have drawn attention to the intricate ways in which bioscientific knowledge production, biotechnology, and bioeconomic valorization strategies mutually shape and reinforce each other in late capitalism, accompanied and to some extent reinforced by the generation of new forms of the individual and collective identities, social relations, networks and communities that Rabinow (1996) dubbed 'biosocialities'.[2] Yet biopolitics and capitalism come into view only in conjunction with biotechnology or biomedicine; the focus is on industries, markets and business strategies organized around biotechnology or biomedicine, that is, on industries, markets and the quest to harness the potential of life processes in the body, body parts or body materials through recent advances in genetics, biochemistry or reproductive medicine. Thus, in the last instance, it is the advent of reproductive medicine and the new genetics that marks the emergence of biocapital. While this strand of research has greatly advanced our understanding of the interpenetration between knowledge production in the life sciences, the formation of new markets and industries, state policies

---

2   For an overview on the discussion concerning the relation between the biosciences, biosociality and the economy, see Gibbon and Novas 2007; for a critique of implicitly techno-determinist assumptions underlying the concept of biosociality see Gerhards 2020, 57.

and institutional arrangements as well as identity and community formation (Gibbon and Novas 2007, 13), it highlights only a particular segment of biopolitics and capitalism and does not discuss the relationship between the two on a conceptual level. A problem arises when biopolitics is conceptually reduced to political or economic activities organized around biotechnology. Despite assertions to the contrary, this stance bears an implicit tendency towards technological determinism if and when it takes late-20th century advances in genetics, biotechnology and reproductive medicine to be the origin and the driving force behind contemporary biopolitics and its interpenetration with the economy. Such a stance also leaves open two questions: whether and how these advances themselves may be shaped and driven by a logic of biopolitics and how this relates to the logic of capitalism. Relatedly, a technology-centred conception of biopolitics tends to overlook or play down biopolitical strategies not necessarily organized around the life sciences but operating through various forms of social, employment, family or immigration policies, through urban planning, social work, birth control campaigns and the like on state, sub-state and global levels, thus ignoring much of what Foucault termed the biopolitics of the population. While Nikolas Rose in 2007 still assumed, at least for late modern liberalism, that state-led interventions on the level of the population were a matter of the past and that biopolitics had become individualized and molecularized, the return of the camps, the selective closing of borders, the rehabilitation of population policy (Schultz 2019) and openly eugenic discourses (Wehling 2010; 2019) leave no doubt that this is no longer true—if it ever was. A technology-centred concept of biopolitics falls short of capturing these persistent yet ever-changing practices, discourses and social technologies of selectively managing the size, structure and qualities of human groups and populations.

7.3   Biopolitics as Self-Government

Government-centred approaches, by contrast, do not focus on matters of science and technology but rather on the relationship between biopolitics, liberalism and technologies of government. Liberalism in this literature, is basically conceived as a political rationality operating through ideas, technologies and mechanisms of governing at a distance (Dean 2002; Larsen 2007; Lemke, Krasmann et al. 2000; Tellmann 2017). It enrols individuals, families, neighbourhoods and other collectivities in programmes of self-government and self-improvement, particularly with regard to health, fitness, sexuality, procreation and other aspects of bodily life. It thereby shifts responsibility for public health, wellbeing and security from the state to individuals, families, groups, neighbourhoods or other collectivities. Biopolitics, in this context, comes as a set of mechanisms for promoting self-government and self-improvement, or, as its inverse, a set of mechanisms for disciplining those deemed incapable thereof. Thus, biopolitics and liberalism ultimately converge on the terrain of disciplining and responsibilizing individuals. Biopolitics, in short, operates as an instrument of (neo-)liberal government. From this perspective, however, it remains somewhat unclear what, if anything, is the added value of concepts such as biopower and biopolitics. If biopower and biopolitics basically denote technologies of discipline and responsibilization, then why not retain these concepts? What, in short, is the 'bio' in biopolitics, and why does it matter?

More recently, Ute Tellmann has suggested approaching this question on a more systematic level. The Foucauldian tradition, Tellmann holds, tends to assume that the biopolitics of the population coincides with a liberal economic governmentality, thus establishing a metonymic nexus between population, biopolitics and economic government that is, however, never submitted to closer theoretical examination (Tellmann 2011, 61). She suggests investigating this nexus by taking a closer look at the work of Thomas R. Malthus. Going back to Malthus, she argues, allows us to reconstruct the missing link between biopolitics and liberal economics that is constituted by the connection between population and scarcity (Tellmann 2017). The notion of scarcity, she holds, assumes a key position in modern economy, defining its boundaries both in terms of economic discourse and in terms of a separate sphere in society. After all, it is reference to the problem of scarcity that sets the economic sphere apart from the sphere of politics (Tellmann 2017, 204). Starting from Malthus, according to Tellmann, we can reconstruct the biopolitical origins of modern economics founded on the inherently racist and colonialist distinction of civilized human life and savage life. The key to understanding this nexus, she argues, is the third element in the connection: time. While savage life is caught up in a timeless present, unable to think ahead, consuming and procreating excessively through times of abundance without providing for the future, civilized life breaks the cycle of abundance and scarcity, resists the temptations of excessive consumption and procreation, and allows for economic progress to take place. Thus, in Malthus, savage life and its lack of futurity are responsible for scarcity and misery among the whole of the population. Thus, for Tellmann, the missing theoretical link between biopolitics and capitalism is to be found in the nexus between scarcity and futurity and this notion of the population. Biopolitics basically denotes the difference between savage and civilized life, coinciding with a difference between a timeless present on one hand and the quest for a better future on the other. It thus also marks a corresponding historical leap. In that sense, biopolitics coincides with the birth of modern liberal economy; it disciplines uncontrolled needs and desires for the sake of eventual fulfilment in the future, thus substituting immediacy for futurity. By doing so, biopolitics constitutively implies a hierarchy of human life, a value differential between savage, present-oriented and civilized, future-oriented life.

Tellmann draws attention to two important features of biopolitics to which I will return later: the relationships among the modern market economy, biopolitics and future-oriented temporality, as well as the value differential ascribed to different forms of human life. However, concerning the issue of biopolitics and capitalism, a few questions remain open. In particular, the focus here is on the relation between biopolitics and liberalism, not biopolitics and capitalism; Tellmann does not use the term capitalism. The meaning of liberalism, however, remains somewhat vague, oscillating between liberal political rationality, market economy and classical political economic discourse. Unlike the concept of capitalism, it does not denote a particular form of society with a particular mode of production and particular forms of social relations. Further, Malthus does not have much to say about biopolitics *after* a modern liberal economy has been established. Is biopolitics still taking place? Has savage life been replaced by civilized life once and for all, so that the biopolitical makes only a single appearance in history? Or does savage life, rather, form a subterraneous layer of human life that continues to threaten the liberal order? In that case, the role of biopolitics in liberalism would be that of a permanent force of repression. Both assumptions—biopolitics as a singular event and biopolitics as a permanent force of repression—lack, I would argue, the peculiar, distinctively modern features of biopolitics and its relation to capitalism. While I agree with Tellmann that both biopolitics and capitalism are inherently future-oriented, I would object that the future toward which they are oriented is not one in which needs are met and scarcity is overcome. Concerning the connection between capitalism and biopolitics, I posit that there is more to learn from Marx than from Malthus: namely that what drives the dynamics of capitalism is *not* the problem of scarcity but the logic of accumulation.

In sum, government-centred approaches tend to reduce capitalism to liberalism while technology-centred approaches tend to reduce biopolitics to biotechnology. None addresses the relationship between biopolitics and capitalism more specifically or on both a theoretical and conceptual level. In order to do so, I suggest a return to Foucault and Marx and their respective conceptualizations of biopolitics and capitalism. I argue that, notwithstanding the obvious differences, there are some remarkable convergences between their analyses of biopower/biopolitics and capitalism, and that these concern above all the investigation of power, life and time under conditions of modernity and the nexus between them. As regards power, both Marx and Foucault study first and foremost the productive face of power, its productive way of operating. This does not mean that power for them is not repressive, but that its repressivity becomes intelligible only through studying its productivity. Further, for both Marx and Foucault, life is a key resource for this type of power. In fact, life is a genuinely modern resource in that it is *the* resource that can be simultaneously used/exploited and improved/increased. Life is the subject, the resource and the product of modern productive power. And finally, for both Marx and Foucault, time is key. Time in modernity, or rather temporality, is the mode of existence of (bio-)power and capital. Both (bio-)power and capital share a performative ontology in that they exist only in action, only when and insofar as they are being performed. Moreover, as I will show, capital and biopower/biopolitics share an inbuilt temporality that is not sufficiently captured by the concept of futurity. This temporal structure is characterized by an ongoing, unlimited process of ever-increasing productivity, thus directed at the future but not at future fulfilment. Instead, it is a permanent, unlimited process of maximizing and optimizing that cannot possibly come to a meaningful end.

7.4   Power and Productivity

Marx' *Critique of Political Economy* and Foucault's work on biopolitics belong to the highest ranks of social theory[3], seeking to capture the epochal features of modern sociality. Neither is content to study merely a single segment of society: Marx does not study 'the economy' but the ensemble of social relations

---

3   For discussions of Foucault's studies on biopolitics as work in social theory, see Braun and Gerhards 2019 and Geisler and Struwe 2019.

in "societies in which the capitalist mode of production prevails" (Marx 1990, 125). And biopolitics in Foucault does not denote a particular policy domain, defined e.g. by reference to medicine or biology (Braun and Gerhards 2019; Wehling 2008), but a historically specific mode of social integration, one that promises to integrate the individual into the social order in a way that benefits both at the same time (Braun and Gerhards 2019; Foucault 2000a; 1994a).[4]

For both Marx and Foucault, productivity, not repression or deprivation, is key to understanding power in the modern world. In their view, it is pointless to battle the forces of repression without tackling the forms through which social relations, social thought and the ways of being a social agent are being shaped and created. This does not mean that repression, extraction, misery and deprivation are insignificant in their analyses; they do not, however, hold the key to understanding and ultimately overcoming the dominant forms of social thought and practice in the present. The key is how we produce and reproduce these forms and how they are imbued with power.

As is well known, the concept of power that Foucault introduces in *The Will to Knowledge* goes beyond the preoccupation with repression, misery and deprivation, highlighting, rather, the productive dimensions of power. Power, he insists, is not just the lid that holds down our boiling-up desires and unduly constrains the forces of sexual and political liberation. Rather, it is a variable constellation of forces within which subjectivities are forming and being formed. For Foucault, the belief that sexual liberation, truth telling and self-exposure will free us from power and allow us to flourish both personally and politically, is itself a historically specific effect of power. Instead, he insists, power produces truth, sexuality, subjects, and the relations between them, and it is precisely the question of *how* they are produced that concerns him. As long as we stay focused on the negative operations of power—such as the

---

4   Jacques Bidet (2016) also reads Foucault as a social theorist, placing him on a par with Marx in that both, he argues, highlight two equally constitutive poles of instrumental reason that dominate the modern social order: capital and organisation. Both rely on respective privileges that allow the dominant class to exercise power, namely the privilege of property and the privilege of elite competencies. Power is here essentially conceived as power over: managerial power over workers, medical power over the ill, university power over students (Bidet 2016, 96). While I agree with Bidet that both Marx and Foucault theorize the modern social order in terms of instrumental reason, I will not highlight the more Weberian conception of "power over" in Foucault but rather seek to bring to the fore the shared logic of capital and biopolitics, their common, inbuilt dynamics towards increasing human productivity.

questions of how truth is being distorted or obscured, how sexuality is being repressed, and how we all are being alienated from our true selves—as long as we focus on this, Foucault argues, we are trapped in a humanist mindset, tying ourselves to some hidden essence, some lost origins that prevent us from truly trying something new. Rather than searching for the truth lost, Foucault suggests, there is more to gain from understanding how truth is being produced. Only if we realize that the alleged nature of man, the essence of the state, or the subject are nothing but historically contingent ways of thinking and acting, will it be possible to do things differently, to live differently and possibly feel differently. Hence, Foucault assumes, focusing on the productive operations of power will potentially give us more freedom to not merely bemoan repression but think and do things differently.

Now, on the one hand, the shift from a 'negative' towards a 'positive' concept of power is clearly deployed against Freudo-Marxism and its preoccupation with sexual repression respectively liberation. Foucault consistently distances himself from what he sees as totalizing approaches, approaches claiming to deduce the effects of social and political power relations from certain economic or political categories, for instance, seeking to deduce "the status of the mad, the sick, children, delinquents, and so on, in our kind of society" from the category of the state, or the category of the state from the category of the commodity and so forth. "[T]hen I reply: Yes, of course, I am determined to refrain from that kind of analysis" (Foucault 2008, 78). Instead, he suggests to approach "our kind of society" through a critical history of the present that would focus on the genealogy of practices and problematizations and the struggles around them.

On the other hand, however, this shift was clearly inspired by Marx:

> I will make a presumptuous comparison. What did Marx do when in his analysis of capital he came across the problem of the worker's misery? He refused the customary explanation which regarded this misery as the effect of a naturally rare cause or of a concerted theft. And he said substantially: given what capitalist production is, in its fundamental laws, it cannot help but cause misery. Capitalism's *raison d'être* is not to starve the workers but it cannot develop without starving them. Marx replaced the denunciation of theft by the analysis of production. Other things being equal, that is approximately what I wanted to say. It is not a matter of denying sexual misery, nor is it however one of explaining it negatively by a repression. The entire prob-

lem is to grasp the positive mechanism which, producing sexuality in this or
that fashion, results in misery. (Foucault 1977, 153f.)

In a word, Marx developed a positive, non-juridical concept of power that
serves as a model for Foucault. In a less well-known text dating back to a
1976 talk at the University of Bahia, Foucault explicitly refers to Marx' *Critique
of Political Economy* as assembling the elements constituting this specifically
new, modern type of power. What are these elements? First, Foucault insists,
there is not *one* power for Marx, but different types of domination or subjugation that each have emerged from specific local and historical contexts and
show specific technologies and mechanisms. He mentions the workshop, the
army and the slave plantation to underline the scope of variety. "Society is an
archipelago of different powers" (Foucault 2012[1976], 4). Second, for Marx, according to Foucault, the formation of sovereignty does not come first and society second, as the juridical conceptions by Grotius, Pufendorf and the contract
theorists would have it. The reverse is true: The regional powers come first
and state power second. Third, and most importantly, these regional powers
do not primarily operate by means of restriction and prohibition; they do not
primarily operate juridically: "The original, essential and permanent function
of these local and regional powers is, in reality, being producers of the efficiency and skill of the producers of a product" (Foucault 2012, 5).

Note that it is not primarily the product that is being produced here but
"the efficiency and skill of the producer". In Marxian terms, this would be
the productivity of living labor. In Foucauldian terms, productive power is
biopower in that it turns the body and the population into a resource whose
vital forces are to be increased and enhanced. Both Marx and Foucault, thus,
are concerned with a type of power directed at shaping, increasing and enhancing the vital forces of the human, at maximizing human skills, capacities, efficiency and functionality. Put differently, what distinguishes modern, productive power from other types of power is that its mechanisms and
technologies are directed at shaping, enhancing, optimizing and maximizing the productive life forces of the human. Moreover, for both Marx and
Foucault, technology is crucial to this form of power, although their attention is on different types of technology: big machinery in Marx and social and
political technologies in Foucault. Still, technology is of the essence as it is
through technology, or technologies, that human skills, capacities, efficiency
and functionality are increased and improved. Therefore, these technologies
themselves become the subject of constant optimization; they are constantly

being refined, improved, made more efficient. This would be the fourth characteristic element of productive power that Foucault finds in Marx:

> these mechanisms of power, these procedures of power, it's necessary to regard them as techniques, which is to say as procedures that were invented, perfected, that were unceasingly developed. There is a veritable technology of power, or better still, of powers, which have their own history. Here, once again, we can easily find between the lines of the second volume of *Capital* an analysis, or at least the outline of an analysis, which would be the history of the technology of power, such as it was exercised in the workhouses and factories. (Foucault 2012, 6)[5]

Hence, Foucault says: Technologies of discipline precede the historical formation of capitalism; capitalism is not the origin of these technologies of power; rather, it is the effect of their proliferation and intensification at different sites and in different settings. The workhouse comes first; capitalism comes second. And although technologies of discipline and control as developed in the workhouse, but not only there, eventually proved functional for capitalism, the type of power they manifest was not brought into being by capitalism. This might also be the place to note that, in the course of the 20th century, it turned out that biopolitical rationality was not confined to capitalist societies. The prisons, penitentiaries, and psychiatric institutions, not to speak of the camps under Stalinism and in many state socialist regimes, provide ample evidence of that. Moreover, as we saw in Chapter 2 of this book, it was not uncommon for biopolitical rationalities to be linked to welfarist rationalities, as in the case of socialist or social reform movements that promoted eugenic policies as a means to build a functioning welfare state. In short, biopolitics and capitalism share the logic of increasing the forces of life as a means of increasing human productivity and functionality, but that does not mean that this logic is the exclusive property of capitalist society. Rather, we can say that welfarist, socialist and capitalist biopolitics share a modern, productivist rationality that may operate within different economic and political regimes.

To summarize, we have seen that Foucault is not at odds with Marx, but in fact agrees with him regarding the heterogeneous origins, the historicity

---

5   Jacques Bidet, however, has noted that Foucault referred erroneously to Volume Two of *Capital* here and that the editors of the talk repeated this error. In fact, Foucault referred to Marx' historical accounts of factory discipline in the chapter on machinery and large-scale industry in Volume One (Bidet 2016, 22).

and the distinctively productive nature of modern power. So far, however, the commonalities we have seen concern only the historical accounts presented in *Capital*, not Marx' more original, distinctive analytical approach, namely form analysis. On the form-analytical level, one would expect more fundamental differences between Marx and Foucault, given that form analysis was in fact Marx' original way of seeking to capture and expose the totality of power relations that characterize capitalist society. To be sure, it is not a homogeneous, monolithic totality with which Marx presents us; it is a fractured, distorted, even hostile totality constituted by inherent antagonisms and contradictions and subject to struggle and contestation, but it is a totality nonetheless, meaning that the critical, historically specific forms characterizing the capitalist mode of production—such as commodity, money, value, wage labor, or capital—are necessarily implicating and co-reproducing each other. While Marx seeks to expose the 'laws' that govern this type of society and the mechanisms that tie these forms to one another, constantly reproducing this 'wrong' form of sociality, Foucault rejects "the inhibiting effect specific to totalitarian theories, or at least [...] all-encompassing and global theories" (Foucault 2003, 6). He deliberately claims to replace them in favor of what he calls local critique. All-encompassing theories, and he mentions Marxism and psychoanalysis here, may be useful for local critiques if and only if:

> ...the theoretical unity of their discourse is, so to speak, suspended, or at least cut up, ripped up, torn to shreds, turned inside out, displaced, caricatured, dramatized, theatricalized, and so on. (Foucault 2003, 6)

It is at this point that Foucault parts company with Marx. He does not seek 'laws' that necessarily tie any form to any other, nor does he attempt to capture the totality of any social formation. The new type of theory that may emerge from local critique, he proclaims, "does not need a visa from some common regime to establish its validity" (Foucault 2003, 6). Whether or not Foucault—particularly in his work on biopolitics and biopower—complies with his own stipulations and actually avoids any totalizing move, and whether it is at all possible to articulate critique without theorizing social totality, is debatable (see e.g. Geisler and Struwe 2019). In the following pages, I do not discuss this question on a general level but point out that, notwithstanding these theoretical–political differences, Foucault's conception of power, as manifested in his analysis of biopolitics and biopower, shows remarkable commonalities with Marx' conceptual analysis of value accumulation as the essence of capital. To allow these commonalities to emerge, it is necessary to first revisit Marx' analysis of capital accumulation as the heart of capitalism.

7.5   Enhancing the Forces of Life

The main focus and the starting point of *Capital* is, importantly, wealth, not scarcity. More precisely, Marx starts from the *form* of wealth and wealth production in capitalist society. Hence the much-quoted introductory phrase of *Capital*:

> The wealth of societies in which the capitalist mode of production prevails appears as an 'immense accumulation of commodities';[6] the individual commodity appears as its elementary form. (Marx 1990, 125)

Wealth, with its specific form and production, is the subject of analysis in *Capital*. More precisely, the subject under study is wealth in capitalist society. In the course of analysis, it results that wealth in capitalist society may well appear as an accumulation of commodities; this is not wrong, but it is incomplete. In fact, the specific form of wealth in societies with capitalist mode of production is the accumulation *of value*, with accumulation not meaning 'a greater amount of' but the *process* of accumulation. Value, in *Capital*, is not a thing or a quality, such as color or weight, nor is it a substance. I follow the interpretation of Michael Heinrich (2004) here, who emphasizes that Marx in *Capital* explicitly abandons the idea that value is created when isolated producers spend private labor-time on the production of a certain use-value, so that from the moment of production, value resides in the labor product. This notion goes back to classical political economy and assumes that value-creation was a universal, ahistorical feature of human labor as such. In *Capital*, Marx departs from this ahistorical, humanist assumption and demonstrates that value and, consequently, value creation, are features of labor only under the conditions of a fully developed capitalist mode of production. Labor products, according to this reading, do not have value prior to and independent of the act of being exchanged; accordingly, the value of a commodity is not determined by the quantity of labor expended on it. Otherwise, a slow and clumsy worker would automatically generate more value than a swift and skilful one (Marx 1990, 129). Rather, the magnitude of value of commodities

---

6   Marx quotes his earlier text, *Zur Kritik der Politischen Ökonomie*, here (Marx 2015, 15).

is determined by the 'socially necessary labor-time' that is required on average to produce "any use-value under the conditions of production normal for a given society and with the average degree of skill and intensity of labor prevalent in that society" (Marx 1990, 129). This, however, cannot be determined in advance, not least because it is subject to constant change. Therefore, Marx argues that value is determined in the act of exchange. In the act of exchange, the producers actively compare the products of their labor, abstracting from the particular content of that labor. "They do this without being aware of it" (Marx 1990, 166f.).[7] The common parameter according to which commodities are compared to one another is the expenditure of labor-time, that is, abstract labor or labor *sans phrase*. Value has no existence independent from this act of comparison in and through the act of exchange; the act must be performed for value to exist.

In societies with a capitalist mode of production, commodities are regularly produced for the market, which presupposes a certain level of division of labor, and exchanged against money, meaning that the reproduction of society is critically mediated through exchange. Under these conditions, producers, in and through the act of exchange, do not merely relate the products of their private labor to each other; rather, they relate the fragment of social labor represented in their labor products to the total labor of society (Heinrich 2004, 55). Value, therefore, is essentially a social relation, a particular form of organizing social life that dominates capitalist society. It assigns certain positions to its members and imposes certain imperatives on them, above all the imperative to sell their labor power if they are owners of nothing but this and to accumulate value if they are owners of means of production.

When the capitalist mode of production is fully developed, Marx argues, and the dominant form of production is production for the market, the logic of the market requires participants to strive for accumulation, for the valorization of value, if they want to maintain their economic existence. Ultimately, therefore, wealth in capitalist societies takes the form of an endless, perpetual, self-propelling process of value accumulation. Accumulation is end-less in that is has no endpoint, no point of sufficiency, no ends in the sense of attainable objectives. It is this uncanny, self-propelling, end-less mode of existence that, for Marx, imbues capital with 'life' and makes it life-like:

---

7   The German original is even more pointed here: "Sie wissen das nicht, aber sie tun es" (Marx 1972, 88).

> But capital has only one sole driving force, the drive to valorize itself, to create surplus-value, to make its constant part, the means of production, absorb the greatest possible amount of surplus labour. Capital is dead labour which, vampire-like, lives only by sucking living labour, and lives the more, the more labour it sucks. (Marx 1990, 342)

Capital, for Marx, is feeding on life; it is consuming life in the form of living labor. Under conditions of capitalism, the production process is at the same time a process of consumption—consumption of living labor—and, potentially, of the production of surplus value. Thus, labor is extracted, even wasted, and made productive at the same time. This is possible because living labor's potential to create value is not limited to creating the value of the goods necessary to maintain its existence. Provided that surplus value can be realized on the market, it can be reinvested to further increase the productivity of labor and make some additional profit. Thus, capital does not simply consume and waste labor but rather assimilates it to its own vampire-like form of existence, transforming labor into its own antagonist, capital. As if under a spell, living labor is forced to feed both capital accumulation and an increase in the forces of production.

We can now see how capital accumulation begins to resemble biopolitics, how biopolitics resembles capital as analyzed by Marx, and in what sense Foucault may have taken inspiration from this analysis. Biopolitics, in Foucault, displays the same logic that characterizes the logic of capital accumulation: the logic of a productive type of power that grows and proliferates while exploiting the forces upon which it is feeding. Both capital and biopolitics, in other words, manifest the same historically new and distinctively productive type of power that marks the era of Western modernity. It is a power

> ...working to incite, reinforce, control, monitor, optimize, and organize the forces under it: a power bent on generating forces, making them grow, and ordering them, rather than one dedicated to impeding them, making them submit, or destroying them. (Foucault 1980, 136)

Biopolitics and biopower, for Foucault, are particularly dominant manifestations of this new, productive type of power that co-emerged with modernity, a type of power geared towards preserving and enhancing human life, its forces, strength and productivity, of "improving and enhancing the functionality of biological human life" (Wehling 2008, 251).

Yet the potential to increase the life forces and productivity of the individual is limited, not least by human mortality. Increasing human productivity on the level of the population is not limited in the same way. While individual bodies are necessary for the process to proceed, while they may form targets of improvement strategies, while without the existence and functionality of individuals no accumulation or biopolitics could take place, the individual is nothing but a moment within an overarching process that proceeds on the supra-individual level. Biopolitics "is a technology in which bodies are replaced by general biological processes" (Foucault 2003, 249). On these grounds, Foucault points out, an overall policy of improving, maximizing and optimizing the life, fitness and productivity of the population may be compatible with a politics of selection, racism and elimination as executed by the Nazi state (Foucault 2003, 254ff.). In Nazi biopolitics, taking the lives of some—the inferior, the weak, the deficient, unfit or unproductive or racially unworthy—was a mechanism for improving life on the level of the master race:

> The more inferior species die out, the more abnormal individuals are eliminated, the fewer degenerates there will be in the species as a whole, and the more I—as species rather than individual—can live, the stronger I will be, the more vigorous I will be. I will be able to proliferate. (Foucault 2003, 255)

Nazi biopolitics also demonstrates that biopolitics is by no means restricted to liberalism. It thereby poses a challenge to government-centred approaches as discussed above. If biopolitics is basically understood as a feature of liberal governmentality, one can either stretch the term 'liberalism' so far as to include Nazism[8] or bracket out Nazi biopolitics as an inexplicable exception to the rule. Both solutions are theoretically unsatisfactory. The problem arises, I suggest, from the equation of modern economic rationality with liberalism. Once we shift the focus from liberal government to the modern logic of increasing and improving human productivity, non-liberal or even anti-liberal totalitarian biopolitics is no longer a contradiction in terms.

Note that, for Nazi biopolitics, the master race was not an existing entity, nor was it co-extensive with the German nation; the master race was something to be actively created, and improving its life was a concerted, future-

---

8   In this vein, Nikolas Rose (2004, 23) asserts that, even in Nazi Germany, atrocities were committed "in the name of freedom", albeit the freedom of the Aryan people. Still, in my opinion, this stretches the liberal idea of governing through freedom too far.

oriented effort to be executed through policies that included selective family allowances as well as forcible sterilization and organized mass murder. All these measures were designed to improve the strength, health, and purity of the coming master race. Anyone who would not conform to this vision constituted a threat or a burden that needed to be eliminated. Hence, taking life was a means of making life; destroying life in the present was a means of optimizing life in the future. Death

> now presents itself as the counterpart of a power that exerts a positive influence on life, that endeavours to administer, optimize, and multiply it, subjecting it to precise controls and comprehensive regulations. (Foucault 1980, 137)

Like capital, biopolitics in its extreme form maximizes life on the supra-individual level by turning the living into the dead. Conversely, capital in Marx assumes a life-like, self-sustaining, proliferating form of life through feeding upon living labor and turning it into dead labor.

7.6   The Time of Capital and Biopolitics

Temporality figures prominently in Marx and Foucault. To summarize the foregoing, the significance of temporality concerns three major aspects: an emphasis on the historicity of the present, an ontology of performance, and the diagnosis of a particular temporal dynamics which I will term 'the dynamics of end-less progression'. Let us recapitulate these three aspects of temporality:

Historicity: The point of critique for Marx and Foucault is to expose the fundamentally historical, contingent status of the prevailing forms of social thought and practice in the present. [9] They deploy historical analysis as a way to undermine the belief in alleged universals and render contestable the mechanisms that create the appearance of ahistorical universality and immutability. Critique, understood thus, may enable contemporaries to contest

---

9   For Foucault's model of critique in comparison to that of Horkheimer and Adorno, see Vogelmann 2018. Much of what Vogelmann states about the inherent nexus of diagnosis, critique and social change in Horkheimer and Adorno, I would add, in fact hearkens back to Marx.

these mechanisms and ultimately replace them with more emancipatory practices and social relations. Neither value nor wage labor, nor the resulting form
of wealth as an accumulation of commodities, is a timeless universal; on the
contrary, these are rather recent ways of organizing social life. The same can
be said for the notion of life and the imperative to enhance it, the notion of
sexuality and the imperative to liberate it, the notion of the population and
the imperative to improve it. Realizing the fundamentally contingent character of such alleged universals, according to Marx and Foucault, may enable us
to conceive of things differently and ultimately do things differently. Wealth,
for instance, must not necessarily take the form of an accumulation of commodities. This is in truth a poor, reductive and destructive form of wealth.
We should replace it with a different, a more sustainable, a more just and inclusive one that acknowledges and values nature and human faculties as its
sources. Rather than an accumulation of commodities, we could, for instance,
consider solidarity to be the form of wealth we want to achieve.

Ontology of performance: Foucault states explicitly that power "is something
that is exercized and that it exists only in action" (2003, 14). Power is neither
an entity nor an instrument or structure; thus, it is never static or fixed. In
order to exist, it must be actively performed. Similarly, Marx conceives of
value as existing only in action. Value must be realized, and it can be realized
only through the act of exchange; if this does not take place, value does not
exist. Moreover, all of the major forms analyzed by Marx turn out to be the
prevailing way of doing something: commodity, exchange value, value, money,
and wage labor are all historically specific forms of organizing social life. They
exist only in action: commodities, value, and wage labor must all be produced,
exchanged, realized, valorized, reproduced, or accumulated in order to be
what they are. This means, in turn, that they will cease to exist when we invent
other ways of organizing social life.

End-less progression: Capital and biopolitics share a temporal structure that
can be described as the dynamics of end-less progression. The mode of existence of both capital and biopolitics, as shown above, is that of an ongoing
process that is simultaneously endless and directed: Capital accumulation and
biopolitics are end-less in that they have no attainable ends and no conceivable end-point. Yet they are directed, namely towards maximization and optimization: an increased accumulation of value and an optimized functionality
of life. In addition, it can be said that both capital accumulation for Marx
and biopolitics for Foucault proceed through using *and* increasing the productive forces of life: The valorization of value includes the use of living labor,

the production of surplus value, the realization of surplus value on the market—and, in the interest of sustaining one's economic existence, investing at least part of the surplus value to further increase the productive forces of living labor through deploying more efficient technology. Thus, exploiting life in the form of living labor and constantly increasing its productivity ultimately form two facets of the same historically unprecedented dynamic. Again, we see the resemblance between capital in Marx and biopolitics and biopower in Foucault, both allowing the extraction the forces of life at the same time as their increase, optimization and maximization.

Above, I argued that the concept of biopolitics captures a specifically modern way of integrating the individual and the social whole—"omnes et singulatim", all and one—as Foucault put it (1994a). Biopolitics, in this sense, provides a set of social and political technologies that supposedly benefit the individual and the social order at the same time. Yet this promise relies on the underlying temporal structure of end-less progress. After all, it is only the presupposition of constant, irreversible and inexorable progress towards the better that may render at least some credibility to the abovementioned promise, allowing for the constant deferring of its fulfilment into the future.[10] In fact, the present constantly fails to deliver, and a harmonious integration of all and one is nowhere in sight. Against this continuous experience, the promises of modernity, capitalism, and biopolitics rely on the stipulation of progress. Progress will bring increased productivity, which will bring improved living conditions, which will bring increased productivity and so forth. Modernity, in short, relies on the—joint and constant—improvement of life and productivity *in time*, or at least the promise thereof. Marx and Foucault expose this nexus, which is why they shift our attention from repression to productivity and towards a new type of power that constantly seeks to optimize the functionality and the productive forces of life. The problem is that optimizing the forces of life coincides with reproducing social relations of exploitation and subjugation as well as norms and standards of functionality, usefulness, productivity and fitness. The counterpart of enhancing life is the devaluation of those who do not meet these standards or are deemed not to meet them. Thus, the imperative of optimizing life fuels the notion of life that is not good enough, that does not meet the standards of fitness and functionality, that

---

10   Again, I thank Peter Wehling for making this point and for reminding me of Walter
      Benjamin's critique of the idea of irreversible, inexorable progress in empty, homoge-
      nous time (Benjamin 1980, 258).

is not strong, healthy, useful, fit or happy enough. Optimizing life implies the construction, problematization, and devaluation of 'deficient life', a construction which, in turn, fuels the demand for technoscientific investments to 'solve' these 'problems' and optimize life further.

7.7   Conclusion

What, then, can be learnt about the relationship between biopower and capitalism from revisiting Marx and Foucault? How can we capture it by re-reading one in light of the other? In any case, this reading does not support a deterministic conception according to which capitalism could have caused biopower and biopolitics or vice versa. It also does not support a functionalist conception indicating that biopower and biopolitics have emerged because they perform certain necessary functions for capitalism or vice versa. Neither of these constructions can be historically or theoretically substantiated, at least not on the basis of Marx or Foucault. On the other hand, stating a mere coincidence, a random overlap of two unrelated phenomena, would also fail to harness the theoretical potential of such a reading. Rather, I suggest, we can discern a common core of biopower and capitalism, a certain logic that they share but that distinguishes them sharply from previous modes of production and types of power, respectively. The key to understanding this logic, I suggest, is a new and distinct connection of power and temporality that was brought about by modernity and is characterized by the co-constitution of productive power and a future-oriented, yet end-less movement that I have termed the dynamics of end-less progression. What distinguishes productive power from repressive, extractive, banning types of power is essentially its capacity to turn human life into a resource that can be used and harnessed and increased at the same time. This is what biopower and capital do: they simultaneously harness and increase the forces of human life. This does not mean that the forces of life need be understood in a bio-realist or vitalist way, as an independent, ahistorical reality. It is the converse: life is that which can be simultaneously harnessed and increased. As such, it is a fundamentally historical phenomenon and contingent on productive power.

In short, productive power is the type of power geared at increasing the functionality, productivity, efficiency and performance of human life, that is, at increasing the production of productivity. Yet to avoid misunderstandings, it must also be stated that productive power does not necessarily improve or prolong the lives of individuals, nor does it necessarily harness the potential of any individual. Using, wasting, damaging or even discarding the life of individuals is not incompatible with the logic of capital and biopower—in principle or in practice. At the macro-level, the level of the population, of society, of the master race, or of whatever collectivity is constructed as a reference, the forces of life may well be increased and optimized regardless of the damage done to individual lives. This constitutes a certain tension, however, within the logic of productive power. On the one hand, it is the claim and the promise of modern biopower and capitalism alike to serve the benefit of "omnes et singulatim" at once. Increasing productivity, functionality and efficiency at the macro-level will automatically benefit the lives of the individuals, and, conversely, increasing the productivity, functionality and efficiency of individuals will benefit society at large. On the other hand, the epoch of biopower and capitalism did not put an end to misery, poverty, insecurity and suffering, at least not for all and not for long; the claim of improving life for each and all is constantly refuted by lived experience. Hence the necessity of constant progression: If life has not yet improved for each and all, it is because we have not done enough to improve the forces of life, to increase the production of productivity. We must increase, improve, optimize, and possibly accelerate them further. We must comply with the imperative of constant improvement. With Marx, we can see the absurdity of this logic; it is not only that producing productivity also produces misery and exploitation, but that feeding the process also becomes an end in itself. Living labor becomes a means of propelling productivity instead of productivity becoming a means of serving human needs. Moreover, within the confines of this logic, there is no room to ask *which* needs productivity should actually serve and at what cost, and what kind of society with which mode of production would be needed to achieve these ends. With Foucault, in turn, we can see that improving life operates as a norm, and a norm implies the existence of the abnormal. Thus, improving life also entails producing deficient life, life that does not meet the standards, that is not productive, not functional, not fit enough. The imperative of improving life thus implies the degradation of human lives considered deficient, abnormal, unworthy according to norms and standards that are never stable—because there is always room for improvement.

Acknowledgments

This book took shape over many years and within many different working contexts. In the order of creation, I wish to give special thanks to the following people for their comments, ideas and support:

Chapter 6 benefitted greatly from participating in the Jewish studies reading group we had during my time at the Henry M. Jackson School of International Studies at the University of Washington in Seattle from 2004 to 2006. In particular, I would like to thank Richard Block and Michael Rosenthal for their substantial comments, inspiration and encouragement.

Chapter 3 draws on work that Svea L. Herrmann, Ole A. Brekke and I did together within a research project on eugenics and restorative justice at Leibniz University of Hanover from 2008 to 2011. My thanks go to the German Research Association for funding this work and to Svea and Ole for the wonderful collaboration. I owe an infinite debt of gratitude to Svea for her substantive contribution to this chapter as well as others which she read and commented on and over and above this for her support and friendship over so many years. My special thanks also go to Margaret Hamm for valuable background knowledge and for allowing me to use the archive of the Association of Victims of "Euthanasia" and Forced Sterilization.

Chapter 2 began to take shape during my research fellowship at the Centre for Baltic and Eastern European Studies (CBEES) at Södertörn University Huddinge near Stockholm in 2010, and I am thankful to Teresa Kulawik for making this possible and for many inspiring conversations then and after.

Chapter 5 originated during my time at the Department for Political Science at the University of Vienna from 2015 to 2017. My thanks go especially to Birgit Sauer for her personal and professional support and encouragement and to Marion Löffler und Karin Bischof for inviting me to present and publish this work and providing valuable comments.

Chapters 1, 4 and 7 were written over the past two years, in 2019 and 2020, when I was based at the Center for Risk and Innovation Studies (ZIRIUS) and the Department for Social Sciences at the University of Stuttgart; I am deeply grateful to Cordula Kropp for granting me the freedom to work on the book and for the many constructive and stimulating conversations we had.

Chapter 7 benefited greatly from the small reading group on critical theory of biopolitics that I had with Peter Wehling in 2019 and 2020. I owe a great debt of gratitude to him for his substantial thoughts, his kind and competent encouragement and his comments on this chapter as well as on Chapter 1.

In 2020, our group merged into another one on biopolitics and the Corona crisis, together with Sabine Könninger and Susanne Schultz. I am thankful to Sabine, Susanne and Peter for this common effort of providing companionship and orientation in a situation of crisis and confusion. Chapter 1 benefited strongly from our discussions.

My thanks also go to Helene Gerhards, who read various draft chapters and provided valuable comments. Special thanks go to Amari Barash for her thoughtful and thorough language editing and to Esther Braun for her careful help with the bibliography. Most of all, I am grateful to my wonderful children David and Esther for the love and joy they bring to my life, for their trust and empathy, and for their attentive views of the world that they so generously share with me.

Parts of this book have been published before in slightly different form. I would like to thank the publishers for permission to make use of the following articles:

Marginal Justice: The Persecution of So-called 'Asocials' and the Politics of Historic Justice in the Federal Republic of Germany. Parliaments, Estates and Representation, 38(1), 2018, 104-120, revised as Chapter 5.

Biopolitics and Temporality in Arendt and Foucault. Time and Society, 1(1), 2007, 5-23, revised as Chapter 6.

List of Abbreviations

AKG	Gesetz zur Allgemeinen Regelung durch den Krieg und den Zusammenbruch des Deutschen Reiches entstandener Schäden (Allgemeines Kriegsfolgengesetz)	General Act Regulating Compensation for War-Induced Losses
B90/ Die Grünen	Bündnis 90/Die Grünen	Alliance 90/The Greens
BEG	Bundesgesetz zur Entschädigung für Opfer nationalsozialistischer Verfolgung (Bundesentschädigungsgesetz)	Federal Indemnification Act
BErgG	Bundesergänzungsgesetz zur Entschädigung für Opfer der nationalsozialistischen Verfolgung	Federal German Supplementary Law
BEZ	Bundes der „Euthanasie"-Geschädigten und Zwangssterilisierten	Association of Victims of "Euthanasia" and Forced Sterilization
BGH	Bundesgerichtshof	Federal Court of Justice
BMBF	Bundesministerium für Bildung und Forschung	Federal Ministry of Education and Research

BMF	Bundesministerium der Finanzen	Federal Ministry of Finance
BMJ	Bundesministerium der Justiz	Federal Ministry of Justice (and Consumer Protection)
BR	Bundesrat	Upper House of Parliament
BRD	Bundesrepublik Deutschland	Federal Republic of Germany (FRG)
BT	Bundestag	Lower House of Parliament
BT Drs.	Bundestagsdrucksache	Parliamentary Publication
BT PLP	Plenarprotokolle des Bundestags	Minutes of Plenary Proceedings of the Lower House of Parliament
BVerfG	Bundesverfassungsgericht	Federal Constitutional Court
BVerfGE	Entscheidungen des Bundesverfassungsgerichts	Decisions of the Federal Constitutional Court
CDU	Christlich Demokratische Union Deutschlands	Christian Democratic Union
CSU	Christlich Soziale Union Deutschlands	Christian Socialist Union
DDR	Deutsche Demokratische Republik	German Democratic Republic (GDR)
FDP	Freiheitlich Demokratische Partei Deutschlands	Free Democratic Party
Gestapo	Geheime Staatspolizei	Secret State Police
GG	Grundgesetz für die Bundesrepublik Deutschland	Basic Law for the Federal Republic of Germany
GzVeN	Gesetz zur Verhütung erbkranken Nachwuchses vom 14. Juli 1933	Law for the Prevention of Offspring with Hereditary Diseases
MdB	Mitglied des Bundestages	Member of the Parliament

NER	Nationaler Ethikrat	National Ethics Council
NS-AufhG	Gesetz zur Aufhebung national-sozialistischer Unrechtsurteile in der Strafrechtspflege und von Sterilisationsentscheidungen der ehemaligen Erbgesundheits-gerichte	Law to Annul Unjust Sentences Imposed During the National Socialist Administration of Criminal Justice (NS Annulment Act)
NSDAP	Nationalsozialistische Deutsche Arbeiterpartei	National Socialist German Workers' Party
OLG	Oberlandesgericht	Higher Regional Court
RStGB	Reichsstrafgesetzbuch	Imperial Criminal Code
RMI	Reichsminister des Innern	The Reich's Minister of the Interior
SPD	Sozialdemokratische Partei Deutschlands	Social Democratic Party of Germany
SS	Schutzstaffel (Gliederung der NSDAP)	Protection Squadron
StGB	Strafgesetzbuch	Criminal Code
StrReha-HomG	Gesetz zur strafrechtlichen Rehabilitierung der nach dem 8. Mai 1945 wegen einvernehmlicher homosexueller Handlungen verurteilten Personen	Act on the Criminal Rehabilitation of Persons Convicted of Consensual Homosexual Acts after 8 May 1945
WD	Wissenschaftliche Dienste des Bundestags	Research Services of the Lower House of Parliament

References

AbilityWatch (2020). *Verfassungsbeschwerde Triage*. Retrieved 25 Nov 2020 from https://abilitywatch.de/menschistmensch/.

Adams, M. B. (Ed.) (1990). *The Wellborn Science: Eugenics in Germany, France, Brazil and Russia*. Oxford: Oxford University Press.

Agamben, G. (1998). *Homo Sacer: Sovereign Power and Bare Life*. Stanford, CA: Stanford University Press.

Agamben, G. (2020). Giorgio Agamben zum Umgang der liberalen Demokratien mit dem Coronavirus: Ich hätte da eine Frage. *Neue Züricher Zeitung* 15 April 2020.

Ahrens, J. (2020). Theorising—Praise of Biopolitics? The Covid-19 Pandemic and the Will for Self-Preservation. *The European Sociologist* 45(1). Retrieved 25 Nov 2020 from https://www.europeansociologist.org/issue-45-pandemic-impossibilities-vol-1/theorising-praise-biopolitics-covid-19-pandemic-and-will.

Alex, A. (2015). Die vergessenen Opfer der Nazis Geschichte: Wie viele »Asoziale« und »Kriminelle« wurden tatsächlich ermordet? *ak* (610), 33.

Allen, A. (2002). Power, Subjectivity, and Agency: Between Arendt and Foucault. *International Journal of Philosophical Studies* 10(2): 131-149.

Allen, A. T. (1988). German Radical Feminism and Eugenics, 1900-1908. *German Studies Review* 11(1): 31-56.

Allen, A. T. (2000). Feminism and Eugenics in Germany and Britain, 1900-1940: A Comparative Perspective. *German Studies Review* 23(3): 477-505.

Allen, G. (1976). Genetics, Eugenics and Society: Internalists and Externalists in Contemporary History of Science. *Social Studies of Science* 6(1): 105-122.

Arbour, L. (2006). *Economic and Social Justice for Societies in Transition*. Center for Human Rights and Global Justice Working Paper Number 10, 2006. New York: Center for Human Rights and Global Justice.

Arendt, H. (1958). *The Human Condition*. Chicago, IL: University of Chicago Press.

Arendt, H. (1968). *The Origins of Totalitarianism*. San Diego, CA: Harcourt.

Arendt, H. (1970). *On Violence*. San Diego, CA: Harcourt.

Arendt, H. (1981). Es gibt nur ein einziges Menschenrecht. In O. Höffe (Ed.), *Funk-Kolleg Praktische Philosophie/Ethik: Reader zum Funk-Kolleg* (pp. 152-166). Frankfurt: Suhrkamp.

Arendt, H. (1993). *Between Past and Future*. New York, NY: Penguin.

Arendt, H. (1996). *Elemente und Ursprünge totaler Herrschaft: Antisemitismus, Imperialismus, totale Herrschaft*. Munich: Piper.

Arendt, H. (2005). On the Nature of Totalitarianism: An Essay in Understanding. In H. Arendt, *Essays in Understanding 1930-1954: Formation, Exile, and Totalitarianism* (pp.328-360). New York, NY: Schocken.

Ayaß, W. (1988). "Ein Gebot der nationalen Arbeitsdisziplin". Die "Aktion Arbeitsscheu Reich" 1938. *Beiträge zur nationalsozialistischen Gesundheits- und Sozialpolitik* 6: 43-74.

Ayaß, W. (1995). *"Asoziale" im Nationalsozialismus*. Stuttgart: Klett-Cotta.

Ayaß, W. (1998). *"Gemeinschaftsfremde". Quellen zur Verfolgung "Asozialer" 1933-1945*. Koblenz: Bundesarchiv.

Ayaß, W. (2005). "Asoziale" im Nationalsozialismus. Überblick über die Breite der Maßnahmen gegen soziale Außenseiter und die hieran beteiligten Stellen. In D. Sedlaczek, T. Lutz, U. Puvogel, and I. Tomkowiak (Eds.), *"minderwertig" und "asozial": Stationen der Verfolgung gesellschaftlicher Außenseiter* (pp. 51-64). Zürich: Chronos.

Balint, J., J. Evans and N. McMillan (2014). Rethinking Transitional Justice, Redressing Indigenous Harm: A New Conceptual Approach. *The International Journal of Transitional Justice* 8(2): 194–216.

Barkan, E. (1992). *The Retreat of Scientific Racism: Changing Concepts of Race in Britain and the United States between the World Wars*. Cambridge: Cambridge University Press.

Bashford, A. and P. Levine (Eds.) (2010). *The Oxford Handbook of the History of Eugenics*. Oxford: Oxford University Press.

Bastian, T. (2000). *Homosexuelle im Dritten Reich*. München: C. H. Beck.

Bastrup, O. R. E. and A.G. Sivertsen (1996). *En landevei mot undergangen - Utryddelsen av taterkulturen i Norge*. Oslo: Universitetsforlaget.

Benhabib, S. (1996). *The Reluctant Modernism of Hannah Arendt*. Thousand Oaks, CA: SAGE Publications.

Benjamin, W. (1968). *Illuminations: Essays and Reflections*. New York, NY: Schocken.

Benjamin, W. (1980). Über den Begriff der Geschichte. In S. Unseld (Ed.), *Walter Benjamin. Illuminationen. Ausgewählte Schriften* (pp. 251-261). Frankfurt: Suhrkamp.

Bidet, J. (2016). *Foucault with Marx*. London: Zed Books.

Bland, L. (1995). *Banishing the Beast, English Feminism and Sexual Morality, 1885-1914*. London: Penguin.

BMF (2012). *Entschädigung von NS-Unrecht: Regelungen zur Wiedergutmachung*. Berlin: Bundesministerium der Finanzen.

BMJ (2016). *Eckpunktepapier zur Rehabilitierung der nach 1945 in beiden deutschen Staaten wegen einvernehmlicher homosexueller Handlungen Verurteilten*. Berlin: Bundesministerium der Justiz und für Verbraucherschutz.

Bock, G. (1986). *Zwangssterilisation im Nationalsozialismus: Studien zur Rassenpolitik und Frauenpolitik*. Opladen: Westdeutscher Verlag.

Bock, G. (2004). Nazi Sterilisation and Reproductive Policies. In D. Kuntz and S. Bachrach (Eds.), *Deadly Medicine: Creating the Master Race* (pp. 61-87). Washington D.C.: United States Holocaust Memorial Museum.

BR Drs. 189/15 (Beschluss) (2015). *Beschluss des Bundesrats*, 10 July 2015.

Braun, K. (2001). (K)Eine Denkerin der Vermittlung? Gesellschaftstheorie und Geschlechterverhältnis im Werk von Hannah Arendt. In G. A. Knapp and A. Wetterer (Eds.), *Soziale Verortung der Geschlechter: Gesellschaftstheorie und Feministische Kritik* (pp. 132-156). Münster: Westfälisches Dampfboot.

Braun, K. (2017). Öb es tatsächlich dazu kommt, ist nach wie vor offen und bleibt abzuwarten."Der Kampf des BEZ um die Anerkennung der ËuthanasieGeschädigten und Zwangssterilisierten als Verfolgte des Nationalsozialismus und die Antworten der Politik. In M. Hamm (Ed.), *Ausgegrenzt! Warum? Zwangssterilisierte und Geschädigte der NS-Ëuthanasie in der Bundesrepublik Deutschland* (pp. 199-221). Berlin: Metropol.

Braun, K. and S. L. Herrmann (2015). Unrecht zweiter Ordnung. Die Weitergeltung des Gesetzes zur Verhütung erbranken Nachwuchses in der Bundesrepublik. In S. Begalke, C. Fröhlich and S. A. Glienke (Eds.), *Der halbierte Rechtsstaat: Demokratie und Recht in der frühen Bundesrepublik und die Integration von NS-Funktionseliten* (pp. 223-241). Baden Baden: Nomos.

Braun, K. and H. Gerhards (2019). Leben, Zeit, Regierung. Eine sozialtheoretische und konstruktivistische Neubestimmung des Konzepts Biopolitik. In H. Gerhards and K. Braun (Eds.), *Biopolitiken. Regierungen des Lebens heute* (pp. 3-40). Wiesbaden: Springer.

Braun, K., S.L. Herrmann and O.A. Brekke (2014). Sterilisation Policies, Moral Rehabilitation and the Politics of Amends. *Critical Policy Studies* 8(2): 203-226.

Broberg, G. and M. Tydén (1996). Eugenics in Sweden: Efficient Care. In G. Broberg and N. Roll-Hansen (Eds), *Eugenics and the Welfare State: Sterilisation Policy in Denmark, Sweden, Norway, and Finland* (pp. 77-149). East Lansing, MI: Michigan State University Press.

Broberg, G. and N. Roll-Hansen (Eds.) (1996). *Eugenics and the Welfare State. Sterilisation Policy in Denmark, Sweden, Norway, and Finland.* East Lansing, MI: Michigan State University Press.

Brunner, J., N. Frei and C. Goschler (2009). Komplizierte Lernprozesse: Zur Geschichte und Aktualität der Wiedergutmachung. In: N. Frei, J. Brunner, and C. Goschler (Eds.), *Die Praxis der Wiedergutmachung in Deutschland und Israel* (pp. 9-47). Göttingen: Wallstein.

BT 3 (1961). *Protokoll der 34. Sitzung des Ausschusses für Wiedergutmachung*, 13 April 1961.

BT Drs. 1/2366 (1951). *Antrag der Fraktion des Zentrums. Entwurf eines Bewahrungsgesetzes*, 22 June 1951.

BT Drs. 4/650 (1962). *Entwurf eines Strafgesetzbuches (StGB).*

BT Drs. 10/4040 (1985). *Antrag des Abgeordneten Ströbele und der Fraktion Die Grünen. Gesetzentwurf zur Regelung einer angemessenen Versorgung für alle Opfer nationalsozialistischer Verfolgung in der Zeit von 1933 bis 1945*, 17 October 1985.

BT Drs. 10/4638 (1986). *Antrag der Fraktion der SPD, Bestandaufnahme, Bericht und Prüfung von verbesserten Leistungen an Opfer nationalsozialistischer Verfolgung von 1933 bis 1945*, 14 January 1986.

BT Drs. 10/4750 (1986). *Antrag der Abgeordneten Ströbele u.a. Nichtigkeitserklärung des GzVeN vom 14. Juli 1933 und der nach diesem Gesetz ergangenen Entscheidungen*, 29 January 1986.

BT Drs. 10/6287 (1986). *Bericht der Bundesregierung über Wiedergutmachung und Entschädigung für nationalsozialistisches Unrecht sowie über die Lage der Sinti, Roma und verwandter Gruppen*, 31 October 1986.

BT Drs. 11/141 (1987). *Antrag der Abgeordneten Frau Dr. Vollmer und der Fraktion Die Grünen, Gesetzentwurf zur angemessenen Versorgung für alle Opfer nationalsozialistischer Verfolgung in der Zeit von 1933 bis 1945*, 6 April 1987.

BT Drs. 11/143 (1987). *Antrag der Abgeordneten Frau Dr. Vollmer u.a. Nichtigkeitserklärung des Gesetzes zur Verhütung erbkranken Nachwuchses vom 14. Juli 1933 und der nach diesem Gesetz ergangenen Entscheidungen*, 6 April 1987.

BT Drs. 11/223 (1987). *Gesetzentwurf der Fraktion der SPD. Entwurf eines Gesetzes zur Errichtung einer Stiftung "Entschädigung für NS-Unrecht"*, 5 May 1987.

BT Drs. 11/1392 (1987). *Beschlussempfehlung und Bericht des Innenausschusses*, 30 November 1987.

BT Drs. 11/1413 (1987). *Antrag der Fraktion der SPD. Richtlinien der Bundesregierung für die Vergabe von Mitteln an Opfer von NS-Unrecht*, December 1987.

BT Drs. 13/1193 (1989). *Antrag der Abgeordneten Volker Beck (Köln), Winfried Nachtwei, Dr. Antje Vollmer und der Fraktion BÜNDNIS 90/DIE GRÜNEN, Errichtung einer Bundesstiftung "Entschädigung für NS-Unrecht"*, 25 April 1989.

BT Drs. 14/2984 (neu) (2000). *Antrag der Fraktion der SPD sowie der Fraktion BÜNDNIS 90/DIE GRÜNEN: Rehabilitierung der im Nationalsozialismus verfolgten Homosexuellen*, 21 March 2000.

BT Drs. 16/1171 (2006). *Antrag der Abgeordneten Volker Beck u.a. Nichtigkeitserklärung des Erbgesundheitsgesetzes*, 5 April 2006.

BT Drs. 16/2307 (2006). *Kleine Anfrage der Abgeordneten Dr. Ilja Seifert u.a. Nichtigkeitserklärung des Erbgesundheitsgesetzes*, 25 July 2006.

BT Drs. 16/3811 (2006). *Antrag der Abgeordneten Dr. Jürgen Gehb u.a. Ächtung des Gesetzes zur Verhütung erbkranken Nachwuchses vom 14. Juli 1933*, 13 December 2006.

BT Drs. 16/5450 (2007). *Beschlussempfehlung und Bericht des Rechtsausschusses*, 23 May 2007.

BT Drs. 16/9405 (2008). *Kleine Anfrage der Abgeordneten Ulla Jelpke, Katja Kipping, Monika Knoche, Jan Korte, Volker Schneider (Saarbrücken), Dr. Ilja Seifert, Jörn Wunderlich und der Fraktion DIE LINKE. Gedenken und Erinnerung an die Aktion "Arbeitsscheu Reich" 1938*, 30 May 2008.

BT Drs. 16/9887 (2008). *Antwort der Bundesregierung auf die Kleine Anfrage der Abgeordneten Ulla Jelpke, Katja Kipping, Monika Knoche, weiterer Abgeordneter und der Fraktion DIE LINKE - Drucksache 16/9405 -*, 1. July 2008.

BT Drs. 16/10944 (2008). *Antrag der Fraktion DIE LINKE. Rehabilitierung für die Verfolgung und die Unterdrückung einvernehmlicher gleichgeschlechtlicher Handlungen in der Bundesrepublik Deutschland und der Deutschen Demokratischen Republik und Entschädigung der Verurteilten*, 13 November 2008.

BT Drs. 16/11440 (2008). *Rehabilitierung und Entschädigung der nach 1945 in Deutschland wegen homosexueller Handlungen Verurteilter*, 17 December 2008.

BT Drs. 17/1493 (2010). *Kleine Anfrage der Abgeordneten Ulla Jelpke et al. Gedenkort für Jugendkonzentrationslager für Mädchen und junge Frauen Uckermark*, 23 April 2010.

BT Drs. 17/1721 (2010). *Antwort der Bundesregierung auf die Kleine Anfrage der Abgeordneten Ulla Jelpke et al.*, 17 May 2010.

BT Drs. 17/8729 (2012). *Antwort der Bundesregierung auf die Kleine Anfrage der Abgeordneten Ulla Jelpke, Dr. Ilja Seifert, Jan Korte, weiterer Abgeordneter und der Fraktion DIE LINKE*, 27 February 2012.

BT Drs. 19/14342 (2020). *Antrag der Fraktionen CDU/CSU und SPD. Anerkennung der von den Nationalsozialisten als äsozialeünd "Berufsverbrecher"Verfolgten*, 22 October 2019.

BT PLP 1/163 (1951). 18 September 1951.

BT PLP 2/191 (1957). 7 February 1957.

BT PLP 11/151 (1989). 21 June 1989.

BT PLP 14/140 (2000). Stenographischer Bericht 140. Sitzung, 7 December 2000.

BT PLP 18/240 (2017). Stenographischer Bericht 240. Sitzung, 22 June 2014.

Buckley-Zistel, S. and R. Stanley (Eds.). (2012). *Gender in Transitional Justice.* New York, NY: Palgrave Macmillan.

Bucur, M. (1994). In Praise of Wellborn Mothers: On Eugenicist Gender Roles in Interwar Romania. *East European Politics and Societies* 9: 123-142.

Bundespräsidialamt (1985). *Speech by President Richard von Weizsäcker during the Ceremony Commemorating the 40th Anniversary of the End of War in Europe and of National-Socialist Tyranny on 8 May 1985 at the Bundestag, Bonn.* Retrieved 14 August 2020 from https://www.bundespraesident.de/SharedDocs/Downloads/DE/Reden/2015/02/150202-RvW-Rede-8-Mai-1985-englisch.pdf?__blob=publicationFile

Burgi, M., & Wolff, D. (2016). *Rehabilitation of homosexual men convicted pursuant to section 175 of the German Criminal Code.* Berlin: Federal Anti-Discrimination Agency.

Buruma, I. (1994). *The Wages of Guilt: Memories of War in Germany and Japan.* London: Farrar, Straus and Giroux.

BVerfGE 6 (1957). *Homosexuelle. Bundesverfassungsgericht Urteil*, 10 May 1957.

Caplan, A. L., G. McGeen and D. Magnus (1999). What is Immoral About Eugenics? *British Medical Journal* 319: 1284.

Center for Genetics and Society (2020). *Disability Rights, Triage and Countering Eugenics in a Time of Pandemic.* Retrieved 25 Nov 2020 from https://www.geneticsandsociety.org/biopolitical-times/disability-rights-triage-and-countering-eugenics-time-pandemic.

Center for Public Integrity (2020). *State policies may send people with disabilities to the back of the line for ventilators.* Retrieved 25 Nov 2020 from https://pub

licintegrity.org/health/coronavirus-and-inequality/state-policies-may-se
nd-people-with-disabilities-to-the-back-of-the-line-for-ventilators/.

Cleminson, R. (2000). *Anarchism, Science and Sex. Eugenics in Eastern Spain, 1900-1937*. Oxford: Peter Lang.

Cleminson, R. (2008). Eugenics Without the State: Anarchism in Catalonia, 1900–1937. *Studies in History and Philosophy of Science Part C: Studies in History and Philosophy of Biological and Biomedical Sciences* 39(2): 232-239.

Control Council Law No. 1 (1945). Repealing of Nazi Laws, 20 September 1945.

Conze, W. and A. Sommer (1984). Rasse. In O. Brunner, W. Conze and R. Koselleck (Eds.), *Geschichtliche Grundbegriffe* 5: 135-178.

Cooper, M. (2008). *Life as Surplus: Biotechnology and Capitalism in the Neoliberal Era*. Seattle, WA: University of Washington Press.

Corntassel, J., and C. Holder (2008). Who's Sorry Now? Government Apologies, Truth Commissions, and Indigenous Self-Determination in Australia, Canada, Guatemala, and Peru. *Human Rights Review* 9(4): 465-489.

Cunningham, M. (2004). Prisoners of the Japanese and the Politics of Apology: A Battle over History and Memory. *Journal of Contemporary History* 39(4): 561-574.

Davis, L. (2020). In the Time of Pandemic, the Deep Structure of Biopower Is Laid Bare. *Critical Inquiry blog* (26 June 2020). Retrieved 25 Nov 2020 from https://critinq.wordpress.com/2020/06/26/in-the-time-of-pandemic-the-deep-structure-of-biopower-is-laid-bare/.

De Greiff, P. (2006). Introduction. Repairing the Past: Compensation for Victims of Human Rights Violations. In P. De Greiff (Ed.), *The Handbook of Reparations* (pp. 1-18). Oxford: Oxford University Press.

Dean, M. (2002). Liberal Government and Authoritarianism. *Economy and Society* 31(1): 37-61.

Deutscher Bundestag (1987). *Wiedergutmachung und Entschädigung für nationalsozialistisches Unrecht. Öffentliche Anhörung des Innenausschusses des Deutschen Bundestages am 24. Juni 1987*. Bonn: Deutscher Bundestag.

Die Grünen im Bundestag and Fraktion der Alternativen Liste Berlin (Eds.) (1986). *Anerkennung und Versorgung aller Opfer nationalsozialistischer Verfolgung. Dokumentation parlamentarischer Initiativen der GRÜNEN in Bonn und der Fraktion der Alternativen Liste in Berlin*. Berlin.

DIVI (2020). *Entscheidungen über die Zuteilung intensivmedizinischer Ressourcen im Kontext der COVID-19-Pandemie. 2. überarbeitete Fassung vom 17.04.2020.* Retrieved 25 Nov 2020 from https://www.divi.de/joomlatools-files/docm

an-files/publikationen/covid-19-dokumente/200417-divi-covid-19-ethik-empfehlung-version-2.pdf.

Dorr, L. L. (1999). Arm in Arm: Gender, Eugenics, and Virginia´s Racial Integrity Acts of the 1920s. *Journal of Women´s History* 11(1): 143-166.

Dowbiggin, I. (2008). *The Sterilisation Movement and Global Fertility in the Twentieth Century.* Oxford: Oxford University Press.

Duarte, A. (2005). *Biopolitics and the Dissemination of Violence: The Arendtian Critique of the Present.* Retrieved 11 August 2010, from http://www.hannahare ndt.net/index.php/han/article/view/69/101

Engs, R. C. (Ed.) (2005). *The Eugenics Movement: An Encyclopedia.* Westport, CT: Greenwood Press.

Eschebach, I. and A. Ley (Eds.) (2012). *Geschlecht und Rasse in der NS-Medizin.* Berlin: Metropol.

Etzemüller, T. (2000). Review of Koch, Lene, *Racehygiejne i Danmark 1920-56* and Runcis, Maija, *Steriliseringar i folkhemmet.* H-Soz-u-Kult, H-Net Reviews, Retrieved 11 August 2020 from http://www.h-net.org/reviews/showrev.p hp?id=15930

Evangelische Akademie Bad Boll (Ed.) (1987). *Vergessene Opfer: Wiedergutmachung für die Betroffenen der Zwangssterilisation und des nationalsozialistischen Euthanasie-Programms.* Bad Boll: Protokolldienst der Evangelischen Akademie.

Federal Ministry of Finance (2019). *Compensation for National Socialist Injustice. Indemnification Provisions.* Berlin: Federal Ministry of Finance.

Ferdinand, U. (2009). Der "faustische Pakt" in der Sozialhygiene Alfred Grotjahns (1869-1931). Sozialhygiene und ihre Beziehungen zur Eugenik und Demografie. In R. Wecker, S. Braunschweig, G. Imoden, B. Küchenhoff and H. J. Ritter (Eds.), *What is National Socialist about Eugenics? International Debates on the History of Eugenics in the 20th Century* (pp. 173-186). Wien: Böhlau.

Feyen, M. (2009). "Wie die Juden"? Verfolgte "Zigeuner" zwischen Bürokratie und Symbolpolitik. In N. Frei, J. Brunner, and C. Goschler (Eds.), *Die Praxis der Wiedergutmachung. Geschichte, Erfahrung und Wirkung in Deutschland und Israel* (pp. 323-355). Göttingen: Wallstein.

Foucault, M. (1977). Power and Sex: An Interview with Michel Foucault (Interviewed by Bernard-Henri Levy). *Telos* 32: 152-161.

Foucault, M. (1980). *The History of Sexuality. Vol. I: An Introduction.* New York: Vintage Books.

Foucault, M. (1988). The Political Technology of Individuals. In L. H. Martin, H. Gutman and P. H. Hutton (Eds.), *Technologies of the Self: A Seminar with Michel Foucault* (pp. 145–62). Amherst, MA: University of Massachusetts Press.

Foucault, M. (1994a). Omnes et Singulatim: Towards a Criticism of 'Political Reason'. In J. D. Faubion (Ed.), *Power: Essential Works of Michel Foucault 1954-1984*, Vol. 3 (pp. 298-325). New York: The New Press.

Foucault, M. (1994b). *The Order of Things. An Archaeology of the Human Sciences.* New York: Vintage Books.

Foucault, M. (1997). What Is Enlightenment? In P. Rabinow (Ed.), *Essential Works of Michel Foucault, 1954–1984, Vol. 1* (pp. 303–19). New York: The New Press.

Foucault, M. (2000a). Governmentality. In J. D. Faubion (Ed.), *Power: Essential Works of Michel Foucault, 1954–1984, Vol. 3* (pp. 201–22). New York: The New Press.

Foucault, M. (2000b). The Political Technology of Individuals. In J. D. Faubion (Ed.), *Power: Essential Works of Michel Foucault, 1954–1984, Vol. 3* (pp. 403-417). New York: The New Press

Foucault, M. (2003). *Society Must Be Defended. Lectures at the College de France 1975-1976.* New York, NY: Picador.

Foucault, M. (2007). *Security, Territory, Population. Lectures at the College de France, 1977-78. Edited by Michel Sennelart.* New York: Palgrave Macmillan.

Foucault, M. (2008). *The Birth of Biopolitics. Lectures at the Collège de France 1978-1979.* Basingstoke: Palgrave Macmillan.

Foucault, M. (2012). The Mesh of Power. *Viewpoint Magazine 2.*

Franks, A. (2005). *Margaret Sanger's Eugenic Legacy: The Control of Female Fertility.* Jefferson, NC: McFarland and Company.

Friedlander, H. (1995). *The Origins of Nazi Genocide. From Euthanasia to the Final Solution.* Chapel Hill, NC: The University of North Carolina Press.

Friedlander, H. (2004). From "Euthanasia" to the "Final Solution". In D. Kuntz and S. Bachrach (Eds.), *Deadly Medicine: Creating the Master Race* (pp. 155-183). Washington D.C.: United States Holocaust Memorial Museum.

Galton, F. (1865). *Hereditary Talent and Character.* Originally published in Macmillan's Magazine 12, 157-166; 318-327, Retrieved 2 July 2020, from http://psychclassics.yorku.ca/Galton/talent.htm

Galton, F. (1907). *Inquiries into Human Faculty and its Development.* London: Dent and Dutton.

Garton Ash, T. (2002). Mesomnesie - Plädoyer für ein mittleres Erinnern. *Transit* 22: 32-48.

Gedenkstätte Hadamar (2020). *Stellungnahme von Gedenkstätten zur Erinnerung an die nationalsozialistischen Euthanasie-Verbrechen. Warum wir die Diskussionen über die intensivmedizinische Versorgung von Senior*innen sowie Menschen mit Vorerkrankungen oder Behinderungen (Stichwort: Triage) in der Corona-Pandemie mit Sorge betrachten.* Retrieved 25 Nov 2020 from http://www.ged enkstaette-hadamar.de/webcom/show_article.php/_c-605/_nr-34/i.html.

Geisler, F. and A. Struwe (2019). Biopolitik als Theorie der Gesellschaft. In H. Gerhards and K. Braun (Eds.), *Biopolitiken: Regierungen des Lebens heute* (pp. 43-66). Wiesbaden: Springer.

Gems, D. (1999). Review Essay. Politically Correct Eugenics. *Theoretical Medicine and Bioethics* 20(2): 199-211.

Gerhards, H. (2020). Patientenpolitiken. Zur Genealogie eines kollektiven Subjekts. Unpublished PhD dissertation manuscript.

Gerhards, H. (2020a). Biopolitik, oder: Wie man etwas für's Leben in der Pandemie lernt. In M. Florak, K.-R. Korte, and J. Schwanholz (Eds.), *Coronakratie: Demokratisches Regieren in Ausnahmezeiten* (pp. 245-253). Frankfurt a.M./New York: Campus.

Gerodetti, N. (2005, April). *Biopolitics, Eugenics and the Use of History.* Paper presented at ECPR Joint Sessions of Workshops, University of Granada.

Gerodetti, N. (2006a). Eugenic Family Politics and Social Democrats: "Positive" Eugenics and Marriage Advice Bureaus. *Journal of Historical Sociology* 19(3): 217-244.

Gerodetti, N. (2006b). From Science to Social Technology—Eugenics and Politics in Twentieth Century Switzerland. *Social Politics* 13(1): 59-88.

Geulen, C. (2007). *Geschichte des Rassismus.* München: C.H. Beck.

Gibbon, S., and C. Novas (Eds.) (2007). *Genetics, Biosociality and the Social Sciences: Making Biologies and Identities.* London: Routledge.

Giessler, H. (1981). Die Grundsatzbestimmungen des Entschädigungsrechts. In Bundesminister der Finanzen in Zusammenarbeit mit W. Schwarz (Eds.), *Das Bundesentschädigungsgesetz, Teil 1 (Die Wiedergutmachung nationalsozialistischen Unrechts durch die Bundesrepublik Deutschland, Bd. 4)* (pp. 1–116). München: Beck.

Gordon, L. (2002a). *The Moral Property of Women: A History of Birth Control.* Urbana, IL, University of Illinois Press.

Gordon, N. (2002b). On Visibility and Power: An Arendtian Corrective of Foucault. *Human Studies* 25(2): 125–45.

Goschler, C. (2003). *The Politics of Restitution for Nazi Victims in Germany West and East (1945-2000)*. Occasional Papers, Institute of European Studies, UC Berkeley. Retrieved August 17, 2020 from https://escholarship.org/uc/ite m/7bz5801b

Goschler, C. (2005). *Schuld und Schulden: Die Politik der Wiedergutmachung für NS-Verfolgte seit 1945*. Göttingen: Wallstein.

Goschler, C. (2009). Disputed Victims: The West German Discourse on Restitution for the Victims of Nazism. In M. Berg and B. Schaefer (Eds.), *Historical Justice in International Perspective* (pp. 93-110). Cambridge: Cambridge University Press.

Graf, G. (1950). Zur Sterilisationsfrage. *Berliner Gesundheitsblatt* 1(1).

Grau, G. (2011). *Lexikon zur Homosexuellenverfolgung 1933-1945. Institutionen - Kompetenzen - Betätigungsfelder*. Berlin: Lit Verlag.

Grau, G. (2014). Die Verfolgung der Homosexuellen im Nationalsozialismus. Anmerkungen zum Forschungsstand. In M. Schwartz (Ed.), *Homosexuelle im Nationalsozialismus* (pp. 43-52). München: Oldenbourg.

Grekul, J., H. Krahn and D. Odynak (2004). Sterilizing the "Feeble-minded": Eugenics in Alberta, Canada, 1929-1972. *Journal of Historical Sociology* 17(4): 358-385.

Grossmann, A. (1995). *Reforming Sex: The German Movement for Birth Control and Abortion Reform*. Oxford: Oxford University Press.

Guse, M. (2005). Haftgrund: "Gemeinschaftsfremder". Ausgrenzung und Haft von Jugendlichen im Jugend-KZ Moringen. In D. Sedlaczek, T. Lutz, U. Puvogel, and I. Tomkowiak (Eds.), *"minderwertig" und "asozial": Stationen der Verfolgung gesellschaftlicher Außenseiter* (pp. 127-156). Zürich: Chronos.

GzVeN (1933). *Gesetz zur Verhütung erbkranken Nachwuchses vom 14. Juli 1933*. Retrieved 2 July 2020, from http://www.documentarchiv.de/ns/erbk-nws.h tml

Haave, P. (2000). *Sterilisering av tatere 1934-1977. En historisk undersøkelse av lov og praksis*. Oslo: Norges forskningsråd (Området for kultur og samfunn).

Haave, P. (2001). Zwangssterilisierung in Norwegen - eine wohlfahrtsstaatliche Politik in sozialdemokratischer Regie? *NORDEUROPAforum* 11(2): 55-78.

Hansen, B. S. (1996). Something Rotten in the State of Denmark: Eugenics and the Ascent of the Welfare State. In G. Broberg and N. Roll-Hansen (Eds), *Eugenics and the Welfare State: Sterilisation Policy in Denmark, Sweden, Norway, and Finland* (pp. 9-76). East Lansing, MI: Michigan State University Press.

Hansen, R. and S. King (2001). Eugenic Ideas, Political Interests, and Policy Variance. Immigration and Sterilisation Policy in Britain and the U.S. *World Politics* 53(1): 237–263.

Harnack, E-W. (1959). *Die strafrechtliche Zulässigkeit künstlicher Unfruchtbarmachung.* Marburg: Elwert.

Hebenstreit, R. (1983). Härteausgleich nach § 171 BEG. In BMF (Ed.), *Das Bundesentschädigungsgesetz. Zweiter Teil* (pp. 467-501). München: C. H. Beck.

Heinrich, M. (2004). *An Introduction to the Three Volumes of Karl Marx's Capital.* New York: Monthly Review Press.

Helmreich, S. (2008). Species of Biocapital. *Science as Culture* 17(4): 463-478.

Hennig, V. (1999). *Zur Wiedergutmachung von Zwangssterilisationen im Nationalsozialismus: Eine Dokumentation.* Berlin: Frieling.

Herlitzius, A. (1995). *Frauenbefreiung und Rassenideologie.* Wiesbaden: Deutscher Universitäts Verlag.

Herzog, D. (2005). *Sexuality and German Fascism.* New York: Berghahn Books.

Hietala, M. (1996). From Race Hygiene to Sterilisation: The Eugenics Movement in Finland. In G. Broberg and N. Roll-Hansen (Eds), *Eugenics and the Welfare State: Sterilisation Policy in Denmark, Sweden, Norway, and Finland* (pp. 195-258). East Lansing, MI: Michigan State University Press.

Hitzel-Cassagnes, T. and F. Martinsen (2014). *Recht auf Wiedergutmachung. Geschlechtergerechtigkeit und die Bewältigung historischen Unrechts.* Opladen: Barbara Budrich.

Hockerts, H. G. (2001). Wiedergutmachung in Deutschland. Eine historische Bilanz 1945 - 2000. *Vierteljahreshefte für Zeitgeschichte* 49(2): 167-214.

Hörath, J. (2017). *»Asoziale« und »Berufsverbrecher« in den Konzentrationslagern 1933 bis 1938.* Göttingen: Vandenhoeck and Ruprecht.

Incesu, L. and G. Saathoff (1988). Die verweigerte Nichtigkeitserklärung für das NS-Erbgesundheitsgesetz - Eine 'Große Koalition' gegen die Zwangssterilisierten. *Demokratie und Recht* 16: 125-132.

Initiative Uckermark (2009). *Initiative für einen Gedenkort ehemaliges Jugend-KZ Uckermark e.V.: International Antifascist Feminist Working Camp at the Site of the former Youth Concentration Camp Uckermark. Reader.* Retrieved 30 July 2020, from http://www.gedenkort-kz-uckermark.de/assets/downloads/b aucamps/2009_Reader_baucamp.pdf.

Irmer, T. (2013). *Zur Geschichte des Arbeitshauses Rummelsburg in der NS-Zeit, Vortrag, Deutsches Historisches Museum.* Retrieved 30 July 2020, from https: //www.dhm.de/archiv/ausstellungen/zerstoerte-vielfalt/docs/Vortrag_Ir

mer_Zur_Geschichte_des_Arbeitshauses_Rummelsburg_in_der_%20NS-Zeit.pdf

Irmer, T., B. Reischl and K. Nürnberg (n.y.). *Das Städtische Arbeits- und Bewahrungshaus Rummelsburg in Berlin-Lichtenberg.* Gedenkstättenrundbrief, 144 (pp. 22-31). Retrieved 30 July 2020, from https://www.gedenkstaettenfor um.de/nc/gedenkstaettenrundbrief/rundbrief/news/das_staedtische_arb eits_und_bewahrungshaus_rummelsburg_in_berlin_lichtenberg/?zoom= 1

Isaac, J. C. (1996). A New Guarantee on Earth: Hannah Arendt on Human Dignity and the Politics of Human Rights. *American Political Science Review* 90(1): 61-73.

Johnson, P. (2010). 'An Essentially Private Manifestation of Human Personality': Constructions of Homosexuality in the European Court of Human Rights. *Human Rights Law Review* 10(1): 67-97.

Johnson, P. (2013). *Homosexuality and the European Court of Human Rights.* London: Routledge.

Kevles, D. J. (1985). *In the Name of Eugenics: Genetics and the Uses of Human Heredity.* New York, NY: Knopf.

Kinkel, K. (1987). *Stellungnahme zum Antrag auf „Nichtigkeitserklärung des Gesetzes zur Verhütung erbkranken Nachwuchses" vom 14. Juli 1933 und der nach diesem Gesetz ergangenen Entscheidungen.* Bonn: Bundesministerium der Justiz.

Kitchin, R. (2020). Civil liberties or public health, or civil liberties and public health? Using surveillance technologies to tackle the spread of COVID-19. *Space and Polity* DOI:10.1080/13562576.2020.1770587: 1-20.

Klausen, S. and A. Bashford (2010). Fertility Control: Eugenics, Neo-Malthusianism, and Feminism. In A. Bashford and P. Levine (Eds.), *The Oxford Handbook of The History of Eugenics* (pp. 98/115). Oxford: Oxford University Press.

Klee, E. (2013). *Das Personenlexikon zum Dritten Reich.* Frankfurt: Fischer.

Kline, W. (2001). *Building a Better Race. Gender, Sexuality, and Eugenics from the Turn of the Century to the Baby Boom.* Berkeley, CA: University of California Press.

Koch, L. (2000). *Tvangssterilisation i Danmark 1929–67.* Copenhagen: Gyldendal.

Koch, L. (2004). The Meanings of Eugenics: Reflections on the Government of Genetic Knowledge in the Past and in the Present. *Science in Context* 17(3): 315-331.

Koch, L. (2006). Eugenic Sterilisation in Scandinavia. *The European Legacy* 11(3).

Koch, L. (2009). How Eugenic was Eugenics? Reproductive Politics in the Past and the Present. In R. Wecker, S. Braunschweig, G. Imboden, B. Küchenhoff and H. J. Ritter (Eds.), *What is National Socialist about Eugenics? International Debates on the History of Eugenics in the 20th Century* (pp. 23-39). Wien: Böhlau.

Koselleck, R. (1989). *Vergangene Zukunft. Zur Semantik Geschichtlicher Zeiten*. Frankfurt: Suhrkamp.

Koselleck, R. (2003). *Zeitschichten. Studien zur Historik*. Frankfurt a.M.: Suhrkamp.

Koselleck, R. (2004). *Futures Past—On The Semantics of Historical Time*. New York, NY: Columbia University Press.

Kristeva, J. (2001). *Hannah Arendt*. New York, NY: Columbia University Press.

Kulawik, T. (2006). *Eugenics and the Making of Universal Citizenship in Sweden. The Social Democratic State Revisited*. Paper presented at the Annual Meeting of the Society for Social Studies of Science, November 1-5, 2006, Vancouver.

Kulawik, T. (2009). *Rethinking Bodily Citizenship in the Era of Reprogenetics. Comparative Insights*. Paper prepared for the First European Conference on Gender and Politics (ECPG), 21-23 January 2009, Queen's University Belfast.

Ladd-Taylor, M. (1997). Saving Babies and Sterilizing Mothers. *Social Politics* 4(1): 136-153.

Lamp, S. (2006). "It Is for the Mother": Feminists' Rhetorics of Disability During the American Eugenics Period. *Disability Studies Quarterly* 26(4).

Larsen, L. T. (2007). Speaking Truth to Biopower: On the Genealogy of Bioeconomy. *Distinktion: Scandinavian Journal of Social Theory* 8(1): 9-24.

Laughlin, H. H. (1925). Eugenics in America. *Eugenics Review* 17(1): 28-35.

Lauré al-Samarai, N. and S. Lennox (2004). Neither Foreigners Nor Aliens: The Interwoven Stories of Sinti and Roma and Black Germans. *Women in German Yearbook: Feminist Studies in German Literature and Culture* 20: 163-183.

Lazare, A. (2004). *On Apology*. New York, NY: Oxford University Press.

Lemke, T., S. Krasmann and U. Bröckling (2000). Gouvernementalität, Neoliberalismus und Selbsttechnologien. Eine Einleitung. In T. Lemke, S. Krasmann, and U. Bröckling (Eds.), *Gouvernementalität der Gegenwart. Studien zur Ökonomisierung des Sozialen* (pp. 7-40). Frankfurt: Suhrkamp.

Leonard, T. C. (2003). "More Merciful and Not Less Effective": Eugenics and American Economics in the Progressive Era. *History of Political Economy* 35(4): 687-712.

Leonard, T. C. (2005). Retrospectives. Eugenics and Economics in the Progressive Era. *Journal of Economic Perspectives* 19(4): 207-224.

Lombardo, P. (n.y.). *Eugenic Laws Against Race Mixing*. Image Archive on the American Eugenics Movement. Retrieved 30 July 2020 from http://www.eugenicsarchive.org/html/eugenics/essay7text.html

Lombardo, P. (n.y.). *Eugenic Laws Restricting Immigration*. Image Archive on the American Eugenics Movement. Retrieved 30 July 2020 from http://www.eugenicsarchive.org/html/eugenics/essay9text.html

Lombardo, P. A. (1996). Medicine, Eugenics, and the Supreme Court: From Coercive Sterilisation to Reproductive Freedom. *Journal of Contemporary Health Law and Policy* 13(1): 1-25.

Lorenzini, D. (2020). Biopolitics in the Time of Coronavirus. *Critical Inquiry blog* (2 April 2020). Retrieved 25 Nov 2020 from https://critinq.wordpress.com/2020/04/02/biopolitics-in-the-time-of-coronavirus/.

Ludi, R. (2005). *Who is a Nazi Victim? Constructing Victimhood through Post-War Reparations in France, Germany, Switzerland*. UCLA Center for European and Eurasian Studies. Occasional Lecture Series 3. Retrieved 30 July 2020 from http://escholarship.org/uc/item/6mp7c78d.

Ludi, R. (2006). The Vectors of Postwar Victim Reparations: Relief, Redress and Memory Politics. *Journal of Contemporary History* 41(3): 421-450.

Ludi, R. (2012). *Reparations for Nazi Victims in Postwar Europe*. Cambridge, NY: Cambridge University Press.

Lynn, R. (2001). *Eugenics: A Reassessment*. Westport, CT: Praeger Press.

Marx, K. (1972). *Das Kapital: Kritik der Politischen Ökonomie*. Erster Band. Berlin: Dietz.

Marx, K. (1990). *Capital: A Critique of Political Economy. Volume I*. London: Penguin Books.

Marx, K. (2015). Zur Kritik der Politischen Ökonomie. In Marx-Engels-Werke Vol. 13 (pp. 6-160). Berlin: Dietz

Mazumdar, P. M. H. (2002). "Reform" Eugenics and the Decline of Mendelism. *Trends in Genetics* 18(1): 48-52.

McCann, C. R. (1994). *Birth Control Politics in the United States 1916-1945*. New York, NY: Cornell University Press.

Michon, P. (2002). Strata, Blocks, Pieces, Spirals, Elastics and Verticals: Six Figures of Time in Michel Foucault. *Time and Society* 11(2/3): 163–92.

Micklos, D. and E. Carlson (2000). Engineering American Society: The Lesson of Eugenics. *Nature Reviews Genetics* 1: 153-158.

Milchman, A. and A. Rosenberg (Eds.) (1998). *Postmodernism and the Holocaust*. Amsterdam: Rodopi.

Miller, Z. (2008). Effects of Invisibility: In Search of the 'Economic' in Transitional Justice. *The International Journal of Transitional Justice* 2(3): 266-291.

Minow, M. (1998). *Between vengeance and forgiveness: facing history after genocide and mass violence*. Boston: Beacon Press.

Mottier, V. and N. Gerodetti (2007). Eugenics and Social Democracy: Or, How the European Left Tried to Eliminate the "Weeds" from its National Gardens. *New Formations* 60 (Eugenics Old and New): 35-49.

Mottier, V. (2008). Eugenics, Politics and the State: Social Democracy and the Swiss "Gardening State". *Studies in History and Philosophy of Science Part C: Studies in History and Philosophy of Biological and Biomedical Sciences* 39(2): 263-269.

Nachtsheim, H. (1950). Zur Frage der Sterilisation vom Standpunkt der Erbbiologen. *Berliner Gesundheitsblatt* 1(1): 603-604.

Nachtsheim, H. (1952). *Für und Wider die Sterilisierung aus eugenischer Indikation*. Stuttgart: Thieme.

Nachtsheim, H. (1964). Notwendigkeit einer aktiven Erbgesundheitspflege. *Gesundheitspolitik* 6.

Neukamp, F. (1951). Ist das Erbkrankheitsgesetz ein Nazigesetz? *Berliner Gesundheitsblatt* 2(1): 250-252.

Newsletter Behindertenpolitik (2006). Nr. 23, März 2006. Retrieved 23 December 2020 from http://www.martinseidler.de/newsletter/newsletter_2 3.pdf.

Ojakangas, M. (2016). Biopolitics in the political thought of classical Greece. In S. Prozorov and S. Rentea (Eds.) *The Routledge Handbook of Biopolitics* (pp.23-35): London: Routledge.

OLG Hamm (1954). 29.1.1954 - 9 W 231/53; Schadensersatz für Unfruchtbarmachung. *Neue Juristische Wochenschrift* 14/15: 559.

Ordover, N. (2003). *American Eugenics: Race, Queer Anatomy, and the Science of Nationalism*. Minneapolis, MN: University of Minneapolis Press.

Otsubo, S. and J. R. Bartholomew (1998). Eugenics in Japan: Some Ironies of Modernity, 1883–1945. *Science in Context* 11(3-4): 545-565.

Palmer, N., P. Clark and D. Granville (Eds.) (2012). *Critical Perspectives in Transitional Justice*. Cambridge, Antwerp, Portland: Intersentia.

Paul, D. B. (1984). Eugenics and the Left. *Journal of the History of Ideas* 45(4): 567-590.

Pedersen, S. (1993). *Family, Dependence, and the Origins of the Welfare State: Britain and France, 1914-1945*. Cambridge: Cambridge University Press.

Ploetz, A. (1895). *Die Tüchtigkeit unserer Rasse und der Schutz der Schwachen*. Berlin: S. Fischer.

Pommerin, R. (1979). *Sterilisierung der Rheinlandbastarde. Das Schicksal einer farbigen deutschen Minderheit 1918-1937*. Düsseldorf: Droste.

Portschy, J. (2020). Times of Power, Knowledge and Critique in the Work of Foucault. *Time and Society* 29(2): 392-419.

Pretzel, A. (2002). Sonderstrafrecht gegen Homosexuelle. In A. Pretzel (Ed.), *NS-Opfer unter Vorbehalt: homosexuelle Männer in Berlin nach 1945* (pp. 23-42). Münster: LIT Verlag.

Rabenschlag, A. J. (2008). Für eine bessere "Bevölkerungsqualität": Ein Vergleich bevölkerungspolitischer Konzepte in Schweden 1920–1940. *NORDEUROPAforum* 18(1): 47-67.

Rabinow, P. (1996). *Essays on the Anthropology of Reason*. Princeton: Princeton University Press.

Rabinow, P. and N. Rose (2006). Biopower Today. *BioSocieties* 1(2): 195-217.

Reilly, P. R. (1991). *The Surgical Solution. A History of Involuntary Sterilisation in the United States*. Baltimore: John Hopkins University Press.

Reilly, P. R. and M. Shaw (1983). The Virginia Racial Integrity Act Revisited: The Plecker-Laughlin Correspondence: 1928–1930. *American Journal of Medical Genetics* 16(4): 483-492.

Reimesch, C. (2003). *Vergessene Opfer des Nationalsozialismus? Zur Entschädigung von Homosexuellen, Kriegsdienstverweigerern, Sinti und Roma und Kommunisten in der Bundesrepublik Deutschland*. Berlin: WiKu-Verlag.

Rentea, S. (2017). Introduction. In S. Prozorov and S. Rentea (Eds.), *The Routledge Handbook of Biopolitics* (pp. 1-19). London and New York: Routledge.

Reynolds, L. (2005). *The Genetic Modification of the Agro-food System and the Transformation of the Biopolitical*. Paper presented at ECPR Joint Sessions of Workshops, University of Granada.

Richardson, A. (2003). *Love and Eugenics in the Late Nineteenth Century: Rational Reproduction and the New Woman*. Oxford: Oxford University Press.

Riechert, H. (1995). *Im Schatten von Auschwitz: Die nationalsozialistische Sterilisationspolitik gegenüber Sinti und Roma*. Münster: Waxmann.

Rinscheid, A. (2013). Entkriminalisierung ohne Individualisierung? Eine komparativ-historische Fallstudie zur Entkriminalisierung von Homosexualität in BRD und DDR. *Zeitschrift für vergleichende Politikwissenschaft* 7(3): 251-275.

Roll-Hansen, N. (1996). Norwegian Eugenics: Sterilisation as Social Reform. In G. Broberg and N. Roll-Hansen (Eds), *Eugenics and the Welfare State: Sterilisation Policy in Denmark, Sweden, Norway, and Finland* (pp. 151-194). East Lansing, MI: Michigan State University Press.

Romer, L. P. and V. Laterza (2020). Coronavirus, herd immunity and the eugenics of the market. There is a clear element of eugenics in the proposals to pursue herd immunity as a strategy against the pandemic. *Aljazeera* (14 April 2020). Retrieved 25 Nov 2020 from https://www.aljazeera.com/opinions/2020/4/14/coronavirus-herd-immunity-and-the-eugenics-of-the-market/.

Rose, N. (2001). The Politics of Life Itself. *Theory, Culture and Society* 18(6): 1-30.

Rose, N. (2006). Will Biomedicine Transform Society? *Kritikos* 3(Aug 2006).

Rose, N. (2007). *The Politics of Life Itself. Biomedicine, Power, Subjectivity in the Twenty-First Century.* Princeton, NJ: Princeton University Press.

Rose, N. and P. Miller (1992). Political power beyond the state: problematics of government. *British Journal of Sociology* 43(2): 172-205.

Rudling, P. A. (2014). Eugenics and Racial Biology in Sweden and the USSR: Contacts Across the Baltic Sea. *Canadian Bulletin of Medical History* 31(1): 41-75.

Runcis, M. (1998). *Stereliseringar i folkhemmet.* Stockholm: Ordfront.

Sandner, G. (2001). Hegemonie und Erinnerung: Zur Konzeption von Geschichts-und Vergangenheitspolitik. *Austrian Journal of Political Science*, 30(1): 5-17.

Sanger, A. (2007). Eugenics, Race, and Margaret Sanger Revisited: Reproductive Freedom for All? *Hypatia* 22(2): 210-217.

Sanger, M. (1920). *Woman and the New Race.* New York, NY: Eugenic Publishing Company.

Sarasin, P. (2020). *Mit Foucault die Pandemie verstehen.* Retrieved 25 Nov 2020 from https://geschichtedergegenwart.ch/mit-foucault-die-pandemie-verstehen/.

Scheulen, A. (2005). Zur Rechtslage und Rechtsentwicklung des Erbgesundheitsgesetzes 1934. In M. Hamm (Ed.), *Lebensunwert-zerstörte Leben. Zwangssterilisation undEuthanasie* (pp. 212-219). Frankfurt a.M.: VAS, Verlag für akademische Schriften.

Schikorra, C. (2005). Schwarze Winkel im KZ. Die Haftgruppe der "Asozialen" in der Häftlingsgesellschaft. In D. Sedlaczek, T. Lutz, U. Puvogel, and I. Tomkowiak (Eds.), *"minderwertig" und "asozial": Stationen der Verfolgung gesellschaftlicher Außenseiter* (pp. 105-126). Zürich: Chronos.

Schmuhl, H-W. (1992). *Rassenhygiene, Nationalsozialismus, Euthanasie. Von der Verhütung zur Vernichtung "lebensunwerten Lebens", 1890 - 1945*. Kritische Studien zur Geschichtswissenschaft Bd. 75. Göttingen: Vandenhoek and Ruprecht.

Schneider, W. H. (1986). L'Eugénisme en France: Le Tournant des Années Trente. *Sciences Sociales et Santé* 4(3-4): 81-114.

Schneider, W. H. (1990). *Quality and Quantity. The Quest for Biological Regeneration in Twentieth-Century France*. Cambridge: Cambridge University Press.

Scholem, G. (1971). *The Messianic Idea in Judaism and Other Essays on Jewish Spirituality*. New York, NY: Schocken.

Schoppmann, C. (1997). National Socialist Policies Towards Female Homosexuality. In L. Abrams and E. Harvey (Eds.), *Gender Relations in German History. Power, Agency and Experience from the Sixteenth to the Twentieth Century* (pp. 177- 187). London: Routledge.

Schultz, S. (2019). Rassistische Zukunftskalkulationen - Zur Biopolitik einer migrantischen Geburtenrate. In H. Gerhards and K. Braun (Eds.), *Biopolitiken - Regierungen des Lebens heute* (pp. 157-182). Wiesbaden: Springer.

Schwartz, M. (1995). *Sozialistische Eugenik. Eugenische Sozialtechnologien in Debatten und Politik der deutschen Sozialdemokratie 1890-1933*. Bonn: Dietz.

Seal, L. (2013). Designating Dependency: The "Socially Inadequate" in the United States, 1910–1940. *Journal of Historical Sociology* 26(2): 143-168.

Selden, S. (n.y.). *Eugenics Popularisation*. Image Archive on the American Eugenics Movement. Retrieved 5 August 2020 from http://www.eugenicsar chive.org/eugenics/list2.pl

Senatsverwaltung für Arbeit, Integration und Frauen (2011). *§ 175 StGB. Rehabilitierung der nach § 175 verurteilten homosexuellen Männer*. Berlin: Senatsverwaltung für Arbeit, Integration und Frauen und Landesstelle für Gleichbehandlung—gegen Diskriminierung.

Simunek, M. (2007). Eugenics, Social Genetics and Racial Hygiene: Plans for the Scientific Regulation of Human Heredity in the Czech Lands, 1900-1925. In M. Turda and P. J. Weindling (Eds.), *Blood and Homeland. Eugenics and Racial Nationalism in Central and Southeast Europe 1900-1940* (pp. 145-166). Budapest: CEU Press.

Sonn, R. D. (2005). "Your body is yours": Anarchism, Birth Control, and Eugenics in Interwar France. *Journal of the History of Sexuality* 14(4): 415-432.

Spektorowski, A. and E. Mizrachi (2004). Eugenics and the Welfare State in Sweden: The Politics of Social Margins and the Idea of a Productive Society. *Journal of Contemporary History* 39(3): 333-352.

Spektorowski, A. and L. Ireni-Saban (2010). Staying Alive: Genetics in the Service of the Welfare "People's Home". *Comparative Political Studies* 43: 1391-1414.

Stegemann, D. (2013). "Arbeitsscheu" und "asozial". *Gen-ethischer Informationsdienst* 220: 16-18.

Stepan, N. L. (1991). *The Hour of Eugenics. Race, Gender, and Nation in Latin America.* Ithaca, NY: Cornell University Press.

Stern, A. M. (2005). *Eugenic Nation. Fraults and Frontiers of Better Breeding in Modern America.* Berkeley, CA: University of California Press.

Stern, A. M. (2005). Sterilized in the Name of Public Health. Race, Immigration, and Reproductive Control in Modern California. *American Journal of Public Health* 95(7): 1128-1138.

Stern, A. M. (2010). Gender and Sexuality: A Global Tour and Compass. In A. Bashford and P. Levine (Eds.), *The Oxford Handbook of The History of Eugenics* (pp. 173-191). Oxford: Oxford University Press.

Stubblefield, A. (2007). "Beyond the Pale": Tainted Whiteness, Cognitive Disability, and Eugenic Sterilisation. *Hypatia* 22(2): 162-181.

Sunder Rajan, K. (2006). *Biocapital. The Constitution of Postgenomic Life.* Durham, NC: Duke University Press.

SZ (2017). "Schandtaten des Rechtsstaats": Das Kabinett billigt die Rehabilitierung verurteilter Homosexueller. Die Opfer sollen individuell entschädigt werden. Reicht das? *Süddeutsche Zeitung*, 22 March 2017.

Szerszynski, B. (2005). *Nature, Technology and the Sacred.* Malden, MA: Blackwell.

Tavuchis, N. (1991). *Mea Culpa: A Sociology of Apology and Reconciliation.* Stanford, CA: Stanford University Press.

Teitel, R. (2000). *Transitional Justice.* Oxford: Oxford University Press.

Tellmann, U. (2011). Ökonomie und Biopolitik. In M. Muhle and K. Thiele (Eds.), *Biopolitische Konstellationen* (pp. 61-81). Berlin: August Verlag.

Tellmann, U. (2017). *Life and Money: The Genealogy of the Liberal Economy and the Displacement of Politics.* New York, NY: Columbia University Press.

Torpey, J. C. (2006). *Making Whole What Has Been Smashed: On Reparation Politics.* Cambridge, Mass.: Harvard University Press.

Tümmers, H. (2009a). Spätes Unrechtsbewußtsein. Über den Umgang mit den Opfern der NS-Erbgesundheitspolitik. In N. Frei, J. Brunner, and C. Goschler (Eds.), *Die Praxis der Wiedergutmachung. Geschichte, Erfahrung und Wirkung in Deutschland und Israel* (pp. 494-530). Göttingen: Wallstein.

Tümmers, H. (2009b). Wiederaufnahmeverfahren und der Umgang deutscher Juristen mit der nationalsozialistischen Erbgesundheitspolitik nach 1945. *Juristische Zeitgeschichte Nordrhein-Westfalen* 17: 173-193.

Tümmers, H. (2011). *Anerkennungskämpfe: die Nachgeschichte der nationalsozialistischen Zwangssterilisationen in der Bundesrepublik.* Göttingen: Wallstein.

Turda, M. (2010a). *Modernism and Eugenics.* Basingstoke: Palgrave Macmillan.

Turda, M. (2010b). Race, Science, and Eugenics in the Twentieth Century. In A. Bashford and P. Levine (Eds.), *The Oxford Handbook of the History of Eugenics* (pp. 62-79). Oxford: Oxford University Press.

Tydén, M. (2010). The Scandinavian States: Reformed Eugenics Applied. In A. Bashford and P. Levine (Eds.), *The Oxford Handbook of the History of Eugenics* (pp. 363-376). Oxford: Oxford University Press.

Villa, D. R. (1992). Postmodernism and the Public Sphere. *American Political Science Review* 86(3): 712–21.

Vogelmann, F. (2018). Biopolitics as a Critical Diagnosis. In B. Best, W. Bonefeld, and C. O´Kane (Eds.), *The SAGE Handbook of Frankfurt School Critical Theory* (pp. 1419-1435). London: SAGE.

Wahl, A. V. (2012). How Sexuality Changes Agency: Gay Men, Jews, and Transitional Justice. In S. Buckley-Zistel and R. Stanley (Eds.), *Gender in Transitional Justice* (pp. 191-217). New York, NY: Palgrave Macmillan.

Waldby, C. (2008). Oocyte markets: Women's Reproductive Work in Embryonic Stem Cell Research. *New Genetics and Society* 27(1): 19-31.

Waldby, C. (2009). Singapore Biopolis: Bare Life in the City-State. *East Asian Science, Technology and Society* 3(2-3): 367-383.

Waldby, C. and M. Cooper (2008). The Biopolitics of Reproduction. *Australian Feminist Studies* 23(55): 57-73.

Waldby, C. and M. Cooper (2010). From Reproductive Work to Regenerative Labour: The Female Body and the Stem Cell Industries. *Feminist Theory* 11(3): 3-22.

WD (2016). *"Asoziale" im Nationalsozialismus, Ausarbeitung WD 1 - 3000 - 026/16.* Berlin: Wissenschaftlichen Dienste des Deutschen Bundestages.

Wecker, R. (2009). Eugenics. A Concept of Modernity? In R. Wecker, S. Braunschweig, G. Imboden, B. Küchenhoff and H. J. Ritter (Eds.), *What is National Socialist about Eugenics? International Debates on the History of Eugenics in the 20th Century* (pp. 23-38). Wien: Böhlau.

Wecker, R., S. Braunschweig, G. Imboden, B. Küchenhoff and J.H. Ritter (Eds.) (2009). *What is National Socialist about Eugenics? International Debates on the History of Eugenics in the 20th Century* (pp. 23-38). Wien: Böhlau.

Wehling, P. (2008). Selbstbestimmung oder sozialer Optimierungsdruck? Perspektiven einer kritischen Soziologie der Biopolitik. *Leviathan* 36(2): 249-273.

Wehling, P. (2010). Biology, Citizenship and the Government of Biomedicine. In U. Bröckling, S. Krasmann, and T. Lemke (Eds.), *Governmentality: Current Issues and Future Challenges* (pp. 225-246). New York: Routledge.

Wehling, P. (2019). Nutzbare Körper und "gesteigerte Menschenhaftigkeit": Biopolitik und Kapitalismus bei Michel Foucault und Walter Benjamin. In H. Gerhards and K. Braun (Eds.), *Biopolitiken - Regierungen des Lebens heute* (pp. 377-399). Wiesbaden: Springer.

Weindling, P. (1993). The Survival of Eugenics in 20th-Century Germany. *American Journal of Human Genetics* 52(3): 643-649.

Weindling, P. (1999). International Eugenics: Swedish Sterilisation in Context. *Scandinavian Journal of History* 24(2): 179-197.

Weingart, P. (1999). Science and Political Culture: Eugenics in Comparative Perspective. *Scandinavian Journal of History* 24(2): 163-177.

Weingart, P., J. Kroll and K. Bayertz (1996). *Rasse, Blut und Gene: Geschichte der Eugenik und Rassenhygiene in Deutschland*. Frankfurt: Suhrkamp.

Weiss, S. F. (1990). The Race Hygiene Movement in Germany 1904-1945. In M. B. Adams (Ed.), *The Wellborn Science: Eugenics in Germany, France, Brazil, and Russia* (pp. 8-68). Oxford: Oxford University Press.

Westermann, S. (2010). *Verschwiegenes Leid: Der Umgang mit den NS-Zwangssterilisationen in der Bundesrepublik*. Wien: Böhlau.

Westermann, S. (2017). "Ein Mensch, der keine Würde mehr hat, bedeutet auf dieser Welt nichts mehr": Zwangssterilisierte Menschen in der Bundesrepublik Deutschland. In M. Hamm (Ed.), *Ausgegrenzt! Warum? Zwangssterilisierte und Geschädigte der NS-Euthanasie in der Bundesrepublik Deutschland* (p. 23-40). Berlin: Metropol.

Wilson, P. K. (2002). Harry Laughlin's Eugenic Crusade to Control the "Socially Inadequate" in Progressive Era America. *Patterns of Prejudice* 36(1): 49-67.

Winter, S. (2014). *Transitional Justice in Established Democracies. A Political Theory* Houndmills, Basingstoke: Palgrave MacMillan.

Wolfrum, E. (2009). Die Anfänge der Bundesrepublik, die Aufarbeitung der NS-Vergangenheit und die Fernwirkungen für heute. In U. Bitzgeio, A. Kruke, and M. Woyke (Eds.), *Solidargemeinschaft und Erinnerungskultur im 20. Jahrhundert. Beiträge zu Gewerkschaften, Nationalsozialismus und Geschichtspolitik* (pp. 363-377). Bonn: Dietz.

Wong, A. (2020). I'm disabled and need a ventilator to live. Am I expendable during this pandemic? *Vox* (4 April 2020). Retrieved 25 Nov 2020 from https://www.vox.com/first-person/2020/4/4/21204261/coronavirus-covid-19-disabled-people-disabilities-triage.

Yamin, P. (2008). The Search for Marital Order: Civic Membership and the Politics of Marriage in the Progressive Era. *Polity* 41(1): 86-112.

Young-ah Gottlieb, S. (2003). *Regions of Sorrow: Anxiety and Messianism in Hannah Arendt and W. H. Auden*. Stanford, CA: Stanford University Press.

Ziegler, M. (2008). Reinventing Eugenics: Reproductive Choice and Law Reform after World War II. *Cardozo Law Journal of Law and Gender* 14: 319-350.

Zimmermann, S. (1988). Weibliches Selbstbestimmungsrecht und auf "Qualität" abzielende Bevölkerungspolitik. *Beiträge zur Feministischen Theorie und Praxis* 11 (21/22): 53-71.

Zinn, A. (2018). *Äus dem Volkskörper entfernt"? Homosexuelle Männer im Nationalsozialismus*. Frankfurt: Campus.

Zur Nieden, S. (2005). Homophobie und Staatsräson. In S. Zur Nieden (Ed.), *Homosexualität und Staatsräson: Männlichkeit, Homophobie und Politik in Deutschland 1900-1945* (pp. 17-51). Frankfurt: Campus.

Zur Nieden, S. (2009). Die Aberkannten. Der Berliner Hauptausschuss Öpfer des Faschismusünd die verfolgten Homosexuellen. In N. Frei, J. Brunner, and C. Goschler (Eds.), *Die Praxis der Wiedergutmachung. Geschichte, Erfahrung und Wirkung in Deutschland und Israel* (pp. 264-289). Göttingen: Wallstein.

Social Sciences

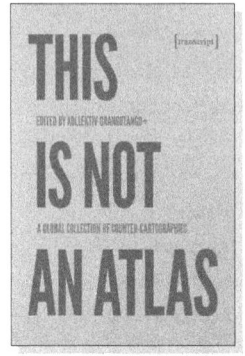

kollektiv orangotango+ (ed.)
This Is Not an Atlas
A Global Collection of Counter-Cartographies

2018, 352 p., hardcover, col. ill.
34,99 € (DE), 978-3-8376-4519-4
E-Book: free available, ISBN 978-3-8394-4519-8

Gabriele Dietze, Julia Roth (eds.)
Right-Wing Populism and Gender
European Perspectives and Beyond

April 2020, 286 p., pb., ill.
35,00 € (DE), 978-3-8376-4980-2
E-Book: 34,99 € (DE), ISBN 978-3-8394-4980-6

Mozilla Foundation
Internet Health Report 2019
2019, 118 p., pb., ill.
19,99 € (DE), 978-3-8376-4946-8
E-Book: free available, ISBN 978-3-8394-4946-2

**All print, e-book and open access versions of the titles in our list
are available in our online shop www.transcript-verlag.de/en!**

Social Sciences

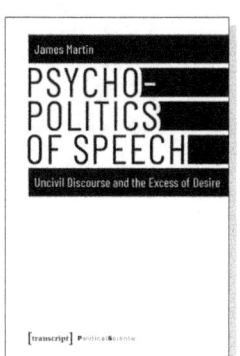

James Martin
Psychopolitics of Speech
Uncivil Discourse and the Excess of Desire

2019, 186 p., hardcover
79,99 € (DE), 978-3-8376-3919-3
E-Book: 79,99 € (DE), ISBN 978-3-8394-3919-7

Michael Bray
Powers of the Mind
Mental and Manual Labor
in the Contemporary Political Crisis

2019, 208 p., hardcover
99,99 € (DE), 978-3-8376-4147-9
E-Book: 99,99 € (DE), ISBN 978-3-8394-4147-3

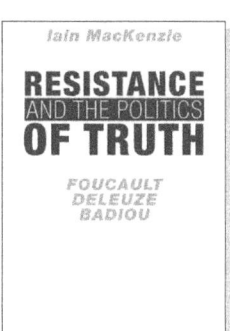

Iain MacKenzie
Resistance and the Politics of Truth
Foucault, Deleuze, Badiou

2018, 148 p., pb.
29,99 € (DE), 978-3-8376-3907-0
E-Book: 26,99 € (DE), ISBN 978-3-8394-3907-4
EPUB: 26,99 € (DE), ISBN 978-3-7328-3907-0

CPSIA information can be obtained
at www.ICGtesting.com
Printed in the USA
BVHW042005151221
624129BV00010B/65